Work Pray Code

Work Pray Code

When Work Becomes Religion in Silicon Valley

CAROLYN CHEN

PRINCETON UNIVERSITY PRESS
PRINCETON AND OXFORD

Published by Princeton University Press
41 William Street, Princeton, New Jersey 08540
99 Banbury Road, Oxford OX2 6JX

press.princeton.edu

Library of Congress Control Number 2021950464
Paper ISBN 978-0-691-22088-8
Cloth ISBN 978-0-691-21908-0
ISBN (e-book) 978-0-691-22087-1

British Library Cataloging-in-Publication Data is available

Editorial: Fred Appel and James Collier
Production Editorial: Jill Harris
Text Design: Karl Spurzem
Cover Design: Karl Spurzem
Production: Erin Suydam
Publicity: Maria Whelan and Kathryn Stevens
Copyeditor: Kathleen Kageff

This book has been composed in Arno with Chalet and Helvetica *for*

August and Julien

Contents

Acknowledgments

I wrote this book, but really it is the collective product of the time, energy, and intellectual labor of many people. First, my heartfelt thanks go to everyone I interviewed. When I began this project, the tech industry was as foreign to me as Mars. Yet my interview respondents—all extremely busy people—graciously took the time to introduce me to their world. They welcomed me to their offices, homes, meditation spaces, social events, gyms, and professional workshops. And they spent hours sharing deeply about their journeys of work and spirit. I was moved by their stories of self-awakening and self-discovery. Our conversations made me critically reexamine the meaning of work in my own life. I hope that I have faithfully conveyed how they find meaning, belonging, and transcendence in their everyday lives.

I could not have written this book without the faithful support of four people in particular. Shari Huhndorf read multiple drafts of the manuscript. I am so grateful to her for our weekly walks and the countless hours she spent with me working through the book's ideas, concepts, and structure. Russell Jeung read the entire manuscript and offered sharp, critical, and insightful suggestions. From the very beginning to the very end, Leslie McCall has been there to help me formulate, reformulate, and sharpen the ideas in this book. E. J. Graff was relentless in her encouragement. She helped me become a better writer.

I am grateful to my colleagues and friends who generously read and engaged with the ideas in this book: Rachel Sherman, David Schoenbrun, Shana Bernstein, Tony Chen, Garner C., Rachael Wong, Brad Chun, Ilana Gershon, Marta Elvira, David Moore, Jennifer Chen, Timmy Chen, Stephen Penningroth, Judy Roberts, Ailey Penningroth,

Bob Williams, Devah Pager, and my editor Fred Appel. My wonderful intellectual community at the Asian Pacific American Religions Research Initiative (APARRI) has supported me every step of the way, especially Khyati Joshi, Grace Kao, Jane Iwamura, Tammy Ho, Sharon Suh, Kirsten Oh, Duncan Ryūken Williams, Pui-Lan Kwok, Jerry Park, Joseph Cheah, Benny Liew, David Yoo, and Jeffrey Kuan.

I benefited from the generosity of many people and organizations in the writing of this book. A grant from the American Sociological Association, sabbaticals from Northwestern University and the University of California, Berkeley, and a visiting position at Stanford's Center for the Comparative Study of Race and Ethnicity supported my research and writing. Suchita N., Sarah P., David C., Gina M., Jon H., and Tim T. shared their observations about Silicon Valley. I am especially indebted to Kathleen T. for her abundant guidance, kindness, and thoughtfulness. Finally, Elizabeth Welch and Sister Patricia Bruno sustained me in body and spirit.

Writing this book was a labor of time, energy, and love for not only me but also my family. My parents, James and Patricia Chen; my sister, Jennifer Chen; my aunt and uncle, Sandy and Luke Hung; and my dear late mother-in-law, Penelope Baskerville, helped care for my children so that I could research and write. Few people are lucky enough to have spouses who are as generous and capacious in mind and spirit as my husband, Dylan Craig Penningroth. Raising two young children, we rarely had uninterrupted time to devote to intellectual conversations. Instead, we perfected the art of scholarly multitasking. Dylan helped me to form and articulate many of the book's concepts and themes while one of us was chopping carrots, washing dishes, folding little people's laundry, weeding, or driving. The ideas from our conversations, scribbled on the backs of old receipts and envelopes, made their way to the pages in this book. At the end, he meticulously and artfully copyedited the book. I'm a better scholar, writer, and person because of him.

I started researching this book when my sons, August and Julien, were toddlers. The book grew up with them. At the end of a day of research and writing, switching gears from the book to the boys was like moving between two different worlds. I was relieved to leave the efficient, productive, and optimized culture of tech for the boys' universe of Harry Potter, Band-Aids, dirt, newts, butterflies, cardboard forts, basketball, and Minecraft. I dedicate this book to them. May they create a world for all of us where magic, wonder, and play thrive, just because.

Work Pray Code

INTRODUCTION

How Work Is Replacing Religion

What happens to us, and what happens to religion, when people worship work? *Work Pray Code* explores how the lives of Silicon Valley tech workers are "transformed"—they say—by the religion that their employers offer on the job. On paper, Silicon Valley is one of the least religious places in America. People there are more likely than other Americans to claim no religious affiliation, or declare themselves to be atheist or agnostic. Given those statistics, I expected Silicon Valley to be a godless place. Instead, I discovered that it is one of the most religious places in America. In the course of my research for this book, I met people like the thirty-two-year-old entrepreneur John Ashton (not his real name),* who left his tight-knit evangelical community in Georgia to move to Silicon Valley—where he traded his Christianity for an even more zealous faith in the eventual IPO of his start-up. As with so many others, John's new faith is sustained by a corporate "faith community," which gives him a strong sense of belonging, identity, and meaning, much like his church back in Georgia.

I also met other people who described profound spiritual transformations, such as the twenty-seven-year-old German engineer Hans Schneider. Emotionally abused by his parents as a boy and bullied by classmates,

* I have changed the names of all interviewees and their companies, as well as characteristics that may make them identifiable.

Hans grew up with a profound sense of worthlessness and self-hate. He finally started "healing" from these wounds when the CEO of his start-up put Hans in a Buddhist mindfulness program at the company's time and expense. Now, not only is Hans "more whole and more spiritual"; he's risen up the ranks to become the head of engineering.

Many others talked to me about their work in spiritual terms. For instance, Doug Robinson calls himself the "head pastor" of the start-up he founded. Management, he claims, is a lot like ministry. With the help of a Buddhist teacher, Doug has developed a professional development program for his team, one that integrates Buddhist-inspired teachings and practices. The program helps employees "connect to their authentic selves," he says, so they can invest their "whole selves" in work. Doug quotes the Buddha more than he does Andrew Carnegie, Peter Drucker, or Tim Ferriss and describes his work as "partnering with the Universe."

Like John, Hans, and Doug, few of the people I met came from Silicon Valley. They described themselves as becoming more "whole," "spiritual," and "connected" after moving there. Most did not identify with a religion, belong to a religious congregation, or attend religious services. Their spiritual transformations didn't happen at a church, temple, mosque, dharma center, or synagogue. Rather, they took place at work.

But tech workers channeling their religious needs into work is only part of the story. The other part has to do with why Hans's CEO paid to send him to a Buddhist mindfulness program. The answer, I came to realize, is that companies have taken up pastoral and spiritual care as a way to make their employees more productive. One human resources director told me that her job was to "nurture the souls" of the employees. One firm I visited sponsors weekly meditation sessions for its employees to make them more focused. Tech companies often hire executive coaches, who serve as what one human resources director described as "spiritual advisers" to senior leaders. These "spiritual advisers" train executives in spiritual practices that help them align their work with their "calling" in life. The benefits packages at several companies I spent time at include the time and funds to allow employees to attend spiritual and religious retreats. Some firms have dedicated positions such as "chief spiritual officer" and "chief mindfulness officer" to manage their employees. In many tech workplaces, meditation rooms are as common as the iconic Ping-Pong table.

What's more, companies are actively bringing religion, particularly Buddhism, to their employees. One firm I visited sponsors weekly "dharma talks," where employees meditate and reflect on the teachings of the Buddha. Google sponsors Search Inside Yourself, a program that brings in Buddhist teachers to teach Googlers meditation, which employees affectionately call "church." The tech giant Salesforce invited over thirty monks from Plum Village, the order of the famous Buddhist leader Thich Nhat Hanh, to chant and teach at the meetings of their annual conferences in 2017 and 2018. At companies such as LinkedIn, Buddhist virtues such as compassion and mindfulness are celebrated as part of a company culture that supposedly gives them a competitive advantage. "The workplace," one tech executive told me, "is the hotbed of spirituality" in Silicon Valley.

It is easy to dismiss all this as simply part of the strange antics of a unique, privileged enclave. Media depictions remind us that Silicon Valley is not the *real* America. And there is some truth to this. Not many American firms, after all, have unlimited vacation, celebrity chefs, pets at work, and Buddhist monks as consultants. While the rest of corporate America is slaving away in colorless cubicles, Silicon Valley tech workers are getting massages, meditating, and playing foosball at work, we are told.

But tech workers in Silicon Valley are not so different from highly skilled professionals in other parts of the country. In surveys, when asked what brings their lives meaning, Americans point to their jobs and careers just as frequently as they do their children and grandchildren.[1] Companies in other sectors and in regions of the country far from Silicon Valley are also trying to attend to their employees' spiritual needs with an eye on the bottom line. Firms such as Taco Bell, Pizza Hut, and Wal-Mart have hired chaplains to help workers deal with spiritual issues.[2] Not only Google but also companies such as Aetna, General Mills, and Goldman Sachs are teaching Buddhist spiritual practices such as mindfulness to optimize employee performance.

Silicon Valley helps us to see a broader trend, one that has eluded scholars of work and religion alike: subtly but unmistakably, *work is replacing religion*. Over the past forty years, work has extracted ever more of the time and energy of highly skilled Americans, crowding out other commitments, especially religion. In 1990, only 8 percent of all Americans claimed no religious affiliation.[3] Today nearly a quarter of them do.[4] The number of "religious nones" has risen fastest in places, like the Bay Area, that have a large high-skilled population. But numbers can lie. As we shall see, high-skilled professionals haven't abandoned religion. Instead, they are looking to the workplace to slake their thirst for belonging, identity, purpose, and transcendence. More and more, companies have become America's new temples, churches, mosques, and synagogues. Work has become a spiritual practice that inspires religious fervor. People are not "selling their souls" at work. Rather, *work is where they find their souls*.

Work Pray Code reveals how tech workers are finding their souls at work. But it's about more than the engineers, programmers, and executives who work at companies like Facebook and Google. Through the lives of Silicon Valley tech workers, the book tells a story of how the expansion of work and the decline of religion is reconfiguring the lives of high-paid skilled workers in late capitalism. This is a familiar tale to scholars and nonscholars alike. Many Americans experience the expansion of work and the decline of religion in their personal struggles for "work-life balance." Work is taking more of their hours and energy, leaving less time for families and friendships. Religion is one of many things in the ledger of "life" that gets sidelined by work. The expansion of work and the decline of religion is also the familiar story social theorists tell about secularization in the West. According to sociologist Max Weber, capitalism forms an "iron cage" of bureaucratic rationalism that "disenchants" the world of the magical "otherworldliness" of religion.[5]

The lives of high-skilled professionals like John, Hans, and Doug suggest that work's influence is indeed expanding. It does so, however, not by extracting and "caging" the human spirit, but by satisfying high-skilled Americans' social, emotional, and spiritual needs. Work, it appears, is fulfilling, not depleting, their souls.

What happens when work is the place where Americans find their souls? The book is organized around three facets of this question. First, it shows how the experience of work changes when companies try to fulfill the social, spiritual, and emotional needs of their employees. Second, it assesses how religion and spirituality adapt when they become a part of work. And third, it explores how the "religion of work" is altering the very social fabric of America. Through the lens of Silicon Valley's tech industry, *Work Pray Code* examines how the meanings of work, religion, and community are transforming in late capitalism.

The Expansion of Work

How did work become a place where highly skilled Americans find their souls? To answer this question, we need to understand how white-collar work has changed in relation to other social institutions, especially religion, in late capitalism. More Americans took on white-collar managerial and professional occupations starting in the 1940s.[6] Writing in 1951, sociologist C. Wright Mills described work very differently from the way that Silicon Valley tech workers like John, Hans, and Doug do. White-collar work, he claimed, was soul crushing. In the big bureaucratic organizations where they worked, white-collar workers "habitually submit to the orders of others," selling their "time, energy and skill to the power of others."[7] Under the oppressive weight of the corporation, workers lost their individuality, freedom, and personhood. The faceless, bureaucratic corporation so squeezed the quintessential American spirit of independence and entrepreneurialism out of employees that Mills characterized that time as the "rise of the little man."[8] "Underneath virtually all experience of work today," he wrote, "there is a fatalistic feeling that work *per se* is unpleasant."[9]

If work crushed the soul, then it was in the world outside of work where white-collar workers found their souls and built their "real" lives, according to Mills. "Work," he wrote, "becomes a sacrifice of time, necessary to building life outside of it."[10] The typical 1950s white-collar worker, who was White and male, worked from nine to five, forty hours a week.[11] Except for executives, work was understood to be contained in one part of a worker's life. This is one big reason the 1950s were also the years American civic participation reached its greatest height. In these organizations outside of work, white-collar workers *recovered* their souls and became something more than another faceless worker in what Mills called the "the great salesroom" of the company.[12] The most important of these were religious congregations. During the 1950s, nearly half of Americans attended religious services weekly.[13] Church memberships grew at a rate faster than the general population.[14] As young, White, middle-class families migrated to the newly developed suburbs, they built their communities around their Protestant and Catholic churches and Jewish synagogues.[15] Through them, they met their friends, found their spouses, raised their children, and created a sense of belonging and identity in the American experiment of suburban living. Through these faith communities they found meaning in life, from baptism at the beginning, to burial at the end, and everything in between. To not participate in religion was to risk both social and existential anomie. In the 1950s, Americans also belonged to multiple social clubs—bowling clubs, poker clubs, softball leagues, workers' unions—but among them religion was the most central to creating community and finding meaning in life.[16] In the 1950s, work was only one of many organizations that the white-collar worker belonged to. Work was reined in, not only by a nine-to-five work culture, but by the nearly compulsory draw of religion.

The forty-hour workweek, and the life associated with it, faded in the late twentieth century, when work expanded, demanding more time and energy, especially from high-skilled Americans.[17] Who worked longer hours changed. In the 1940s, high-school dropouts were more likely than college graduates to work over forty-eight hours a week. By 1980, the situation had switched: college graduates were more likely to work over forty-eight hours a week. And by 2000, over 40 percent of male college graduates did.[18] What's more, those in the top 20 percent of income earners—largely skilled professionals and managers—were *twice* as likely to work long hours than those in the bottom 20 percent.[19]

The experience of one Silicon Valley engineer is now the reality for many professionals: "No one works forty hours a week today. Fifty hours is a good week. Sixty to sixty-five hours is more typical." In a survey of sixteen hundred managers and professionals, business scholar Leslie Perlow found that 92 percent reported working fifty or more hours a week. And one-third logged sixty-five hours or more. But even these hours do not reflect the twenty to twenty-five hours that most reported monitoring their work, but not actually working.[20] We're at a place today where "professionals," according to economist Heather Boushey, "devote most of their waking hours to their careers."[21]

The demands of work ballooned for high-skilled workers as a result of several changes in the late twentieth century and early twenty-first century.[22] For one, the need for professionals grew as the American economy shifted from an industrial to a postindustrial economy. Between 1960 and 2000, professionals increased from about one-tenth to one-quarter of the American working population.[23] With the rise of global competition starting in the 1980s, companies responded by downsizing, creating "mean and lean" companies where employees were expected to do two or three times as much work as before. Mergers, acquisitions, downsizing, deregulation, and "investor capitalism" led to layoffs of white-collar workers but created longer work hours for those who survived the cuts.[24] On top of that, the advent of technologies such as email, smart phones, and video conferencing have intensified and drawn out work. Companies now expect employees to be on call at all times, erasing the distinction between work and home. Work has taken over so much of some lives that according to one study, 26 percent of professionals and managers sleep with their smart phones.[25]

But there is another, less cited reason that professionals started working longer and harder—work became more rewarding and more fulfilling. This is especially true for high-skilled professionals in the last forty years relative to other occupational groups. Since 1980, wages have been stagnant or declining for most Americans, but they've ballooned among the top wage earners, who are largely professionals and managers.[26] The earnings of those in the top ninety-fifth percentile of workers (making more than $150,000 a year) rose at a rate almost four times higher than that of those at the fiftieth percentile.[27]

So too, those in the higher income brackets have grown *even more* satisfied with their jobs in the last forty years. In a study measuring the job satisfaction of Californians in the twenty-year period from 1978 to 1998, workers in the top 20 percent of the income distribution (which includes professionals) became *more satisfied* with their jobs, while all others became less satisfied with their jobs.[28]

To be sure, the picture is not completely rosy for high-skilled professionals. They also struggle with consequences of globalization, downsizing, and the corporate culture: stress, tight deadlines, insecure employment, and difficulty balancing obligations with the family. Many feel that they work too long. Yet still, professionals claim that they "choose" to work overtime and that they find pleasure in their work. According to one study, the vast majority of professionals and managers state that they "usually" work overtime because they "enjoy work and their colleagues" to a far greater degree than do other occupational groups.[29]

What changed to make work so pleasurable and rewarding for high-skilled professionals? The economic transformation of the late twentieth century prompted companies to alter work, making it not only more demanding, but also more fulfilling for some, and less so for others, depending on where workers fit in the "skill divide." According to sociologist Arne Kalleberg, companies took two different management strategies depending on the skill level of their employees.[30] Some maximized profits by "low-road strategies"—reducing wages and deskilling, off-shoring, and subcontracting jobs—in short, minimizing costs by disinvesting in their workers. This has been the fate of many blue-collar jobs that were once "good jobs" offering decent pay, job security, benefits, and dignity. For people working in these jobs, work became more scarce, insecure, and unsatisfying.

Other companies took "high-road strategies" by investing especially in their high-skilled workers: rewarding them with higher wages, more skills and training, and greater autonomy over their work. Instead of treating their highly skilled professionals as "costs to be minimized," companies considered them as "assets" to invest in. Firms taking "high-road strategies" tended to be concentrated in knowledge-intensive industries, such as technology, that faced both global competition and frequent labor shortages.[31]

These companies introduced new incentive structures designed to make work more rewarding for high-skilled workers, despite greater demands and less security. For instance, in the late twentieth century, a growing number of Fortune 1000 firms instituted reward practices such as gainsharing, profit sharing, employee stock ownership plans, stock option plans, "pay-for-performance" programs, and nonmonetary recognition awards for performance.[32] Companies adopted "high-performance work systems" emphasizing mentoring, training, and learning. And they flattened the authority structure, removing middle management to prioritize team work, greater autonomy, and decentralized management.[33]

But to compete in the new global economy, company leaders felt they needed to do more than restructure the financial and professional incentives of work. They needed to transform their organizational cultures to extract the full discretionary effort of their skilled workers—to get employees to invest their *whole* selves—emotionally, socially, and spiritually—into their work. Starting in the 1980s, American firms looked to the Japanese, their fiercest competitors, as a model. Japanese firms had a competitive advantage over American firms, business experts claimed, because they emphasized unity and loyalty and were able to command deep sacrifice and commitment from its employees.[34] Popular best sellers like William Ouichi's *Theory Z: How American Business Can Meet the Japanese Challenge*, argued that American firms should learn from the Japanese by creating similar strong cultures that cultivated belonging, loyalty, and shared goals and values among employees and management.[35]

What kind of organization could inspire that kind of sacrifice, faith, and commitment in its members? There was only one obvious answer in America—religion. In the late twentieth century, corporate managers started shifting their metaphor of employees in the company from cogs in an efficient, well-oiled machine, to something that resembled a faith community: members who *belong* to a shared community, and *believe* in a higher and transcendent goal.[36] In short, the task of modern management in late capitalism changed from organizing work to be more efficient, to making it *more meaningful*.[37]

Today, companies are not just economic institutions. They've become meaning-making institutions that offer a gospel of fulfillment and divine purpose in a capitalist cosmos.[38] Most Fortune 500 companies have adopted key elements of religious organizations—a mission, values, practices, ethics, and an "origin story."[39] Having a strong corporate culture that is meaningful, according to one study, can account for 20–30 percent of the differential in corporate performance when compared to "'culturally unremarkable' competitors."[40] Business leaders ought to take meaning making seriously, another study concludes, because nine of ten people are willing to earn less money for more meaningful work.[41] According to one leading business thinker, "Meaning is the new money."[42]

Contemporary ethnographic studies of professional work frequently allude to the religious nature of work. In a study of women executives, sociologist Mary Blair-Loy demonstrates how work provides a powerful form of meaning to the lives of the women executives. Work, Blair-Loy argues, is a form of devotion. "Schemas of devotion to work are like pseudo-religious articles of faith," she writes, "they promise to provide meaning to life and a secure connection to something outside themselves."[43] The executives in her study "lose" themselves in work. Work "induce[s] a powerful sense of transcendence," Blair-Loy writes.[44] It gives them a sense of identity, independence, recognition, community, and even "euphoria."[45]

Sociologist Gideon Kunda also describes the work of engineers in a Boston tech firm in religious language: "membership in Tech implies heavy involvements and a strong emotional bonding of the individual to the company, characterized in such terms as 'missionary zeal,' 'fierce loyalty,' and 'family affiliation.'"[46] Religious elements such as "ideology" and "ritual" in the company's culture produce what is tantamount to late capitalism's version of Émile Durkheim's collective effervescence, "the collapse of boundaries between the self and the organization," according to Kunda.[47]

The professionals that Blair-Loy and Kunda studied are actually not so different from other workers. When the Pew Research Center conducted an open-ended survey asking Americans what gives their lives meaning, 34 percent answered "career," making work one of the most important sources of meaning to Americans, second only to the family (at 69 percent).[48] What's more, work seems to mean the most to highly paid skilled workers. They are more likely to claim that work gives them a sense of identity rather than something they do for a living.[49] According to Reverend Scotty McLennan, who teaches at Stanford's business school, "business people spend the majority of their waking hours at work, and many of them want to find it meaningful."[50] Looking to work as a primary source of meaning among the highly skilled is an example of what political theorist Kathi Weeks calls "the postindustrial emphasis on work as a practice of self realization."[51] Seen within these larger patterns of American attitudes toward work, it is not strange that Silicon Valley tech workers are finding their souls at work. Rather, it reflects a broader trend of high-skilled Americans turning to work for spirituality and meaning in late capitalism.

Americans today are looking to work in order not only to believe in something, but also to *belong* to something. Stretched for time, busy Americans are finding community at work, and not in faith communities, sports leagues, neighborhoods, or clubs. When sociologist Maria Poarch asked the residents of a middle-class Boston suburb where they found their friends and source of community, the most popular answer was "work."[52] A real estate agent from the study reflected, "I very much belong to a community within my own office, within my own company, within my own industry. . . . Strangely enough I am unbelievably and sadly disconnected from the community that I live in, both because we've lost our religious pulls to one another and there is simply not the time."[53] In another study of professionals and religion, the authors conclude, "For many businesspeople, the corporation is the closest thing that they have to community after family."[54]

With the growth of job insecurity and the "gig economy," the social benefits of work are not equally enjoyed by everyone. Some suggest that work is not the source of community that it once was in the days of secure employment.[55] Yet outside of the family, work is still the major source of friendship for most Americans.[56] When asked where they met the two friends they socialize with most, the majority of working-age Americans answered work.[57] And community is still one of the top things that employees say that they look for in a job.[58] Even outside the workplace, work continues to be the locus of community in places like Silicon Valley, where work-oriented associations, networks, and gatherings such as hack-a-thons and meet-ups organize social life.[59]

To be sure, work has always been an important source of community and friendship. But not until the rise of the modern corporation did management learn to systematically mine the social needs of the human worker for productive labor.[60] Responding to global economic restructuring in the late twentieth century, many American companies redoubled their efforts to design family-like cultures that cultivated community, sociality, commitment, and loyalty from their employees.[61] Community, companies have learned, is good for business. According to a study by Gallup, employees who have close friends at work are more engaged and productive.[62] Even in Silicon Valley, where workers change jobs every three to five years, companies believe it pays to invest in the game rooms, cafeterias, social events, and social clubs that create community. Concerning the social offerings at her large tech firm, one human resources professional said, "I corral and channel [employees'] energy into not just the product, but to *experience* here!" It's no surprise that, in the carefully designed communities of Silicon Valley tech firms, over half of employees say they found their best friends at work.[63]

According to sociologist Arlie Hochschild, companies now meet the social needs of American workers better than families do.[64] Burdened by the overwhelming demands of family life today, the people in her study find pleasure, community, fulfillment, intimacy, and belonging in the "managed cheer" of the workplace rather than the chaos and stress of home. Having supplanted the loving and nurturing functions of the family, she concludes, "work may become their rock."[65] Political scientist Robert D. Putnam agrees: "Professionals and blue-collar workers alike are putting in long hours together, eating lunch and dinner together, traveling together, arriving early, and staying late. What is more, people are divorcing more often, marrying later (if at all), and living alone in unprecedented numbers. Work is where the hearth is, then, for many solitary souls."[66]

In short, over the last forty years, work has expanded in the lives of high-skilled professionals. Work takes more than any other institution today, but it also gives more than any other institution. High-skilled Americans are finding belonging, identity, meaning, and purpose at work. The case of Silicon Valley shows that many companies are happily assuming these expanded functions because they think it's profitable. According to senior human resources leaders at Facebook, "Today more companies are operating in knowledge and service economies. They're not just fulfilling basic needs; they're aiming to fulfill *every* need, providing conveniences like meals and gyms, and competing to be the best places to work." And, the Facebook leaders concluded, "from 1984 through 2011, those that won [the best places to work] outperformed their peers on stock returns by 2.3% to 3.8% per year."[67]

The holistic provisions of companies like Google and Facebook might seem new, but in fact they reflect trends long in the making. The Facebook leaders practically echo a corporate executive quoted in the nearly forty-year-old popular business classic *In Search of Excellence*: "Companies . . . have become sort of a community center for employees, as opposed to just a place to work. . . . They have become . . . mother institutions."[68]

The Decline and Diffusion of Religion

If work has expanded to become an institution that fulfills *every* human need as leaders at Facebook claim, what has happened to the other social institutions that organize human life? Conversely, if highly skilled Americans are giving all their time to work, what are they taking time from? If work expands, what contracts? This is the question that scholars of work and family have been asking for years. Work and family, they maintain, are competing commitments. The expansion of work has come at the cost of the family.[69] This is true, however, not only for the family, but also for other vital social institutions, especially religion.

For most of the twentieth century, religious organizations were the original "mother institutions" in the United States. Even when religion declined dramatically in Western European countries as a result of industrialization, urbanization, and secularism, the United States remained exceptionally religious well into the late twentieth century: over 90 percent of Americans continued to claim a religious identity, and over 90 percent professed to believe in God or a higher power.[70] There's good reason for this. Religion has played a vital *social* function. It has been the primary source of community, belonging, identity, and meaning for Americans.[71] Writing in 1955, sociologist Will Herberg argued that through religion people found their place in American society.[72] Americans organized their personal, familial, and social lives around their religious identities as Protestant, Catholic, or Jew. Religion was so influential that it even determined how much money people made, who they voted for, where they lived, and who they would marry.[73]

But as Americans invest more of their time and energy into work, they are simultaneously disinvesting from the social dimensions of organized religion. As a result, religion has lost the influence it once had over the social lives and identities of Americans. Today, fewer Americans claim a religious affiliation than ever before. The fastest growing religious demographic in American society are people who claim no religious identity, a category sociologists call religious "nones." When the General Social Survey started collecting religious data in 1972, the proportion of "nones" in the American population was 7 percent, and it stayed steady there for about twenty years. But starting in the 1990s, "nones" have increased rapidly, so that in 1990 they were 9 percent, and by 2018, the religiously unaffiliated made up 23 percent of the American population.[74]

So too, fewer Americans are participating in religious organizations. Since the mid-1980s, religious service attendance has slowly declined.[75] In 1990, 35 percent of Americans attended religious services weekly or more compared to 27 percent in 2018.[76] Meanwhile, the number of Americans who never attend services increased dramatically, from 13 percent in 1990 to 30 percent in 2018.[77] Faith communities have felt the pinch. The median number of people involved in congregations has dropped.[78] And so has the time Americans devote to religious organizations. From 2003 to 2018, Americans spent *a quarter less time* participating in religious organizations on the weekends.[79]

To be sure, the expansion of work does not by itself explain religion's decline in the United States. Waning religious participation is a trend that some scholars date to the 1960s, before Americans started "overworking."[80] Moreover, since the mid-1970s, Americans have participated less in all types of civic organizations, not just religious ones.[81] Still, there is clear evidence that when people devote more time to work, they take it partly from the time they might have spent on religious activities. In *Bowling Alone*, Robert Putnam attributes some of the drop in civic participation, including religious participation, to the increasing amount of time that Americans are spending at work. According to the General Social Survey, Americans who overwork attend religious services less. Between 1973 and 2018, of those working forty hours a week, 33 percent attended church once a month or more, compared to 24 percent among those working fifty hours a week.[82]

High-skilled and high-income Americans are especially apt to choose work over religion. An early study of lawyers, professors, and engineers found that men whose careers involved more training and socialization were more strongly bound to their professional community than to their religious community.[83] Several studies show that high wages reduce religious participation by encouraging people to substitute market work for religious activities.[84] In general, high-income Americans rank lowest among nearly all measures of religiosity—attendance, importance, belief, prayer, and so on.[85] What's more, it is the resource-intensive *social* demands of religion that compete with economic activity. A study examining the economic growth and religiosity of different countries found that while religious belief spurs economic growth, economic growth is negatively correlated with time-intensive religious attendance. The authors, economists Robert J. Barro and Rachel M. McCleary, concluded that "more church attendance signifies more resources used up by the religion sector."[86]

What's more, religious decline is most pronounced in what urban studies scholar Richard Florida calls "human capital clusters," geographic areas where knowledge industries concentrate.[87] These are metro areas that have a high proportion of highly skilled professionals: San Jose; Washington, DC; Cambridge, Massachusetts; Austin; and San Francisco. These "human capital clusters" have created their own cultures and institutions, including coffee shops and yoga studios, that support a lifestyle where religious organizations have become peripheral. The religiosity of metro areas is closely associated with occupations and socioeconomic class, Florida finds. Metro areas with higher religiosity tend to have lower incomes and education levels, and "working-class economies." Low-religiosity metro areas, on the other hand, have more college-educated, high-income workers in the knowledge economy.[88] Another study found that counties with higher religious adherence and denser concentrations of religious congregations have a smaller proportion of "creative class" workers and fewer patents.[89]

In the past, upwardly mobile Americans signified their changing status by "moving up" the religious ladder from more demanding to less demanding, higher-prestige denominations: Pentecostals became Baptists; Baptists became Methodists; and Methodists became Episcopalians. But today's highly skilled professionals are choosing to leave religion altogether. The decline of religious affiliation and participation, however, does not mean that religious needs have disappeared. They've just been displaced. As religious studies scholar Kathryn Lofton observes, "Where our social and ritual interests are placed now is not in denominational tradition but workplace culture."[90] Why should time-constrained professionals join a religion when work offers the same social, spiritual, and status-enhancing benefits?[91]

Just when work is replacing religion, religion is moving into the secular world, a trend I call *the secular diffusion of religion*.[92] And it is especially pronounced with Buddhism and Hinduism, whose religious practices are being severed from religious communities, and repackaged for business and therapeutic use. Fewer Americans are participating in organized religion, but they are still engaging in religious practices, largely Asian ones, through secular sources. For instance, meditation, a practice largely inspired by Buddhist and Hindu traditions, has exploded. In 2017, fully one in seven Americans said they meditated,[93] even though only one in seventy say they are Buddhist or Hindu.[94] Most Americans become exposed to Asian spiritual practices such as yoga, meditation, mindfulness, chanting "Om" or other Sanskrit mantras not through Hindu or Buddhist temples, but through secular institutions such as schools, workplaces, hospitals, gyms, and yoga studios, secular websites, and books.[95] Through these secular venues and mediums, Americans learn about Asian religious ideas such as dharma, moksha, enlightenment, and impermanence. They are exposed to Hindu and Buddhist deities such as Ganesh, Kuan Yin Bodhisattva, or the Buddha in yoga studios, spas, or therapists' offices. People don't belong to Asian religions but "consume" them through the "spiritual marketplace" of self-help books, retreats, therapeutic treatments, and self-improvement and motivational seminars and the like.[96] Moreover, there is a class dimension to this type of spirituality.[97] It's particularly prevalent among well-educated Westerners—who can afford the classes, workshops, and retreats.

Today, many high-skilled Americans are learning the Buddhist practice of mindfulness meditation in the workplace. Companies like Aetna, McKinsey, and Nike have embraced mindfulness for its widely touted promises to enhance productivity and focus. One recent study found that 22 percent of American companies incorporate mindfulness practice, a number that although likely inflated, shows how popular the once obscure practice of elite Asian monastics has now become.[98]

To be sure, companies and other secular organizations are not teaching the same Buddhist mindfulness that monks practice in the mountain monasteries of Asia. It's a secularized, Westernized version, repurposed as a therapeutic and self-improvement practice.[99] As one mindfulness entrepreneur put it, it's a Buddhism that's had the religion "steam cleaned" out of it. This doesn't mean the absence or erasure of Buddhism, but the evolution of a new kind of Buddhism, one that has adopted the instrumental logic of work.[100] The corporate teaching of mindfulness is the logical consequence of work replacing religion—*religion is now a part of work*. Buddhism has found a new institutional home in the West, the corporation. Fewer Americans are praying in the pews these days. Instead, more are getting healed, actualized, and enlightened at work, through religious practices borrowed from religions that few of them actually profess.

The spiritual importance of the workplace today represents a monumental shift in the history of modern capitalism. When Max Weber studied the origins of the modern capitalist work ethic, he had to understand the world that seventeenth-century European workers lived in—one that revolved around the Christian church and its teachings. How, he asked, does religion organize people's work lives? Today in the late capitalist West, the spheres of religion and work are reversed. Religion exists in the sacred cosmos of a work-centered world. And to understand religion in the lives of high-skilled Americans, we must look at the institution of work. So instead of asking, as Weber did, how religion shapes work, the more relevant question of our time is: how does work organize people's religious lives?

It *is* strange that Silicon Valley tech workers are "finding their souls" at work. Not because it's a quirky thing that happens only in Silicon Valley. As I've argued, many high-skilled Americans are "finding their souls" at work. It is strange because it goes against our normative assumptions about the boundaries of work and religion. The problem is that these work-life boundaries no longer describe the lives of many high-skilled Americans. We speak incessantly about the need to restore "work-life balance" because we remain under the influence of a deeply ingrained view that work drains the self. But many highly skilled American workers no longer hold that view: work is where they find fulfillment. Rather than ridicule Silicon Valley tech workers for worshipping work, perhaps we should wonder whether they are harbingers of things to come—whether their orientation toward work may already be ours, too.

People finding their souls at work reflects the seismic shift in work and religion that has occurred in the last fifty years. Work has expanded in the lives of the highly skilled, by simultaneously extracting more of their time and energy *and* fulfilling more of their needs that religion once met. Conversely, religion has lost influence, and its power has been diffused through secular sources. Work is simultaneously displacing and absorbing religion.

What do we lose when work replaces religion? Workplace pundits celebrate the integration of practices like meditation and mindfulness into Silicon Valley. These practices have made the workplace more humane and holistic, they claim. And most of the people I spoke to agreed. They are delighted to find personal, social, and spiritual fulfillment at work. What's not to like about a company that "cares" for your mind, body, and spirit? This appears to be a win-win situation: people are happier, and companies are more profitable.

But could work be becoming *too* enchanting and *too* fulfilling? Things look different when we consider the larger social consequences of what I call *Techtopia*—an engineered society where people find their highest fulfillment in work. By taking care of the body, mind, and soul, tech companies have colonized the functions of other social institutions. In the stories that I will share, we see that as people invest more of their selves in work, they invest less of themselves in critical social institutions like the family, neighborhoods, and religion. And as the workplace expands to meet the holistic needs of its employees, the influence of other social institutions, such as religion, decline. At one time, religion was a sanctuary from, and even a prophetic critic of, the crushing instrumentalism of work. Now, not only is the workplace replacing religion, but it's conscripting religion into its service. *Work Pray Code* is a story of what happens when work takes over the institutions that shape our souls.

CHAPTER 1

Losing My Religion . . . and Finding It at Work

This is a story about people who move to Silicon Valley and lose their religion. But it's also about how they find religion someplace else: at work. Early on in my research, as I was interviewing tech professionals, I noticed that some of them said that they used to be religious. Leaving religion wasn't a conscious choice for them. They didn't actively reject it or experience a crisis in faith. Rather, religion had so quietly tiptoed out of their lives that most people could not explain where it went. John Ashton, a thirty-two-year-old entrepreneur from Georgia, is one of these people. In 2010, he moved to Silicon Valley when he was recruited by a start-up. At five-eleven, with his close-cropped brown hair, blue eyes, and earnest smile, John looks like the proverbial White boy next door. Like the rest of the guys at his start-up, he's dressed casually, in bright green Adidas sneakers with neon yellow laces, jeans, a faded Georgia Tech t-shirt, and a light black windbreaker. For him, as for the rest of them, coming to Silicon Valley has been a journey of letting go of the old, and taking up the new.

Back in Georgia, the most important thing to John was his faith. He became a Christian in high school, when he joined the youth group at his best friend's Baptist church. The church was warm and loving, nurturing him through his adolescent years. "It was the first time I experienced a loving community outside of family," John explains. That early experience as a teenager laid a foundation for religious community in his life. From that point on, the church and Christian fellowships were always an anchor in John's life. When he went away to college at Georgia Tech, John joined a Christian frat and became the president in his senior year. Its motto was the Bible verse Ephesians 5:1, "be imitators of God," and it required a commitment to Christian service and godly living. Even though Georgia Tech's frats were known for having lots of alcohol, their frat house was dry. When most college guys were drinking and partying, John and his frat brothers were feeding the homeless and visiting the elderly. Instead of heading to Florida for spring break debauchery, John and his brothers built orphanages in the slums of Mexico. His faith community in high school and college "built character," he says, and they showed him "how to love people in different ways." Once he started working after college, John joined an evangelical church in Atlanta that he describes as "big," "fun," and "crazy." Attending Sunday service "was like going to a rock show." All his friends were a part of the church, and John, who loved music, played guitar in the church band. The church and his faith "grounded" him, he says.

In 2011, John moved from Atlanta to Silicon Valley to join a tech startup. He now refers to church as "a phase of my life" and explains that "it's not a big part of who I am anymore." When he first came out West, John tried out a couple of churches, but nothing felt right. Churches in Silicon Valley, he says, did not have the same "big" and "fun" energy that he experienced in Atlanta. And as the church and his friends in Georgia drifted further and further away, so too did the centrality of religion in his life. In retrospect John admits that during those years in Atlanta, "doubt started creeping in my head that this is the truth and the only thing right and true in the world." But he didn't leave Christianity, and he didn't leave the church because "where we were from, it [church] was just what you did."

John's life is a vivid example of how the soul changes in the process of moving to Silicon Valley. Why did someone so religious leave religion after moving to Silicon Valley? I wondered. Is there something about working in Silicon Valley that makes people lose their faith?

John's story prompts another question. If people like John are leaving religion after moving to Silicon Valley, what has taken religion's place?

Over 75 percent of Americans claim a religious identity. Religion has traditionally served as one of the primary sources of belonging, identity, and meaning for them.[1] This was certainly the case for John in Georgia, who described his church as having been "like a family" and who had found personal meaning and purpose through his religion. What has become John's "loving community outside of family" now that he has stopped going to church? What "grounds" him? If in Georgia going to church was "just what you did," what's "just what you do" in Silicon Valley? If Christianity shapes the soul in Georgia, what shapes the soul in Silicon Valley?

Leaving Home, Leaving Religion

To understand the souls of tech folk like John, the first thing we must remember is that almost no one who works in these companies is actually from Silicon Valley. They are "tech migrants"—immigrants who come to work in the technology industry. They come from far-off places like India, China, Korea, and Germany. Even more come from the far corners of the United States—small towns in Iowa, New Hampshire, Tennessee, Texas, and South Carolina. These details are important. For nothing stirs the young American soul like the journey of leaving home and finding a new one. Westward migration preceded some of the most dramatic moments of religious transformation in American history. The majority of people who were part of the Second Great Awakening in the early nineteenth century were young migrants moving west, according to historian Whitney Cross.[2] So were those drawn to new religious movements in the Bay Area in the 1960s and 1970s.[3] And to the masses of young Irish, Italians, and Germans who came to the United States in the late nineteenth century, migration, according to historian Timothy Smith, was a "theologizing experience."[4] But one important detail separates the spiritual journeys of "tech migrants" today from other migrants in America. In the past, immigrants found community and immortality by building churches, synagogues, temples, and communes. The "tech migrants" of the twenty-first century, however, meet these religious needs by starting companies.

About 80 percent of my research participants moved to Silicon Valley to work in the tech industry. The rest moved for other reasons—to attend school, to be with a partner—but all eventually found jobs in tech. Most tech migrants are single, college-educated White and Asian men in their twenties with engineering or computer science backgrounds. Untethered to familial obligations, they can move at the drop of a hat. They come alone and have at most a few acquaintances in Silicon Valley. In short, they are far from home, alone, young, impressionable, and eager to pour themselves into work. The decision to move to Silicon Valley is an easy one. It is, after all, the mecca of tech. Most have the attitude of Brian Ross, a twenty-seven-year-old Boston-based entrepreneur, who was offered a job in Palo Alto on a Friday, and expected by the company to be at work the next Monday. Despite the compressed timeline, the decision to move from Boston to San Francisco in two days was a "no brainer." He explained, "It's like moving from the minor to the major leagues . . . a chance to upgrade myself so I'm in a place to swing."

Moving may be advantageous to their careers, but it has spiritual costs: it uproots people from the communities that nurture their religion. As a result, religion is one of the traditions that people may leave behind in the process of migration.[5] That's what happened to Ben Green, a twenty-nine-year-old tech entrepreneur. When he lived in New York City working as an investment banker, Ben was deeply involved in a Reformed Jewish synagogue. He observed Shabbat and did not work from sundown on Friday to sunset on Saturday, despite his demanding job. On Saturdays, he'd walk from his home on Forty-Eighth Street to his synagogue on Eighty-Sixth Street without a wallet or a cell phone, observing the Jewish religious law against mechanical devices and commerce on the Sabbath. Ben also took time out of his busy schedule to make regular trips to Israel with members of his synagogue. Since moving to San Francisco in 2010, however, Ben says, the influence of Judaism in his life is "not nearly as strong." He doesn't belong to a synagogue, nor does he observe Shabbat anymore.

South Asian immigrant tech workers also become less religious after moving to Silicon Valley. Most are Hindu and are separated from their families and the larger Hindu culture that nurtured their religion. For instance, Prakash Shankar was a devout Hindu when he lived in India. He practiced yoga every day and had even lived for a time in an ashram and studied under a guru. But after leaving India in 2006, his Hindu world felt very far away, and he stopped practicing altogether. Most of the South Asian immigrant engineers that I interviewed associated religious practice with family and home. They talked about praying as a family in front of the home shrine or watching their parents and grandparents practice yoga and meditate in the morning. Their attachment to these traditions weakened with their distance from their family and the social institutions that supported Hinduism.

People lose their religion in the process of moving, not only because they leave home, but because the Bay Area is one of the least religious regions of the country. According to the 2014 Pew Research Landscape Study, 35 percent of Bay Area residents are religiously nonaffiliated, compared to 24 percent in New York, 25 percent in Los Angeles, and 23 percent in the general population. Moreover, the Bay Area is less Christian than the rest of the United States. Only 35 percent of San Francisco residents identify as Christian compared to 71 percent of the general population. When it comes to weekly religious attendance, the Bay Area trumps all as least religious—only 22 percent of Bay Area residents attend religious services weekly, compared to 32 percent in New York and 34 percent in Los Angeles. Silicon Valley is not alone in having a weak religious culture. Low religiosity is common to what urban studies scholar Richard Florida calls "human capital clusters," or metro areas that have a high concentration of knowledge industries like technology. Places like Seattle and Boston, which have vibrant tech industries, are also among the least religious places in the United States.[6]

The experiences of John and others illustrate the effect of regional religious geographies. John is right when he attributes his Christianity to geography. On belonging to a church, he says, "Where we were from, it was just what you did." In the Bay Area, on the other hand, people say things like "I'm surprised when I learn that someone goes to church regularly," as one engineer told me. People experience a monumental shift in religious culture when they move from a devout region like Georgia to a nonreligious region like the Bay Area.

To be sure, millennials, who are the vast majority of tech migrants, are less religious than previous generations.[7] Yet religious geography affects millennials' religiosity too. Millennials maintain or even increase their religiosity when they move to places with a stronger religious presence. For instance, when millennial Susan Kim, a computer programmer who grew up in a Korean Christian home, moved from Southern California to New York in 2010, she continued going to church. She stopped, however, when she moved from New York to the Bay Area three years later. Similarly, Ben Green, who had been active in the Hillel House during his college years at Yale, became even more observant after he moved to New York City. But like Susan, he dropped his religious practice after moving to the Bay Area.

People have a hard time finding the right religious community in the Bay Area. For example, Ben Green tried to find a synagogue in San Francisco, but couldn't find a rabbi that he "could connect with." "The communities are more intact in the East Coast than they are here," he observes. Jacob Simon also claims that he was "a lot more active" in the Reformed Jewish community when he lived in New York than he is now in San Francisco. Similarly, Arjun Patel, who in Bangalore had been active in the Ramakrishna Mission, known as the Vedanta movement in the West, claims he didn't have the energy to attend the Vedanta Society in San Francisco, blaming the thirty-minute drive and twenty-minute hunt for parking.

Those who were religious emphasized how difficult it was to maintain their religion. Gwen Kowalski says that her family sticks out in the Bay Area because they attend Catholic mass on Sunday mornings. Her children's sporting events and their friends' birthday parties are all scheduled on Sunday morning when their family attends church. It wasn't like that where she grew up in Michigan, she claims. One tech worker and his family decided to move back to South Carolina because of the lack of religion in the Bay Area. Even though his work was thriving, he and his wife wanted their children to grow up in a close-knit church community, something they'd had trouble finding in the Bay Area.

Engineers especially feel their tech workplaces, which claim to want their employees to be "authentic" at work, are hostile to religion. Most people who are religious keep their religion a secret at work. For instance, a vice president at one large firm who belongs to a small religious community says he is "in the closet" at work about his religion. None of the colleagues of another vice president know that he has been the devout follower of a guru for the last twenty-five years. Few of one engineer's colleagues know that he is also a Buddhist priest. Christians also keep quiet about their religion.[8] One entrepreneur claimed that in the twenty-seven years that he's worked in Silicon Valley, he's met only a handful of fellow practicing Christians. A local pastor confirmed this observation, claiming that members of his congregations who work in tech claim they don't know other Christians at work. And Christian tech workers reported that they never brought up religion at work, fearing they'd be ridiculed or shunned in tech's aggressively secular culture.

But look a bit deeper, and Silicon Valley culture isn't quite as secular as it seems.

The Religion of Work

Tech migrants leave their religion when moving to Silicon Valley because of changes in religious geography. First, they are separated from their religious communities. And second, they move to one of the least religious parts of the country. But something else changes when they move to Silicon Valley, something that on the face of it has nothing to do with religion, but that, on closer examination, has everything to do with "being religious" in the new land of Silicon Valley. This new thing is also a source of identity, belonging, meaning, and purpose. It is the religion of work, and it is practiced in surprising ways.

Back in Georgia, John Ashton observes, work was different. "No one cared back there what I did for work or where I went to school. It was just what I did to pay bills." Things are different in Silicon Valley. "Out here, it's your identity," he says. "It's 'this is what my life's about.'" John started coding at the age of ten when his parents sent him to a coding sleepaway camp for a week during the summer. He'd always been a creative kid who tinkered with things—taking apart and reassembling toasters, radios, phones, lawn mowers, anything he could get his hands on. Once he learned to code, he programmed everything in the house, the thermostats and television controls. In high school he turned his basement into an arcade full of video games that he designed and built, charging friends three dollars for entry. John always thought of computers as his hobby, and the things he created as "quirky inventions."

After graduating with an engineering degree from Georgia Tech in 2005, John got a job programming for a bank in Atlanta. It was an easy nine-to-five job, with little supervision, which freed him to work on his many "quirky inventions" both on and off the job. One of his side projects was an application that he developed initially to help himself and other members of the ten-person church band coordinate their scheduling for practices and performances, and organize the collective database of hundreds of scores of music that they used. The app worked like magic for his small team of ten band members. John saw he could develop it for larger working teams. He started connecting with others who were developing similar products at tech fairs like South by Southwest in Austin. That's where he met Darren Tolman, the founder of Harmonize, a well-funded start-up in Silicon Valley that was developing a similar application. When Darren approached John to work for them, John jumped at the opportunity. Joining Harmonize in Silicon Valley was a chance, he explained, "to bring my game to the next level." John's creation was of a type that later became known as enterprise social networking apps.

In Silicon Valley, work took on a new significance and gravity in John's life. Back in Georgia, having an easy job, and thinking of the "quirky" program he designed as a "hobby," gave John the time and energy to cultivate his faith through his church by participating in Bible studies, playing in the band, and volunteering and serving on overseas mission trips. But in Silicon Valley, work wasn't nine to five anymore, and his computer programs were no longer fun, quirky hobbies. In Silicon Valley, John channeled all his devotion into work. Like religion, it demanded his faithfulness and sacrifice. For the first three years at Harmonize, John felt like he was working all the time, weekdays and weekends. He had built systems before, but they weren't products with users that he had to manage. He reflects, "The really interesting thing [that] happened is we started getting users, and that's when I just started putting insane hours to try to keep up with the problems that I created [laughs]. I mean I was doing a lot of work. Every time we had a release like I'd be up till four in the morning or something like that." The app became so popular that the servers were crashing almost every day. They couldn't staff the company with qualified engineers quickly enough. Work was frantic. Of his hours, John explains, "it got pretty bad. It got to the point where I was working probably fourteen hours a day pretty steady." He'd spend ten to twelve hours writing code and then three to four hours reviewing it. John would arrive at work at nine in the morning and stay till eleven at night, eating breakfast, lunch, and dinner there. Then he'd wake up and do the whole thing over again. To stay alert he started drinking drinks that had two to three times the amount of caffeine as Coke and Red Bull, with names like Bawls and Cocaine. Work took up so much time and energy in John's life that he had to sacrifice other things in his life—not just sleep, exercise, and having a social life outside of work, but also religion. In light of work being "pretty crazy," John explains, "finding a church wasn't a priority."

Beyond sacrifice and devotion, work also required something that up till now he'd directed only toward God: faith. John was acutely aware of the competitiveness of the valley. All the smartest engineers in the world congregate in the valley, John explained. They're hoping to beat the odds and "hit the jackpot," which he described as "you either IPO and become the next Microsoft or get acquired by Google or Facebook." But even among the most brilliant engineers, over 90 percent of their startups fail: they run out of money and dissolve. Given the odds, you had to have faith. You had to believe in things yet unseen. "You've got to drink the Kool-Aid," as John put it. "You have to believe your company is one of those one out of ten that's going to make it. . . . Otherwise why the hell would you do this?"

When Darren was recruiting him to Silicon Valley, John remembers, Darren offered him "the Kool-Aid." "I'll never forget this. He looked me right in the eye and said, 'If we do this right, we will change the way the world organizes work.'" Recounting that moment, John laughs and says he immediately thought of Darren, "I like you a lot, but you're crazy." Back in Georgia, John never had to "drink the Kool-Aid." His tinkering made wacky, personal inventions, and not products that would change the world or become the next Facebook. Becoming a tech entrepreneur required John to transform his relationship to his work. He had to become one of those "crazy" people who believed that his invention would change the world.

Work gave John a clear purpose in life, one that was not so different from Christianity—to transform the world one person, or user, at a time. Only John's work did it through technological products, not the Gospel. For entrepreneurs like John, changing the world isn't some idealistic, fantastical dream, but a mandate. Over the course of our conversation, John repeatedly used religious language. Changing the world was a "burden," much as some Christians call spreading the Gospel a burden. "We feel very burdened by, we have to come up with this thing that's going to change the world."

All this talk about believing in work, drinking the Kool-Aid, and the burden of changing the world would have felt strange and "crazy" to John back in Georgia. But in Silicon Valley it was normal. The company made work real, urgent, and immanent in Silicon Valley, just as the church made God real, urgent, and immanent to John in Georgia. Harmonize gave him a sense of community, belonging, and identity, like his church did.[9] John and his coworkers called themselves "Harmonizers." They hired engineers based on whether they could fit into the "Harmonizer" culture of having the capacity to work intensely but also goof off and have fun. John's life revolved around the brotherhood of other Harmonizers, who became his closest friends. He spent more time with them than he'd ever had with his church or Christian fraternity. Not only did they work together, but they ate three meals a day together, played together, and traveled together. In the winter, they rented cabins in Lake Tahoe and went snowboarding. And in the summer, they went camping and to Burning Man. They even made music together. John and a couple of coworkers jammed during their breaks. The start-up took up so much of John's time, energy, and devotion that he had none for anyone or anything else. When I asked him about dating, John said that he wasn't into meeting people online or through a set-up. But with so few women at work, his only chance to date would come from meeting someone randomly in a social setting. And that almost never happened because he was always at work.

For John, work wasn't contained within time and space. It was an omnipresent spirit that had become a part of him and infused everything that he did. Just as John's devotion to God hadn't been confined to Sundays at church, his devotion to work informed every part of him and at all times. John had crafted his Christian life in accordance with the biblical teaching to "be imitators of Christ." Now he crafted his work life to optimize his productivity. He stopped eating carbs to keep himself mentally alert. He practiced intermittent fasting to keep his thinking more lucid. He meditated to improve his focus. He drank coffee before his twenty-minute powernaps each afternoon so that he'd wake up refreshed and ready to work.

John never chose to leave Christianity. He'd had his doubts, like most Christians in a secular age. But he never had a crisis of faith or a break with the religion. Instead, his Christian faith slowly withered and died, like a sapling in the shadows of a giant redwood, choked off from water and light. The god of work was like the God of the Hebrews in Exodus, a "jealous God," who demanded exclusive worship. If believing in God and going to church was "just what you did" in Georgia, then believing in work and "drinking the Kool-Aid" is "just what you did" in Silicon Valley.

Work as a Source of Meaning

Although John had been more religious than most tech migrants, his story illustrates how work takes on the functions of religion, even for those who've never been religious. Silicon Valley firms are not alone in acting as "religions." Scholars have noted the similarities between work and religion in other intense, high-commitment careers, comparing the workplace to a monastery,[10] describing work as a "devotion,"[11] and as a source of "meaning, justification, purpose and even salvation."[12] The "religious" nature of work, however, is particularly intense in Silicon Valley. First, the geographic concentration and dominance of the tech industry creates a shared, homogeneous culture that defines the meaning of work (and life) in one place. Tech culture is not confined to one company but spills out into the general culture of Silicon Valley. Everyone in the Bay Area can feel the dominant presence of the tech industry: from the tech-oriented billboards lining Highway 101; from the ominous white and black double-decker buses checkering the roads that transport tech workers to and from work; and from the exorbitant cost of living pegged to high-tech salaries.

Second, Silicon Valley engineers tend to be young, single, and unattached "migrants," far from home and family, and therefore ripe to be "converted." Explaining his "religious" attachment to his company, one tech migrant from India told me, "I'm an immigrant. I don't have family, community, or a support structure." Immigrants to the United States have traditionally gravitated toward religious organizations because they offer sources of belonging and support that have been displaced in the process of moving.[13] But for the reasons discussed earlier—the regional weakness of religious affiliation in the Bay Area and the disinclination toward religion among millennials, who are the majority of the tech force now—today's tech migrants aren't turning to religion. In fact, when I asked about sources of community, my respondents of all generations responded much as did one tech professional in her early forties: "Community is a challenge around here." Most, especially millennials, could not identify a community outside of work that they felt a part of. Bereft of religious institutions and other sources of community, tech migrants seek "religious" resources through their workplaces.

Much as happened to John, work became more personally meaningful to most of my respondents after they moved to Silicon Valley. Some had worked in demanding industries before coming to Silicon Valley but nevertheless explained that work felt different now. For instance, entrepreneur Chris Hadley had worked at a prestigious management consultant firm in Manhattan, putting in sixty- to-seventy-hour weeks, before joining a start-up in Silicon Valley at the age of twenty-six. Even though tech's hours were comparable to management consulting, the work felt different to Chris. He described it as expressing something essential to who he was, saying, "It was the path that I wanted to follow . . . a side of me so desiring to express itself."

Because Chris was more personally invested in the Silicon Valley start-up than in the management consulting job, he worked all the time. Management consulting also had long hours, but with that job Chris could enforce boundaries to his work. In his start-up life in Silicon Valley, however, work was boundless; as he put it, work "is present in your life a lot of the time." Everyone in the company worked six days a week. And it was easy on his one day off to feel like, "oh, I just need to take care of something—and end up spending hours running analytics, creating reports, and mailing them out." To Chris, work wasn't a place or a thing contained in time or space, but something that had become a part of him. He explained, "I was mentally preoccupied all the time. Even when I wasn't at the office, I was still mentally working," a state that other engineers, especially entrepreneurs, also described.

Entrepreneur Mike Wong is another example of someone who experienced work differently after moving to Silicon Valley at the age of twenty-eight. He described his old job at the Department of Defense as "an obligation" that he had to fulfill because it funded his education. In contrast, the start-up was something that he "wanted to do" even given the high risk of failure and the low pay; he was earning below minimum wage after counting all the hours he worked on his $36,000 salary in 2012. Like Chris, Mike devoted most of his time to working. He was one of several engineers who would code for over sixteen hours in a day, hours he'd never put in for the Department of Defense.

Those who had moved from established firms to start-ups were the most likely to suddenly find work more meaningful. But many tech workers in large firms also found work meaningful. For instance, thirty-five-year-old Roshan Menon, a programmer from India, explained that when he worked in a large firm in New Jersey he had a different attitude toward work:

> I thought of work as just a job. I do my job. I get paid and leave. I've always been an IT guy; it's just fun and games for me. I don't get stressed out about it. You don't bring your worries home. I didn't want to think about work after I was done with work. I wanted to pursue other interests. I never considered work would be somewhere where I'd find any meaning. And, that has changed.

Now that Roshan works for a large Silicon Valley company, he describes himself as someone who takes "ownership" of his work, "that guy who's coming up with new products." Work is no longer just fun and games, nor is it confined to the workplace; it's something he thinks about all the time because, he says, "I really want to make a difference in the world."

People may wish their work to be meaningful and impactful, but 55 percent of American private sector employees consider their jobs "just what they do for a living," according to a study conducted by the Pew Research Center in 2016.[14] Only 4 percent of Americans say that their job or career is the most important source of meaning in their lives.[15] The gap between the ideal and reality of work is widest among millennials who, according to Gallup polls, want to find purpose in their jobs, and yet are the least engaged of all generations in the workforce.[16] In Silicon Valley, however, the vast majority of the people I met were people like John, Chris, Mike, and Roshan: millennials who found their work to be very meaningful and believed that it made a difference in the world. According to a survey conducted by PayScale, over 70 percent of employees at Apple, Google, and Facebook believe they are improving the world.[17] This creates a culture where people *expect* work to be meaningful. That was true for Greg Johnson, a twenty-six-year-old engineer who left his job creating graphics for video games because "it wasn't changing the world." He moved to his current company for its "culture of good." Greg was attracted to its mission of making the internet accessible to everyone, even the poorest, around the world.

When people come to Silicon Valley, they learn to expect their work to "change the world." This is not, however, how they thought of work, or the act of "making things," before Silicon Valley. In narrating their work histories, engineers often compared themselves to craftsmen and described their work as "making things." They told early stories of themselves as children and their love for "making things" with technology such as machines, computer programs, and movies. They said that their passion for "making things"—not making money or changing the world—drew them to engineering.[18] Money, in fact, was a trifling thing. One engineer explained that, to inventors, "Money's like toilet paper. You need it, but you don't want to spend your time thinking about it." "Making things" is a hobby and what engineers do for fun. For instance, on what he does for leisure after work, one engineer told me, "I would go home and write code for fun [laughs], read papers or watch videos from people giving talks about the design of this system or that system." Another engineer told me that in his free time, he learns new programming languages. In fact, people from the design and business side of tech often complain about clueless engineers who care only about building technologically sophisticated systems, but have no idea how the product will change the world and make money.

Once moving to Silicon Valley, engineers learn that "making things" is no longer just a fun "hobby," but that "things" must become "products" that will change the world. Things that were once created in the spirit of play and leisure are now endowed with a higher purpose. They take on the quality of being "sacred," set aside from the ordinary and worthy of devotion. This is what they learn in the hagiography of Silicon Valley: Out of humble dorm rooms and garages, Saint Bill Hewlett, Saint David Packard, Saint Bill Gates, Saint Steve Jobs, and Saint Mark Zuckerberg made things that transformed the world.

Hagiographies aren't just fanciful legends. They offer stories through which the faithful interpret and craft their own lives. It is no different in Silicon Valley's religion of work. Everyone in Silicon Valley is trying to change the world with their products. My interviewees spoke of their products using the language of transcendence and transformation that we often associate with religions. For instance, one entrepreneur described the work networking app his company created as "helping humanity thrive." Another entrepreneur told me that the mission of his digital gift certificate app was to "spread love." Yet another entrepreneur described the social networking app his company built as "leveling the playing field." I found this to be true not only among entrepreneurs in start-ups but also among engineers in large firms.

Having Faith in Work

I was perplexed by such claims. Could technologists really believe that helping people find parking spaces was "doing good," that connecting people to retailers for gift certificates was "spreading love," or that giving internet access to the impoverished farmer in rural Vietnam, who didn't even have reliable electricity, was a way to "level the playing field"? Religions require faith, and this is no different with the religion of work.

In his classic text on work and religion *The Protestant Ethic and the Spirit of Capitalism,* sociologist Max Weber identified religious faith as the source of the modern work ethic. Calvinists in seventeenth-century Europe developed a ceaseless work ethic because they believed that the fruits of their labor were proof that they were predestined for heaven. Three centuries later, faith and salvation are still a feature of work. But in our secular age, without the certainty of what Weber called an "other-worldly" heaven and hell, it's a faith that work offers salvation in *this world*—the assurance of purpose and significance in a capitalist cosmos.[19]

The story of how Cecelia Lau became unmoored during a "crisis of faith" in her company illustrates the importance of faith to work in Silicon Valley. Cecelia, a thoughtful and articulate Asian American woman with a chin-length bob, moved to San Francisco when she graduated from Dartmouth College in 2014. She was one of the few people I spoke to who didn't move because of work. Rather, she moved to follow her boyfriend, who was starting graduate school in chemistry at UC Berkeley. At first, Cecelia worked at a design agency, where she was "not inspired" and felt she "was making the world worse." When she found a new job as a user-experience designer at the medium-sized start-up Guru.com, Cecelia was ecstatic. Guru was a personal motivation app that people could use to track their goals and their progress on their phone. She loved creating a product that helped people achieve their dreams. Working at Guru was nothing like the design agency. Now she had a sense of meaning and higher purpose in her work. "I was working on something that had a positive effect on society," she explained. At Guru she found a community of like-minded "idealistic" people who believed in the work. By then, she had broken up with her boyfriend; deciding that "Guru will be my life," she threw herself into work. Soon, she became like the others: she ate breakfast, lunch, and dinner at work, and her social circle narrowed until it included only other Guru employees.

Everything changed, however, when Guru was sued and found liable for exaggerated claims about their product's effectiveness. Instead of saying that the app would make users more motivated, they could only say that it *might* make users more motivated. The company hadn't hurt any of its users, nor had it intentionally lied to them, as tobacco companies had. But the lawsuit crippled the company precisely because it unraveled the faith of its employees. Cecelia was "crushed." She and others became "disillusioned," prompting a mass exodus from the firm, including her, because they "couldn't bear to be associated with the company." Even now, two years later, Cecelia speaks about the incident with the pain of betrayal in her voice. Reflecting on work after the lawsuit, she said, "It just felt really meaningless for me. It was like it lost this higher purpose that I thought the company had." Cecelia and her coworkers could no longer believe in the work. The experience was so damaging to Cecelia and her "idealistic" Guru coworkers that many of them left tech altogether to pursue careers in nonprofits or attend graduate school.

As Cecelia's story attests, faith is a critical dimension of tech work.[20] People in Silicon Valley may not always use the word "faith," but they know that they need it. This feeling comes out obliquely, mostly in jokes about "drinking the Kool-Aid,"[21] or calling companies, including their own, "cults." But these jokes also hint that their faith is fragile. The tech faithful are susceptible to doubts, fears that their companies will fail or that their products will not change the world—that, ultimately, their work has no meaning. But in tech, as in the world of religion, "faith without works is dead."[22] Faith in work and devotion to work are symbiotic. The more people work, the more they need to "drink the Kool-Aid," and vice versa. In the end, tech workers are not so different from the Calvinists that Weber described in *The Protestant Ethic*. For both, faith in a tenuous salvation fuels their ceaseless work ethic.

Belonging: Companies as Faith Communities

Anyone who drinks the Kool-Aid knows that you can't do it alone. That's why both religions and companies are collective enterprises. They are "faith communities," communities that support the act of faith.[23] On one level, faith communities do this by articulating the articles of faith—the doctrines, creeds, and sacred texts and teachings. For most companies, and many other organizations, these articles of faith are their mission statement and statement of core values. For instance, Google's mission statement is "to organize the world's information and make it universally accessible and useful." Some of the company's professed core values are "don't be a copycat," "be open to change," "embrace transparency." But as religious clergy know, faith is fragile, and few people can "keep the faith" on doctrines, creeds, and teachings alone. They need the human connection and the sense of belonging and community that religions create.

As I've discussed, faith communities have always been important sources of belonging and identity in the United States. This is what the keen French observer of American life Alexis de Tocqueville wrote in 1835 in his classic *Democracy in America*. Over a century later in 1955, the religion scholar Will Herberg rearticulated this claim, arguing that religion, rather than national origin, would be the primary source of identity and belonging for immigrants and their descendants in the United States.[24] Herberg and Tocqueville are still right. But in twenty-first-century Silicon Valley, tech migrants form communities around their faith in companies, not the faiths that grew from Abraham. They talk about "joining" companies. They do not talk about joining congregations.

Tech companies create community through rituals of bonding, much as religions do. These are not the occasional company picnic, outing, or service project, but regular rituals that happen on a daily and weekly basis. For instance, one start-up has social activities every day at 5 p.m.: video games on Monday, Tuesday, and Thursday; board games on Wednesday; and happy hour on Friday. At another start-up where many of the employees are also artists, they have a weekly "hour of art," where people paint, draw, or engage in whatever creative activity they wish. A few start-ups have in-house bars where everyone gathers to drink at the end of the day. Google has its well-known "TGIT," or "thank God it's Thursday," where Googlers gather to watch owners Larry Page and Sergey Brin put on a comedy act, and different teams share what they are doing.

Some firms incorporate "small-group practices," a type of intentional subcommunity that is common in religious organizations.[25] For instance, several smaller companies have weekly sessions where employees gather to "check in" and share about their personal lives. The founder of one start-up even calls this check-in "prayer time." Larger companies build community through various leadership and professional development programs that group employees into small groups, which gather regularly to talk about their personal lives. The organizer of one of these programs calls them "sanghas," the Sanskrit term for a Buddhist monastic community. Other large companies build a sense of belonging and community by forming clubs based on shared interests or backgrounds, such as a hiking club or a Chinese club. On top of that, since most people I spoke to have two or more meals a day at the company, they have several opportunities every day to "break bread."

Tech professionals, for the most part, seem proud to belong to their companies. They take their company identities very seriously. Unprompted, they eagerly talk about their company's mission. They identify with their companies by wearing company t-shirts and sticking the company logo on their computers, water bottles, and backpacks. Some companies have nicknames for their employees. For instance, employees at Google call themselves "Googlers." The employees at one large firm say that they have an online forum devoted to discussing the virtues of their company mission and identity. At another firm, I observed a heated lunchtime debate among a group of engineers over whether an employee who filled two take-home containers with the last of the chicken on the serving dish at the company cafeteria was acting within the "compassionate" character of the company.

The "religious" bonds that employees develop with their coworkers are similar to those of another institution that forges intimate ties: the family. In fact, some, especially those who are alone and far away from home, even call the company their "family." This is the case with Hans Schneider, a twenty-seven-year-old engineer from Germany who was wearing his company t-shirt when I met him. His move to Silicon Valley was the first time he'd left Europe, and he described feeling "insecure." But Hans quickly found a family in the small start-up where he worked, calling his manager, Makenna, his "work mom." When he arrived, he had no place to stay—so he lived with his "work mom" for several months. Along with Doug the CEO, Makenna has taken Hans under her wing, spending time with him after work in the evenings and weekends, introducing him to yoga and meditation, and helping him build confidence and self-esteem. Hans, in fact, is much closer to his American work family than his family in Germany. Throughout his childhood his parents were emotionally distant and unresponsive to the fact that he was bullied in school. But in Silicon Valley, his work family gives him the support that his own family never did. Now, he says of his work colleagues, "I have this awesome family that I go to every day."

Hans was one of several people who underwent a "conversion experience" in their "faith communities" or companies. "Work conversions" are much like religious conversions, except that work converts find new identities and sources of self-worth through the workplace, not religion. Yasamin Ahmadi, an engineer in her late twenties who calls her large firm her "work family," is an example of a "work convert." A tall, personable, and poised woman, Yasamin says that she was shy, quiet, and lacking confidence when she first started at the firm four years ago. "If I had spoken to you four years ago, trust me, we wouldn't be having this conversation. My company has changed my life." Growing up in Iran, Yasamin says that she learned that women should be quiet and obedient. When Yasamin first started working at her company, she'd never speak in meetings out of fear that she'd look stupid. But through the help of her "work family," she's learned to have a voice and speak up. She credits her manager, Stephanie, for seeing her potential to be a strong leader and "never giving up" on her. About Stephanie, Yasamin says, "She's my best friend. She motivates me every step of the way, and she's known me very well, especially when I was going through my difficult times. She's been like a rock supporting me."

As work converts, both Yasamin and Hans expressed feelings of moral obligation and indebtedness to their "work families." Yasamin said, "I can't imagine leaving this company. I know I can get a really good job somewhere else, but I don't know why, I just can't." After a moment's pause, she reflected, "What they've given me these four years I don't think any company can offer me." Hans also expressed feelings of indebtedness to his company. He admitted that his company's technology isn't as cutting-edge as Google's (everyone compared their companies to Google), but Google could never give him his "awesome family."

Hans and Yasamin's stories suggest that, as Arlie Hochschild has argued, the relationships employees develop with their companies resemble the emotional and moral bonds of obligation that we associate with intimate, private institutions such as the family and religion.[26] When work is a source of meaning, purpose, identity, and community, as it is for so many of the people I studied in Silicon Valley, it draws from the same emotional well of devotion and duty typically reserved for family, friends, and religious community. Work in Silicon Valley is what sociologist Lewis Coser calls a "greedy institution." It vies for "exclusive and undivided loyalty," outmuscling family and religion when they get in its way.[27] Yasamin admitted that her sense of duty to her "work family" is even stronger than that to her real family. She claimed that her mother would scold her, "You can say no to me just like that, but you will never say no to your work family!" Yasamin confessed, "That's actually true. . . . I can say no to her just like that but I cannot say no to my company because they have helped me become who I am today." Although Yasamin's mother's observation is about the tension between work and family, it describes a general principle that extends to religion: loyalty to work competes with loyalty to other communities of commitment and moral obligation. The more you give to one, the less you give to another. Moreover, Yasamin's response, "I cannot say no to my company because they have helped me become who I am today," suggests that the reason some tech workers are so devoted to work is not because their companies are so demanding, but because *work is so giving*, a theme I explore further in the next chapter.

"Work conversions" are primarily shifts in belonging and loyalty. Tech migrants who lose their religion in Silicon Valley do so because they change faith communities—instead of belonging to a church, temple, synagogue, or mosque, they belong to work. Most people cannot explain why they are no longer religious because they think of religion as beliefs, rather than religion as belonging. No one left religion because of a crisis of faith or an intellectual disagreement with their religion. Rather, they left their religion because they now belonged to another community of faith—their workplace.

This is what happened to Thomas Kim, a Korean American programmer in his late twenties. When he moved from New York to Silicon Valley, he stopped attending church. In New York Thomas worked at a large firm that he described as "just a job": his hours were nine to five, with a one-hour lunch break. This left ample time and energy to be active in his Asian American church, where most of his friends were. In 2013, Thomas left New York and joined a start-up in Silicon Valley, citing "more opportunities for career advancement." He was right. In his small start-up, where it was always all-hands-on-deck, Thomas quickly moved up the ladder; in three years he assumed the kind of authority that it would have taken him "about twenty years" to earn at his old firm. Thomas described his own transformation as a leader in the start-up. Once, at a tech meeting, he had the exhilarating experience of speaking to a crowd of three thousand people. A shy introvert, Thomas had always been petrified of public speaking. At the meeting though, not only did he survive it, but he "nailed it." The start-up gave Thomas that same sense of self-worth, status, and belonging that the Korean church offered to his displaced immigrant parents when they migrated from Seoul to the United States and converted to Christianity. Thomas was no longer a nine-to-fiver, but someone whose life revolved around work: He worked all the time. All his friends were from work. Church was no longer a part of his life. Even the way Thomas looked had changed. His friends said that when he first moved to Silicon Valley he had thick glasses and wore "dad jeans." When I met Thomas, he sported hip sneakers and architectural glasses frames, had a green streak through his hair, and went by "Tom." Like John, Thomas did not consciously choose to leave Christianity; nor did he have a crisis of faith. Rather, he changed to whom he belonged. Instead of belonging to a church, he belonged to the faith community of work.

Those in ministry know that community is the foundation of belief and faith. The same is true for the faith community of work. Roshan Menon, a programmer at a large firm, underlined the importance of community to belief when I asked him about "drinking the Kool-Aid" at his company. He replied, "I'm not a person who'd go for that. . . . It's just a brand. . . . I couldn't care less." I pressed him on this, because only moments before he had spoken so passionately about believing in the company mission and about his desire to "change the world." He responded, "I'm loyal to the community," speaking of the close bonds that he'd forged with his manager and friends at the firm.

To be sure, tech workers are notorious for continually changing jobs and starting new companies. But community is also a dimension of the job hopping and serial start-up culture of Silicon Valley. When entrepreneurs start new companies, they bring their faithful disciples from earlier faith communities with them. Communities move together. The genealogy of tech companies is similar to the successive spawning of new religious communities through church planting, the development of new ministries, and schisms. Moreover, companies become impersonal and institutional as they grow, engineers complained. Continually joining or founding start-ups is how some engineers create and sustain the high that comes from belonging to a faith community. For instance, the close-knit executive team of one start-up expressed anxiety about achieving their goal of getting acquired. What would happen to their faith community if it got broken up with an acquisition, they wondered. "We'll just start another company," one person responded. In another time or place, the answer to the question might be, we'll start a commune, club, or church. This entrepreneur's response, however, indicates that work is the main way tech workers create and experience community.

When John Ashton says that Christianity was "a phase in my life, not something I do now," he is talking about his life before his conversion. His church now—headphone-clad programmers coding silently in rows of white desks—is very far from his church in Georgia, where they prayed, built orphanages, and sought to be "imitators of God." Coming from the other side, Cecelia, the user-experience designer who left tech, speaks about her former life with a sense of estrangement that's similar to John's about Christianity. The intense culture of the start-up—sharing three meals a day with her coworkers, working around the clock, changing the world—is all so distant and unbelievable to her now in her new life as a writer. When Cecelia and a former colleague who also left tech get together, she says, "we kind of laugh about that time together. Because we're like 'what happened?'" These examples show that you can't drink the Kool-Aid alone.

Nonbelievers versus True Believers in the Religion of Work

For 70 percent of my respondents, work is a vortex that devours everyone in its path. These tech professionals (excluding people in human resources) become "true believers." They join the "faith community of work" and "drink the Kool-Aid."

Who then, are the exceptions, the "nonbelievers"? Who doesn't drink the Kool-Aid? And what relationship do those holdouts have with religion? As it turns out, there is a clear demographic pattern to who becomes a "true believer" and who doesn't. "True believers" tend to be the young, single, and more recent migrants, who are also the majority of the tech workforce. "Nonbelievers," on the other hand, tend to be older workers (forty-plus) and people with families. I found one exception to the pattern. Religious people—people who identify with a religious tradition and belong to religious communities—are "nonbelievers" in the religion of work, regardless of age, family status, or timing of migration.

So what do people who are older, parents, or religious have in common? They are bound to communities outside of work that offer alternative sources of identity, belonging, meaning, and purpose.

Carl Jennings's experience at Zizi, a thirty-person start-up, offers insight into why some people are "nonbelievers." Carl, a quiet man in his mid-fifties with sandy hair and wire-rimmed glasses, preferred to wear slacks and ironed, collared shirts to work. He was hired as the chief financial officer (CFO) of Zizi for his years of experience and expertise. As the CFO, he was one of four people on the executive team, all of whom—except for him—were under the age of thirty-one. Carl was different from the rest. "I'm probably the least idealistic of the four," he admitted. Whereas the other three members of the executive team spoke to me about the company mission with great passion and optimism, Carl struck a more cautious tone, questioning the sustainability of their business model. He spoke softly, occasionally looking over his shoulder, concerned that others might hear him in his typical wall-less start-up office that offers little privacy. Carl's doubts manifested in other ways. He didn't participate in the company daily meditation at 2 p.m. Instead, he attended the weekly Taizé service at his church. Nor did he go on yoga retreats or ski trips with others. He explained: "So, you know, the three of them are single, and they all kind of get together a lot and mingle, and it's a very important part of our culture. People are going out. Other employees coming together for lunches on the weekend. Some going out to the movies together and going to live music together and having dinner at each other's houses, and I do none of that." Carl was also the only person to tell me that he didn't bring work home, even though he worked fifty-to-sixty-hour weeks, like the others I spoke to.

Why was he different?

Carl differed not because he was naturally skeptical or antisocial—but because he was devoted to something else. Explaining why he doesn't bring work home, he answered: "I have very, very strict boundaries. It's like 5:30 on Friday, I turn my phone email off, and I make a personal commitment not to open up my Chrome browser, which has my work email in it. But because of my"—he paused—"I have a wife of thirty-three years. I have three adult daughters." Carl's face softened, and his eyes brightened. "Feeding my marriage is incredibly important to me," he continued. "She's great. I love her. She's a great friend. . . . So my time with her is precious." Carl's heart and soul belong to something other than work—his wife and family. In addition to being a committed father and husband, Carl is an active member of his church, which he called a "great, great community," and plays in the church band every Sunday.

The other three members of the executive team are also involved in things outside of work: yoga and meditation, rock climbing, and cycling. They are a part of social networks; they attend hack-a-thons and meet-ups with other entrepreneurs. But none of them speak about being bound to their hobbies or networks with the sense of love and duty that Carl has for his wife, family, and church. None of their hobbies and networks demand the time, energy, and devotion that work does. Unlike Carl, the three other members of the team can give all of themselves to work. Being devoted to something other than work, however, can be a liability in Silicon Valley. When I ran into Zizi's CEO a couple of years later, he told me that everyone was still working there—except for Carl, who had been "let go."

The example of Carl and his company illustrates the key difference between true believers and nonbelievers in the religion of work. "True believers," who are young, single, and more recent migrants, are unencumbered and have few competing obligations. They are ready and willing converts to the religion of work. This was true for the three other members of the executive team, who were younger and single and had moved to Silicon Valley within the last five years. Carl, on the other hand, was fifty-four and had lived in the Bay Area for over thirty years. Work was a big part of his life, but not his whole life. "Nonbelievers" spend less time engaging in nonwork activities at work such as playing Ping-Pong or meditating. Their friendship networks extend beyond work. This makes "nonbelievers" less likely both to identify with the company, and to stake their sense of meaning and purpose in work. In short, work alone does not define them.

The Exceptionally Religious "Nonbelievers"

Not all young, single, and recent migrants become "true believers." Some religious migrants who are young and single become "nonbelievers"—they stay committed to religion. Why? How do they resist converting to the religion of work?

According to Weber, all world religions share a critical stance of judging this world against an ideal world that should be.[28] This "world-rejecting" dimension of religion offers followers a way to resist, separate from, and, in some cases, even transform "the world." Throughout history, religions have prompted some members to live differently and sometimes apart from "the world." Monasticism, sectarianism, religious communes, and new religious movements are all responses to this tension between religion and the empirical world that is.[29]

Religion does a similar thing in Silicon Valley. It offers its members an alternative sense of identity, belonging, meaning, and purpose to that of "the world" of work. Religiously based faith communities form tight bonds of kinship that act as bulwarks against the vortex of work. But the pull of work is exceptionally strong, and, to resist it, tech professionals must be *exceptionally* religious, and deeply embedded in their faith communities.

Timing is an important factor in determining who stays religious. Religious people tend to become involved in religious communities soon after moving to Silicon Valley, before work can claim them. Several religious people came to Silicon Valley with tight-knit religious networks intact. For instance, when Ed Baratheon, who's been the CFO in several start-ups, first moved to Silicon Valley in his twenties, his home church in Colorado set him up with Christian housemates. Establishing Christian ties early in his Silicon Valley career was critical to maintaining his faith: "I moved in and lived with believers from day one." They supported each other in their faith lives. He says that his Christian housemates "kept me grounded" during his roller-coaster career as a start-up entrepreneur.

Similarly, Jim Ward, a forty-eight-year-old vice president at a large tech firm, is a member of a small religious community, one with chapters worldwide. When he moved to San Francisco in 2005, finding the local chapter was one of the first things that he did. Jim has also lived in Paris, London, and New York, and in each of these places he sought out his religious community, which he describes as "home."

People are more likely to maintain their religions not only if they connect to religious communities soon after moving, but also if their religious interactions are frequent, regular, and personal. For example, although Ed Baratheon spent more than sixty hours a week with non-Christians at his start-up, he socialized with his Christian roommates every night when he went home. Lisa Chu and Mai Nguyen, recent college graduates who work at a large tech firm, also found Christian roommates early on who supported their active religious involvement. Lisa and Mai interact with Christians not only every day in their homes but also through their churches. For instance, Lisa goes to church on Sundays, attends prayer meetings on Mondays and Tuesdays, and hosts a Bible study and dinner at her apartment every Friday.

Protestants belong to especially demanding church cultures, where members are expected to spend a lot of time with each other despite having busy schedules.[30] For example, Lisa Chu, who interacts with fellow church members four days a week, works a relatively modest (for Silicon Valley) fifty hours a week. But people like Stan Li and Howard Chen, who work at least sixty hours a week, also make time to attend church on Sunday and Bible study on Wednesday, and to volunteer. They do this because they feel morally compelled to give to their faith communities. For instance, Howard calls his church "a commitment." He talks about being a deacon and helping with the youth ministry as ways of "serving" the church. Howard describes himself as a "steward" of his time and resources, which, he says, belong to God.

Religious people resist being swallowed by work by plunging into their tight-knit, hermetic religious communities. This is especially true for Protestants. Seventy percent of the close friends of Lisa Chu, who I mentioned sees church members four times a week, come from her church, and *none* are from work. Roger Kao, who leads a Bible study and goes on religious mission trips to Mongolia, claims that "99 percent" of his friends are from church. One person said that all the members of her "singles" Bible study group at her church married one another. The friendship patterns of religious people are nearly a mirror image of the "true believers," who claim the majority of their friends are from work. The two groups are not so different. Members of either can be so intensely bound and committed to their respective communities that they have no time and psychic energy to develop interests in things and relationships with people from outside. Hermetic social ecologies are common traits of other high-commitment institutions such as cults, the military, and monasteries.[31]

Protestants aren't the only highly committed "nonbelievers." Buddhists are too. For instance, Gil Goldman, a Buddhist engineer who moved to the valley in the 1970s and became a monk, has stayed intensely involved in the local Zen community. For the last forty years, he has led the 5:30 a.m. daily zazen at the Zen temple by his house. Similarly, as a Zen priest, Peter Lucas has maintained some of his priestly duties as well as his involvement with the Zen Buddhist community even after starting a software company in the 1990s. One of the few millennials to claim a Buddhist identity, Cecelia Lau attends a weekly dharma talk at her zendo and goes on regular retreats. Like Protestants, she also uses the language of moral obligation to describe her relationship to the zendo, considering it a "duty" to financially support it.

Religion offers members not only communities and identities set apart from work, but also systems of meaning that question and even oppose the Silicon Valley religion of work. Religious people draw from the "world-rejecting" tendencies of their religions to resist work's total claim over them.

Religious people take pains to differentiate themselves from the "true believers" in Silicon Valley. My religious respondents, who are mostly Christian and Buddhist, portray their religion as going against the grain of Silicon Valley work culture. Protestants are particularly apt to say they feel like they are swimming against the tide of Silicon Valley values of wealth, status, and success. Ed Baratheon is an example of this. He insists on driving an old Volvo despite being a successful serial entrepreneur. The valley's preoccupation with money and career, he says, "goes against biblical mandates." His Christianity reins in the rapacious appetite of work. Every morning on the train, he reads the Bible to keep himself on the "right track." "The church and Bible study," he claims, "are a check from drifting too far."

Howard Chen, an entrepreneur who's sold multiple start-ups and retired at the age of fifty, is another Protestant who is "in but not of" the Silicon Valley world of work. He acknowledges that he is "very well off" and that his "biggest spiritual challenge" is to maintain what he calls "Christian stewardship"—using God's gifts responsibly—in the midst of the Bay Area's extreme wealth. He says that living in the "high-tech bubble," it's easy to forget that most of the world does not share his material privilege and to get caught up in the area's status seeking and materialism. "If your friend drives a Tesla, you want one too," he says. Howard wards off the temptations of Silicon Valley by intentionally belonging to a class-diverse community of faith.[32]

Stan Li, the senior director of product development at a large tech firm, who works more than sixty hours a week, admits that maintaining his faith is "a constant struggle." For him, the "struggle" is to resist the Silicon Valley ethos that work is the source of identity and value, an ethos that makes it "easy to derive personal value from work" and "unnatural to put value in anything else." Stan describes both the pressure and the pleasure that comes from being consumed by work: "I felt that pressure to be working all the time by my peers and management. I don't think it was intentional. They were really excited about the product. And when you derive your personal value from work, I understand why you'd want to spend all your time at work." Stan had "troubling experiences" as the child of parents who pressured him to succeed financially and academically. His decision in high school to convert to Christianity was his way of rebelling against his parents' values, of saying, "my self-worth is more than a letter on a piece of paper." Today he faces the same struggle—this time not against his parents but against the Silicon Valley religion of work that would define his value by his success. Stan has to fight against the prevailing religion of work in order to be religious: "I'm always conscious to take myself out of work for church activities." Being religious also means that he doesn't engage in any of work's social activities, such as playing games or joining social clubs, and that he rations his work time so that he can spend his extra time with his church community. Stan's tight and frequent social ties with fellow Christians compete against work's gravitational pull.

Buddhists feel a more subtle tension with the religion of work. Buddhism liberates them from the "attachments" formed by the culture of the capitalist workplace, they say. For instance, Zen priest Gil Goldman claims that Zen "tak[es] the edge off my personal ambition." Buddhism, he maintains, opposes the instrumental logic that dominates work. According to Gil, true Zen practice is detached from trying to achieve any particular outcome: "In Zen practice we do not try to obtain anything. It is an end in itself." He continues, "The main point is to allow the mind to be quiet, to practice letting go of attachments." It is precisely the "grasping" quality of results-oriented behavior so common in tech that causes human suffering.

Cecelia Lau also defines her Buddhism in opposition to the instrumentalism of capitalism. She claims that she began to experience the truth of Buddhism only after letting go of her "attachment" to the "capitalist" worldview that "we're all supposed to be megaproducers and efficient." She reflects, "I'd been so used to being in the system where it's this very quick problem-solution-problem-solution, A-to-B formula. I realized how deeply that permeated my life and the way I viewed the world." Cecelia claims that shifting from an instrumental orientation to one where "the journey is the goal . . . changed my life and the way that I orient to the world." Once she accepted this Buddhist wisdom, she says that she felt free to leave tech and pursue writing more seriously.

Cecelia was one of a handful of my respondents who actually became *more religious* when she converted to Buddhism. Cecelia converted, however, when she became disillusioned and lost faith in work—not while she was fully immersed in her tech world and its beliefs. No longer caught in the vortex of work, Cecelia had the time, space, and energy in her heart and mind to accept a different kind of faith.

Among my religious interviewees, Cecelia is an exception: she left tech. For the rest, religion offers traditions, practices, and communities that orient them to work *differently* from their Silicon Valley peers. Some of these people prioritize religion over work—leaving work early to participate in religious activities, or in one engineer's case, taking two weeks off to do service work in Brazil's *favelas* with his church. Others subsume work into religion by making work a part of their religious practice. That's what Gil Goldman does. He considers the workplace a vehicle toward enlightenment, an idea that is captured in the Buddhist quote he shares with me: "Before enlightenment, chop wood, carry water. After enlightenment, chop wood, carry water." The stress and challenges of work, he says, are opportunities to cultivate Buddhist virtues of equanimity and compassion.

Some Christians also interpret work as a part of Christian practice. One compared tech workers to Israelites in Babylon who, despite being in exile, are called by their God to intermarry and cultivate the land they live in. In other words, despite aiming for heavenly salvation, they are still called to live in and bless the world they are in now. In both Christian and Buddhist interpretations, *work is in service to religion and not the other way around.*

Buddhists and Protestants both feel that they are swimming upstream against the prevailing Silicon Valley religion of work. And no one does it alone. They gain strength from their religious communities and the traditions that support their "countercultural" values and orientations. That's a critical difference from nonreligious people who critique Silicon Valley's religion of work. Nonreligious critics say things like, "I don't want work to be my whole life" or "there's more to life than work." They have interests that take them away from work—cycling, mountain climbing, hiking, yoga, Burning Man, meditation—all of which are common hobbies in the Bay Area. But for them, these are leisure activities that *offer a respite from* work, *rather than resistance to it,* as religion does.[33]

Religions, however, are singular in offering alternative narratives and practices of self and community against Silicon Valley's religion of work. Families can do this, too, but religions are particularly powerful in critiquing the culture of work because they do so in ways that are both systematized—embedded in a sophisticated and coherent tradition of religious teachings, texts, practices, and rituals—and collective—shared with a community that reinforces these alternative values and norms about the meaning of work. Moreover, religious people not only interact regularly with religious communities that think of work differently; they feel morally bound to those communities.

These "religious exceptions" illustrate the extraordinary collective effort that it takes for technologists to resist the religion of work and maintain their religious traditions in Silicon Valley. Young tech migrants who find shelter in the folds of religion are less likely to get pulled into living entirely at work. But being religious is especially challenging in Silicon Valley, where religion's influence is weaker than in other parts of America. Moreover, the workplace claims so much devotion, duty, time, and energy that tech migrants often don't have much left to give elsewhere. It is easier and more natural to assimilate into the faith communities of their companies, which offer a ready and resonant source of identity, community, and meaning.

In one of the most celebrated essays ever written on Silicon Valley, journalist Tom Wolfe attributed the founding of Silicon Valley's tech culture to religion.[34] He traced the discipline, austerity, and zeal of early founder Robert Noyce, who invented the silicon chip in 1959, to his midwestern Protestant roots. Noyce and other early founders eventually "slowly walked away from religion." But religion never walked away from them. Religion, Wolfe writes, was "sewn in the lining of their coats." Intel, the firm Noyce founded, "wasn't a corporation; . . . it was a congregation."

Some things haven't changed much since Robert Noyce. Silicon Valley is still in the business of silicon and the sacred. And the vast majority of Silicon Valley tech workers continue to be migrants—like Noyce was—who find belonging, meaning, and identity in the "congregation" of their companies. But if religion was "sewn in the lining" of tech entrepreneurs' coats back then, they are now more apt to wear it on their sleeves of their hoodies. Silicon Valley firms have taken up the pastoral mantle of spiritual care, the topic I turn to in the next two chapters.

CHAPTER 2

Corporate Maternalism

NURTURING BODY AND SOUL

If work is replacing religion, it's not just because tech workers are looking for religion at work. Companies are actively bringing spirituality into the workplace. That's what I learned from people like Linda Alvarez, a vivacious senior leader in human resources at a large firm I'll call Gateway Tech. "Well-being is not just about the physical," she says, but also an integrated state of physical and spiritual well-being that Linda refers to as "wholeness." Bringing "wholeness" to people is her life passion. Before coming to Gateway, Linda worked at a food retail company with a large, unionized workforce. Her responsibility was making the workplace compliant with union regulations, a job she wasn't excited about. Moving to Gateway, she says, resonates with her life calling to nurture spiritual well-being. There, she creates "an environment where people feel whole when they come to work."

A practicing Roman Catholic who describes herself as an "equal opportunity employer" of all spiritual and religious traditions, Linda is an avid consumer of the Bay Area's abundant spiritual marketplace. She's taken workshops on spiritual healing modalities such as shamanism, reiki, neurolinguistic programming, and the Enneagram. She integrates the knowledge from these workshops into her work at Gateway. Her tidy office is "an invitation to be more fully whole." The well-known Christian Serenity Prayer hangs from her door. On the wall, Linda has a collage of the people and symbols that are most meaningful to her—the Virgin of Guadalupe, the Dalai Lama, a Christian cross, and a Buddhist lotus. The collage encourages others to follow her lead and say, "I fully embrace who I am and I bring it all" to work. When employees come to her office, she hands them mantras from her basket of meditation stones on her desk: Be. Stillness. Breathe.

At Gateway, Linda started a workshop that teaches spiritual practices such as meditation, mindfulness, and journaling. The workshop seeks to give employees time to pause and space to reflect, away from their busy lives—all while they are at work. Linda has converted a conference room into a meditation room, where employees can go to meditate or pray. She has also started a lunchtime meditation program, where employees can sit in meditation three times a week. In these sessions, meditation instructors read from spiritual texts, from poems to religious scriptures, such as the Bhagavad Gita or the Bible.

Gateway Tech is not alone in bringing spiritual care to the tech workplace. Spirituality is now one of the many perks of the Silicon Valley workplace, along with free meals, smoothies, gyms, and massages. Companies such as Google, Apple, Salesforce, and LinkedIn now have dedicated meditation rooms in their buildings.[1] Salesforce's San Francisco office has them on each floor. Many companies are teaching their employees meditation. Perhaps most well-known is Google's Search Inside Yourself, a six-week elective course that Googlers refer to as "going to church." The founder and facilitator of the program, Google engineer Chade-Meng Tan, says the purpose of the course is to "develop high-resolution awareness on demand," which "has the effect of increasing productivity." But the all-star line-up of Buddhist luminaries that Tan brings to Google, such as Jack Kornfield, Sharon Salzburg, and Thich Nhat Han, contemplate productivity less than topics such as the nature of suffering and how to cultivate compassion. The influence of Search Inside Yourself has expanded beyond Google's walls. It is now a freestanding nonprofit organization that teaches meditation to business leaders all around the world.

Other tech companies have followed Google's lead, bringing high-profile spiritual teachers to their campuses. Salesforce's annual megatech conference Dreamforce dedicates one of its three days to the well-being of the soul. Well-known spiritual leaders like Deepak Chopra and Wayne Dyer teach participants how to live mindfully, introducing them to Buddhist concepts such as karma.

Linda Alvarez is one among many human resources professionals I met in Silicon Valley who consider caring for the physical and spiritual well-being of their employees to be part of their job. Why do tech companies care about this? In the previous chapter, I explored how work becomes religion from the vantage point of tech employees. In this chapter, I look at the other side: why companies take on the physical and spiritual care of employees—concerns that typically belong to institutions like the family and religion. What does it look like when company leaders decide to take care of their employees' whole selves? What's in it for them?

The Problem with Burnout

To see why corporations care for the physical and spiritual well-being of their employees, we must first understand one of tech's most pressing problems. When I asked people in human resources what the biggest industry problem might be, their answer was unanimous: "Burnout." One human resources professional even described her job as "taking care of employees so they don't feel burnt out." According to Sarah Kim, the human resources director of a medium-sized start-up who used to work in the clothing industry, burnout is what makes tech companies different. "They expect a lot. So when you work for tech—you're kind of working all the time." She describes the typical workday for engineers at her start-up as "starting at ten in the morning and ending at ten in the evening." Burnout is typical in her start-up, she says, and most employees last for only two years. Another human resource professional at a large firm said of tech culture, "There's no time; you run, not walk, to your meetings," and "you're drinking out of a fire hose." One seasoned human resources director called the problem a "disease of pace" that afflicts engineers at his company, making them the "oldest thirty-year-olds I've ever seen."

Sociologists consider working over fifty hours a week to be "overwork."[2] But in Silicon Valley, working fifty hours is considered a light week. Most engineers have difficulty quantifying their work hours because work is so consuming and uncontained. After scratching their heads, most engineers report that they work somewhere between fifty and sixty hours a week, but that's not including the regular emailing and phone meetings outside of work. In Silicon Valley, overworking is "just what you have to do." Young male engineers often describe their work hours using diminutive qualifiers such as "just" or "only" such as "just sixty hours, but I get to work whenever I want," or "oh, nothing crazy, I only work about fifty-five hours a week." One engineer said that in the first three years of his start-up, he worked fourteen-hour days, seven days a week, and shrugged it off as par for the course. In tech, overwork is a badge of pride.[3] One serial start-up entrepreneur claimed brazenly that he works "anywhere and anytime."

But chronic overwork takes a toll. I heard harrowing stories from burnt-out tech professionals who in their prime of youth should have been healthy and vibrant. Among these tech casualties were a twenty-six-year-old woman whose immune system was so overwrought that she came down with mono; a twenty-nine-year-old man who had a nervous breakdown; a thirty-two-year-old woman who developed a mysterious illness that left her unable to work for a year; and *three* men in their thirties who experienced temporary paralysis for months. In addition, people also reported the more common symptoms of burnout: exhaustion, irritability, inability to focus, and headaches.

Employees *choosing* to work too hard is a strange and rare dilemma in the history of labor management. Throughout the history of modern capitalism, most companies have been trying to get their employees to work faster and longer. Understanding burnout as a problem now reflects a fundamental shift in how companies view their skilled labor in a knowledge economy: as assets to be developed rather than costs to be cut.[4] In an industrial economy, the means of production are machinery and natural resources. In a knowledge economy, however, "the means of production is knowledge, which is owned by knowledge workers and is highly portable," according to management scholar Peter Drucker.[5] That makes educated workers and their skills the company's *most valuable assets.*

Burnout is a problem because it exacts a financial toll on companies, according to human resources professionals. It is the literal depreciation of company assets. Employees who are not well become liabilities. Sick employees cost the company in higher health-care bills and absenteeism. The typical ailments that plague most tech workers, such as stress, anxiety, and lack of sleep, may not require hospitalization but are still deadly. Human resources professionals would often list a litany of costs related to employees who are unwell: increased errors, lack of motivation, depression, and mood contagion. And they declaimed its costs in dollar terms: "One million people miss work each day because of stress"; "job stress costs American companies $300 billion dollars"; "we lose 10 IQ points when we're stressed."[6]

These costs make employee wellness a company problem and not a personal one, according to human resources professionals. Employee burnout is as damaging to tech companies as machine breakdown or depleted natural resources are to manufacturing companies. One person put it this way:

> Your biggest and most expensive and most important asset walks out of the door every day and voluntarily walks back in. The capital of the building, the tools, the infrastructure, the carpet is the least important part. That part behind your forehead is really expensive and very important. How do we take care of the part that carries it around, including the one that allows that to do its best work?

And so when companies "take care" of the person, or "the part that carries" the brain "around," they expect a return on investment (ROI), according to human resources professionals. Workers who are "well," they reported, are more productive, can work longer hours, and are more creative and resilient. One person purported to quote the exact ROI on employee well-being, contending that "organizations that pay attention to the health, wellness, and happiness of their employees have a

27.4 percent average operating margin compared to traditional companies that only have a 14.7 percent margin." Management thinks that caring for employee well-being is profitable.

Burnout, I learned, isn't a result of employees working "too hard." Tech companies expect people to work very hard. Rather, managers see burnout as a result of insufficient self-care, something that happens when employees neglect what Karl Marx called "the reproduction of labor power," things like eating and resting that maintain the worker's ability to work. Employees don't burn out if they have the proper care, which includes not only eating and resting, I was told, but also engaging in interesting hobbies and connecting with friends and "the Universe."

Back in 1867, Marx recognized the quandary of work and the limits of time, a problem we now call "work-life balance." "Within the 24 hours of the natural day a man can expend only a definite quantity of his vital force," he wrote. "During part of the day this force must rest, sleep; during another part the man has to satisfy other physical needs, to feed, wash, and clothe himself. Besides these purely physical limitations, the extension of the working-day encounters moral ones. The labourer needs time for satisfying his intellectual and social wants."[7] The working capacity of humans, Marx explained, is limited by their "physical needs" and "intellectual and social wants." This leaves the tech industry in a bind. If workers spend too much time and energy working, they cannot take care of themselves, and they will deplete company assets. But any time employees take to care for themselves is time they are not working.

Moreover, the problem of employee care is not just one of time, according to human resource professionals. Many believe that left to themselves, most tech workers will run themselves into the ground. They attribute workers' self-neglect to the driven personalities that are drawn to tech. "They work so hard!" the director of wellness at one large firm exclaimed about its engineers. "Their bodies can't sustain that level of work. They aren't forced to work so hard, but they are so aspirational and passionate." The director of wellness at another firm explained that its engineers were "perfectionists" who couldn't stop themselves from working and burning out. Passion, aspiration, and perfectionism—

the qualities that make them good tech employees—also make them prone to self-neglect.[8]

What are companies to do about burnout? Silicon Valley managements' solution is to take the personal care of employees into their own hands.

Corporate Maternalism

Back in 2000, when Google's office was just a living room and Mark Zuckerberg was still in high school, Susan Lamott was the vice president of talent and development of a small tech firm called Tech Pointe—and discovered a small perk that transformed how employees there worked. A former elementary-school teacher and principal, Susan was known for being both caring and capable. She thought that human resources was a lot like being a principal; both jobs were about nurturing a community of growing individuals. Her firm had an intense work culture, where engineers worked around the clock. According to Susan, "people were working too hard." Tempers were flaring, and people were falling asleep at their desks. Employees routinely missed lunch and got home so late that they missed dinner too. As a former school principal, Susan had seen something like this before. And she knew the consequences were serious. Students, often from impoverished backgrounds, would underperform at school because they didn't have enough food and rest. With the stress of poverty—unstable housing, absent parents who are working all the time or looking for work, lack of food—kids would come to school exhausted, with foggy heads and grumbling stomachs. Students couldn't learn under those conditions. The Tech Pointe engineers reminded her of those kids. They might not have been financially impoverished children—but they were time-impoverished adults who couldn't properly take care of themselves. They were burnt out. To Susan, the results were the same: members of the community weren't performing up to their potential.

"Listen, why don't we just bring in lunch, because these people aren't eating lunch, and then they're not going home to dinner, and then everything's getting cattywampus," Susan suggested to the CEO. The firm started providing hot lunches three times a week, a move that Susan compared to Head Start, a program for underprivileged students that among other things, provides free breakfast in school.

No one could have predicted how much free lunch would change everything. People in the company were thrilled. Not only did the meals physically nourish them, but, according to Susan, the meals "spiritually nourished" them. The energy of the company transformed. According to Susan, employees started feeling that "the company cares about me," and their attitudes toward work shifted from "stress" to "I want to produce and drive that engine forward." Susan's free-lunch experiment prompted her to start other programs to promote employee health and happiness, such as yoga classes and community volunteering.

Susan's introduction of hot lunches, yoga, and community volunteering to her firm is an example of *corporate maternalism*, where companies provide for the personal care of their employees to make them happy, healthy, and (therefore) productive. Tech companies have not disrupted the laws of the market. There still is no such thing as a free lunch, really. Corporate maternalism monetizes the nonproductive parts of life that the busy tech worker otherwise has no time for—eating, exercising, rest, hobbies, spirituality, and friendships—and makes them a part of work.

While women are a distinct minority in tech, they do the majority of the work of corporate maternalism—not surprisingly, since women dominate most of the occupations that attend to personal needs.[9] The departments running corporate maternalism include human resources, a traditionally feminized and lower-status corporate profession, along with its affiliate departments such as Wellness, Learning, and Development, and Leadership and Talent Development.[10] These employees are the company "mothers" who care for employees, ensuring that they are in tip-top shape to compete in the race for technological innovation.

Corporate maternalism reflects the relational shift between companies and their high-skilled labor in the knowledge economy. In the past, human resources managed workers defensively by "protecting the company from its employees," as one person put it, by enforcing compliance. Now human resources "protect" the company by caring for its most valuable assets, its high-skilled employees. Susan Lamott illustrates this change in her view of a "great HR organization." According to her, the problem with most human resources departments is that they are mired in the old way of doing things. They are merely concerned with "bean counting and 'Did you get your compensation papers in?'" She identifies "the conundrum of a great HR organization" this way: "How do you nourish people's souls when they are working so hard to make the corporation more money?" Susan isn't alone in thinking about how to "nourish people's souls." I was struck by the maternal language others in human resources used. They describe their jobs using words such as "care," "support," and "nurture." "Taking care of you so you can work," is a typical description. "Give [employees] avenues to bring out their best potential and to take care of their bodies" is how another describes her role in the company.

Elizabeth West has worked in human resources in Silicon Valley for over twenty years. She notes that the changes in nomenclature for human resources reflect the change in focus from employee compliance to employee personal development. As she puts it, "Human resources used to be called 'personnel,' and then 'human resources,' and now it's called 'learning and development.'" To move away from the sterile and mechanical term "human resources," many companies are opting for more humane titles such as "people operations" and "people development." Those shifting terms reflect how at one time tech companies treated employees as "resources" like machines, but now treat them like "plants that need to be watered and nurtured," as one human resources professional put it.

At one time engineers disdained the staff in human resources, most of whom lack the requisite engineering background to garner respect in tech. One retired executive said that in the 1990s, the engineers in his company referred to "HR" as "human remains." Throughout the history of the male-dominated modern corporation, human resources has been considered low status and compensated accordingly.[11] Although this is still generally true, corporate maternalism has made human resources more likable to employees. Many tech workers I interviewed acknowledge and reciprocate the maternal affections of human resources, using words like "coddle," "care," and "pamper" to describe the work that they do. When Cecelia Lau, a user-experience designer, moved from a traditional design firm to a tech firm, she says she felt "coddled" and exclaimed, "Oh wow, this is comfortable!" "The ones taking care of getting the Safeway and Costco deliveries, keeping the fridge stocked" is how one male engineer describes human resources, a position that he observed is largely done by "women and gay men." Another engineer explained that HR arranges weekend entertainment by getting hard-to-come-by theater and concert tickets for employees. Jack Liu, an engineer in his early thirties, reflected on the head of human resources, who does happen to be a gay White man:

> They kind of become mom. They take care of us. They're the ones who get us all the food. They're the ones to tell us that we didn't put the dishes in the dishwasher and we should, right? Every day at 3 p.m. there's chopped vegetables, and we have this thing that's a picture of Darth Vader, and it says, "Luke, eat your vegetables." And then there's always fresh-cut fruit in the morning, and that doesn't come out of nowhere. I know they spend a lot of time doing that. . . . He just takes care of us and he does a really good job, like knowing that we'd get a giant kick out of the Darth Vader thing.

To Jack, human resources staff are like "mom," who takes "care of us." They take care of the domestic chores of cooking and cleaning, disciplining children, and even cajoling them into eating their vegetables. The care is so personalized that the head of human resources even knows to tack up a kitschy poster of Darth Vader.

The Personal Is the Professional

Over its history, modern capitalism has offered different versions of corporate care. Most notably, starting in the 1880s, companies like the Pullman Car Company and Ford Motors practiced what scholars call "industrial paternalism."[12] Companies provided employees with lunchrooms, recreational facilities, theaters, and housing. Industrial paternalism was also a program of forced assimilation for a largely immigrant and working-class labor force. At Ford Motors, company "social workers" inculcated habits of "clean living" that conformed to those of the White, Protestant middle class and enforced them by docking pay.[13] By the 1920s, most companies had abandoned these totalistic and controlling practices because they were unpopular with employees. In the middle of the twentieth century, companies like Kodak and Sears also took care of their employees by offering generous benefits and lavish lifestyle amenities such as cafeterias, bowling alleys, and swimming pools. These provisions were a form of social engineering, designed to make employees identify with management rather than unions.[14]

Corporate maternalism is Silicon Valley's twenty-first-century version of corporate care, replacing the coercive style of earlier management with the holistic therapeutic approach of California mind-body-spirit. Corporate maternalism is based on the principle that I call *the personal is the professional.* That's the widely accepted idea among Silicon Valley human resources professionals that human workers are "integrated" and "whole people"—not automatons who leave their selves at home—and that because of this, their personal lives bear on their professional performance. Human resources professionals in tech, many of whom are interested in Asian spirituality and mind-body practices, see *the personal is the professional* as a more humane and enlightened approach in a cold, hard tech world dominated by machines, numbers, and, not coincidentally, men. Susan Lamott, the human resources innovator we heard from earlier, draws from her experience in weaving to compare the "whole person" to "the whole cloth, the whole tapestry." She believes it's important to understand that there's a seamless connection among the threads of physical, mental, and spiritual well-being and productivity.

Most people today would probably agree that some parts of our personal lives affect our work performance. It's difficult to concentrate when we are hungry or sleep deprived. The stress from a fight with a family member or friend distracts us from doing our best work. The absence of close and meaningful relationships can leave us feeling unmotivated at work. The idea that companies are at least partially responsible for the personal care of their employees is embedded in legislation such as the Family and Medical Leave Act of 1993 and company benefits such as health care, retirement, and disability. Many Silicon Valley firms that I observed use a holistic approach to apply *the personal is the professional* to all of life. They take care of not only health care and retirement, but also meals, exercise, hobbies, personal relationships, and spirituality. In this context, spirituality is just one of many dimensions that make up the "whole person."

The "WQ Test," or Well-Being Quotient Test, of the start-up Star Bright is an excellent example of *the personal is the professional* at work. Every Friday afternoon, Greg Hopkins, the company's thirty-year-old founder and CEO walks around the office reminding every employee to take it. The WQ Test is an anonymous online survey that asks employees to rate their level of satisfaction from 1 to 10 on various dimensions of their lives, such as health, love, spirituality, work and career, money, and personal development. The company is "the team," and they collectively win or lose together. The team achieves what Greg calls "happy happy" when the team collectively scores an average of eight or above. Taking the test is not required, but it is strongly recommended. While the individual scores are anonymous, the survey tracks who submits ratings—and Greg keeps tabs on this. It's no surprise, then, that participation is "at about 100 percent." Rubbing his hands in excitement, Greg reports, "We were at 8 last week. We went up to 8.5 this week! It makes me so physically elated and happy when our numbers are high!" Self-care is a mandate at Star Bright. "Everyone knows that if you're not taking care of yourself, you're not playing for the team," Greg says.

On Monday mornings, the team reviews its score at their weekly check-in. For an hour, they sit in a circle and share how what's going on in their lives is reflected in the survey. At one Monday meeting, Vijay, an engineer in his twenties with curly black hair and thick glasses, tells the team about a recent date. Greg is pleased and hoots and claps loudly. He tells me later that he's so happy for Vijay, who has suffered from low self-esteem because he hasn't had much of a romantic life. Vijay is shy, Greg says, and he doesn't know how to ask women out. Greg arranged for Vijay to work with an executive coach who helped him build his confidence as a leader, which included developing the skills to ask women on dates—something I learned is not unusual in corporate coaching. It worked. Vijay tells me that, since working with the coach, his life has changed: "I'm going on a couple [of] dates every week!"

In addition to increasing Vijay's "love" rating, the company also helped raise his "spirituality" rating. Star Bright encourages its rising leaders to attend an all-expense-paid weekend retreat with the Landmark Forum retreat, a spiritual/self-help program that Greg calls "cheap enlightenment." Vijay says that the retreat helped him confront the childhood trauma of feeling like a failure against his parents' impossibly high expectations. "I'm so much more of a whole person, in terms of emotional intelligence and being in touch spiritually," Vijay claims. "Spirituality is one of the areas where I rate a ten every week."

Vijay's romantic and spiritual well-being have been a boon for the company, according to Greg. "When Vijay started dating, it was like such a breakthrough!" Vijay's newfound confidence in his personal life has transferred into his professional life. He claims that he's more assertive, poised, and articulate. Vijay's been promoted to lead engineer and now comes to work confident, energized, and full of new ideas, according to both him and Greg.

While the WQ Test is an extreme example of how tech companies intervene in their employees' personal lives, it vividly illustrates the assumption behind the idea that *the personal is the professional*: that people produce and perform their best when their bodies, minds, and spirits are in the optimal condition, and that it therefore is in the corporation's interest to care for and "optimize" the personal dimensions of its employees' lives. That includes their diet (those ubiquitous "free" lunches and snacks), their exercise regimen, their hobbies, their family relationships, their romantic lives, and their spirituality. To be sure, companies vary widely in how intimately and comprehensively they apply *the personal is the professional*. But none of the human resources professionals I interviewed challenged this assumption. This has profound implications.

First, *the personal is the professional* challenges traditional workplace assumptions that separate the personal self from the professional self. The vast majority of my respondents, both inside and outside of human resources, dismissed the idea that there is a distinction between "work" and "life." Gwen Lewis, a forty-year-old pragmatic and no-nonsense head of learning and development at a medium-sized tech firm, described the integration between the professional and personal in her own life. "It feels like, 'well, you can run on your own or get your own gym membership.' That's your 'personal life.' And my feeling is [pause] you don't check who you are—physically, mentally, spiritually—at the door when you walk into work."

Patrick Sullivan, an executive at a large firm, also rejects the idea that our lives can be separated into different boxes labeled "work" and "life" and "spirituality." He says that his spirituality "is just a dimension of who I am . . . and so for me it makes no sense that that does not show up at work." Similarly, personal issues, like a bad day at home, bleeds into a bad day at work and vice versa: "Your issues show up at work." Mike, the CEO of a start-up, says, "My life is now. I'm at work. I'm living. If you think that you're not living when you're at work, you're selling yourself short." Similarly, Makenna, a member of the executive team of another start-up, says, "There is no such thing as life and work. It's one big life!"

Second, *the personal is the professional* has radical implications for the role that corporations play in employees' personal lives. We see this in Vijay's experience. Star Bright's CEO believes the company reaped returns on its investment in Vijay's romantic and spiritual life, areas that, outside Silicon Valley, have no obvious bearing on his work. Anne Simmons, a veteran in leadership and development, explains the approach this way: "You build a person, and it shines through all areas of their life." Like others in the industry, she compares the work that her unit does to the coaching of high-performance athletes who make certain that their athletes' diets, sleep, emotions, and spirituality are in the optimal states to compete. She quotes former Chicago Bulls coach Phil Jackson, one of America's most famous Buddhists, as saying, "My approach is to relate to a player as a whole person, not just a cog in a basketball machine." Anne interprets this as meaning that you cannot separate athletic performance from the personal dimensions of a player's life—and by extension, that you cannot separate on-the-job performance from personal well-being.

That philosophy helps explain corporate maternalism's relentless focus on the physical care of employees. For instance, in addition to offering three meals a day to make healthy eating easy and convenient, companies teach employees how to eat nutritiously. At one company the cafeteria tables were dotted with standing flyers that offer "tips for a healthy life," reminding employees to drink eight glasses of water a day. In another example, I listened in on the conversation of a group of engineers discussing how the company had rearranged the snack counter to encourage healthy eating. They made the fruit and nuts easily accessible at the front of the counter but put the "unhealthy snacks" such as candy and cookies in jars with screw tops at the back. Another engineer told me that his start-up generally provides fruits and vegetables and no unhealthy snacks like chips. At another start-up, the CEO offered me a sandwich bag full of trail mix and dried fruit that, he claimed, the company secretary "loves to make" every morning for the employees. And during my visit to another company, a member of the wellness department showed me a small glass room in the center of the cafeteria where a chef stood behind a counter surrounded by male employees in their twenties. "That's where we hold classes on mindful eating and cooking," he explained. "We teach people how to eat mindfully, so they learn to savor their food and eat with intention. We also . . . teach them to cook so they don't eat junk over the weekends."

The personal is the professional also mandates attention to the interior care of employees. Stan Mitchell, director of wellness at a firm with a "sustainable high performance" program, blames burnout on the workers' own psyches, not the company's expectations. Drawing on a survey the company conducted, he argues that the primarily young male engineers in his firm are "driven to perform by internal pressure and not from their managers," an observation echoed by others in human resources in various tech firms.[15] Stan explains that many of his firm's engineers feel insecure there. In high school and college, these young men were often the best programmers in the room. But in Silicon Valley, they are just like everyone else. "They are perfectionists," he says, "who fear they aren't as good as their coworkers." Employees get burnt out,

Stan maintains, not because of the workload, but because employees place on themselves impossible and fear-driven expectations. Stan thinks his job in the wellness department is to help these young men develop skills to manage their fears. His department teaches engineers mindfulness, reflection, emotional self-awareness, self-regulation, and resilience, so that they can "sustain high performance" *all* the time.

Another firm calls its program the Well-Being Journey. Here, employees participate in an anonymous well-being assessment based on questions such as, "My relationship with my spouse, partner, or closest friend is stronger than ever," "My life has an important purpose or meaning," "Did you smile or laugh a lot yesterday?," and "Did you exercise at least twenty minutes yesterday?" After identifying their well-being weaknesses, employees are encouraged to participate in the company's most relevant workshop offering. Those include More Time for You; Live Well, Find Your Balance; and Resilience: Finding Your Inner Strength. These workshops teach practices such as meditation, mindfulness, and journaling with the aim of cultivating self-awareness and offering employees time to pause and space to reflect, away from their busy lives—all while at work. The company believes its program helps employees find balance and inner strength to smile more, and have strong intimate relationships, all qualities that, according to the theory, will affect workers' professional performance.

Yet another firm manages the holistic care of employees under the title "personal sustainability." This medium-sized firm's CEO hired Stephanie Twain, a gentle woman in her forties who is a licensed chaplain, to serve under the vague title of "director of consulting services" and to train employees in "personal sustainability." Stephanie acts as a chaplain by going on regular walks with employees, ministering and comforting them in times of trouble. She's created collective rituals for the group during difficult times, such as when an employee has a death in the family. She leads a meditation every Thursday called "sit in bliss," where employees who are "always on" can gather together and "flop on the floor and become human again." During "sit in bliss," Stephanie offers a brief reflection, often drawing from various religious traditions.

"Sit in bliss" is a form of spiritual care that helps employees recuperate from the demands of intellectual work and "become human again" so that they can return to those demands and "personally sustain" high levels of work performance.

Companies provide spiritual care, but not because they are spiritual institutions like churches, synagogues, or temples, whose goal is the spiritual development of the member. Rather, they attend to the spirit for the reason they attend to body and mind: to ensure that the human worker can produce at his or her highest capacity. Corporate maternalism's spirituality is instrumental—a means to an end, not an end in itself.

Other secular institutions attend to the spiritual for instrumental reasons, too. Hospital chaplains and military chaplains provide spiritual care that serves the institution's mission. Hospitals' spiritual care promotes healing so patients can recover and leave the hospital. Military spiritual care rehabilitates broken soldiers so that they can return to the battlefield. In tech companies, spiritual care restores busy and burnt-out technologists so that they can produce optimally, day in and day out. One human resources professional put it bluntly: "We help you to work more and to work better."

MATERNAL BONDS

The philosophy that *the personal is the professional* is what human resources professionals are conveying in their regular invitations to "bring your whole self to work." The more that employees bring their whole selves to work, the more they invest in the company's success. Human resources professionals understand that when the company meets its employees' personal needs, the employees are less likely to spend their time and energy elsewhere. And, more subtly, corporate maternalism changes the nature of the employee's relationship to work. When employees receive the company's maternal care, they are not just financially connected to their companies, but also physically, socially, and spiritually connected to work. As Gwen, the head of leadership and development we met earlier, put it, "If you bring more of yourself to work then you are probably going to bring more to your work." HR professionals think this changes *the way* people work, as we saw in chapter 1. Gwen emphasized that she herself used the "amazing expensive benefit" of on-site day care. For her, its most obvious benefits—making work convenient and possible for women with young children—were merely "ancillary." The real benefits, in her view, have to do with the way it connects employees to the company. She explains, "When I was bringing my kids in, I could say, 'I'm going to be five minutes late because I'm dealing with a temper tantrum,' and someone is going to probably pick up on that and say, 'I've got it, I'll let other people know you're late.' Or they know your children because they come to your desk or they come to lunch. They form a relationship with them. And it changes the meaning of your work. Your children understand your work and your friends at work. They feel a part of it. And it just connects you more deeply to that place."

Susan Lamott, the former school principal, concurs. She started a community service day at her company to help people bring their "whole selves" to the workplace. The company had an Ocean Beach clean-up day, where employees spent the day picking up trash on Ocean Beach, with lunch provided by the company. At the feedback session afterward, she says, "People were ecstatic. Not just, 'Yeah, that was nice,' but ecstatic, like 'I finally feel like I've given something back to my community,' or 'I nourished myself at a spiritual level.'"

When Susan first suggested the community service day to company executives, some objected, arguing that volunteering had nothing to do with business—and that people could volunteer on their own free time, not on company time. Susan noted that people didn't have the free time to do it on their own—and argued that the benefits to the company would be exponential when employees could "spiritually nourish" themselves *through* and *with* the company. Susan reasoned that "people want to serve others in a different way, other than just the grind of their job." She argued that it was advantageous to the company to recognize this dimension in people, and to "feed" it. When that side of the employee was "nourished," Susan explained, "it fed the production and furthered the company. When it was not nourished, it created psychological issues for people, like 'Who am I?' 'Where do I give?' 'Where do I fit in?'" Most important, Susan emphasized, "they feel like a chunk of them is not there at work." She shrugged. "If I don't feel like I'm a whole person at work, how much are you really getting out of me?"

Gwen and Susan argue that corporate maternalism doesn't benefit the company by merely mitigating worker burnout, but by binding workers emotionally, socially, and spiritually to the company. Susan articulates this clearly: When the company takes care of the whole person, it gets the whole person. This is one of the ways that organizations with high demands, like cults and communes, command the commitment of their members.[16] As Gwen claims, the *meaning* of work changes when employees invest their whole selves in the workplace. Work is not merely the contractual exchange of labor for wages—but, as I showed in chapter 1, it becomes charged with emotional, social, and spiritual meaning. Tech workers *identify* with work. They *want* to work. They *need* work. Practices like corporate maternalism reflect the late capitalist shift in the control of labor, a move away from practices of overt coercion and toward the creation of strong work cultures that can induce genuine consent to the will of management.[17]

Corporate maternalism is the latest version of a long effort to obscure the relations of power between company and employee, and the contractual nature of work. These efforts seek to recast what Karl Marx perceived as an employment relation that was inherently oppositional—recast it away from the world of contract, wages, and timesheets, with their tangible rewards and consequences, to a more personal, private, and cooperative (nonoppositional) relationship defined by intangibles such as commitment and loyalty. In the early to mid-twentieth century, the owners of companies like Kodak and Sears used above-union wages, lavish lifestyle amenities, and generous benefits to get workers to identify with management, rather than join a union.[18] This is also why the metaphor of the company as family is so popular in modern capitalism.[19] In non-economic institutions like the family and religion, members' commitment and loyalty are unconditional and unlimited.

The Efficient Consolidation of Life@Work

Corporate maternalism not only provides for the personal care of employees but consolidates it in the physical workplace, to optimize work productivity. Companies offer all kinds of "scientifically based" workplace interventions to enhance work efficiency. "In human resources," said one person, "we are always trying to see how we can get people to be more productive. Like letting everyone have meetings where you stand up instead of sit down, so that they can go faster." Another person said he had custom designed a distinct office scent to condition a Pavlovian response: when employees smell it, they will instinctively start working. Still others described the cost/benefit analysis that goes into every detail of creating the tech work experience, such as the sugar content of snacks, the amount of carbohydrates in the lunch, the distance of the snacks from work stations, the placement of water fountains, the color of the walls, and so on—seeking to apply every second of the tech worker's time efficiently toward work. Tech companies also turn going to the bathroom into productive time. One company posted management tips on the inner door of the bathroom stall, a program it called "learning on the loo." And at another company's bathroom stall, they posted instructions on how to upgrade a popular computer application. Even allowing engineers to have flexible schedules feeds workplace productivity. "We can't work them 24/7 unless we give them flexibility," one human resources professional said matter-of-factly.

This overarching concern for efficiency tries to upend the modern work-life dichotomy and to centralize all the functions of work, home, religion, and neighborhood under one roof. A typical tech campus is designed to enable busy engineers to meet all their personal needs so that they can devote their full attention and energy to work. The workplace is supposed to be their home, gym, dance studio, art studio, garden, bar, restaurant, meditation hall, library, laundry room, game room, dentist office, and therapist office (and even more), all rolled into one. In the Silicon Valley workplace, work and life are no longer separate and opposing spheres because *life happens at work*.

In fighting the notion that work and life occupy distinct spaces and times, tech companies are reviving a much older way of organizing society. In agrarian societies, work and life were integrated for both women and men.[20] The farm was both home—where people ate, slept, and played—and workplace—where people labored and participated in the economic system. Industrialization began to impose stark boundaries between work and life, particularly for men. Work became confined to a particular space, time, and logic—the factory, with its rhythm governed by the values of efficiency and productivity. Life—defined as activities that don't contribute to production—happened outside of the factory in the home, church, neighborhood, bowling alley, baseball diamond, saloon, hair salon, and so on. Those places operated by their own logics of aesthetics, emotions, and ethics—the pursuit of health, beauty, happiness, holiness, justice, family, pleasure, community, intimacy, and so on. Today's tech company is returning to the undifferentiated spheres of its preindustrial predecessor, however, by making life a part of work.

For instance, most tech companies feed their employees, a trend that is growing with other companies around the country.[21] Large companies have their own gourmet cafeterias where they provide breakfast, lunch, and often dinner, which is free or heavily subsidized. Smaller companies hire caterers. And both large and small companies have kitchens stocked with drinks and snacks. Most tech professionals report that they eat two or three meals a day at work. They rely so much on work for meals that tech companies have displaced local restaurants in Silicon Valley.[22] Sarah Kim, head of human resources at a medium-sized start-up, explains the calculations behind the "free" food:

> There are studies that show that employees lose about an hour a day getting food when they go out of the office, grab food, and come back. So it ends up being cheaper for the company to pay for food and keep them in house. So we offer free food all the time—breakfast, lunch, and dinner. The food is brought in every day.

Sarah explains how this logic also applies to chores. Instead of being diverted to "life's chores," employees can devote their time and attention to work:

> You make it really easy for employees to continue working. So like dry cleaning. There are times when I used to rush out of the office to go home because my dry cleaners is going to close at six, or whatever. And so by not having to worry about that and offering it—it's like, "Okay, that's one less thing I have to worry about. I can just go to the office."

Another human resources professional readily agreed. "It's a way to keep your employees on-site. If they're not out running errands like dry cleaning or getting the oil changed on their car, they're at work coding and working." To keep employees "coding and working," the services that the company offers to support "life" are extensive. Here Linda Alvarez, a human resources director at a large firm, explains the reasoning behind the plethora of lifestyle services at her company:

> These are . . . busy people with busy lives, and the idea is to make it a little less busy for you. So things like, you know, you can get your hair cut on-site. You can get a dentist appointment, you can get your car washed, you can get all your dry cleaning, and you know, shirts pressed. You can go to the gym. We have walking trails. We have healthy food selections in the cafeteria. So the list goes on and on and on around providing services.

And companies outsource the chores they cannot bring on-site, like housecleaning, dog walking, babysitting, and gardening. One company has a subsidized concierge service that charges employees only $5 an hour to have someone run errands for them. Another company gives employees a $2,000 annual stipend for what one engineer called "me stuff": housecleaning, gardening, manicures, and haircuts. Notably, these services mostly benefit salaried "core" employees. Janitors and other contract workers have busy lives too. But they are paid hourly, and their companies don't pay them while they are running errands and getting their teeth cleaned.

Corporate maternalism brings into the workplace leisure activities and hobbies that are typically done at home or in the neighborhood. Many tech offices are designed with an "office-as-home" aesthetic that one tech employee described to me as "flipping the private and public."[23] If you're feeling sleepy you can take a nap in one of the nap pods or cubby holes. If you're hungry, grab a snack from the perpetually well-stocked kitchen. The days of the cubicle and corner office are gone. Now, employees all work in one big room with moveable desks, write-able surfaces, couches, coffee tables, and lounge chairs. Enclosed offices are few and far between. At one company, client and company meetings take place in what resembles a family room, bright purple whimsical couches and blue bean bags in the center of a sea of desks and computers. The work-at-home aesthetic invites employees to hark back to the hallowed early start-up days, when the office was someone's living room or garage, and there was no distinction between work and life. For instance, the shoe-less policy at the offices of Gusto.com is a holdover from the company's early days, when it conducted its affairs in its founder's living room, shoeless. Now five hundred employees strong, they've continued the homey feel.

Corporate maternalism makes leisure and hobbies convenient for the busy tech worker. Ping-Pong and pool tables are now standard pieces of furniture in the tech office. I frequently saw guitars lying around offices. Explaining the keyboard and guitar in the conference room of one start-up, its CEO explained, "Because we work long hours, we want to make hobbies complementary to work." One of his employees even wrote a company-provided guitar into his employment contract. Now, instead of taking time from work to play his guitar, he can do it at work. For the artistic, places like Facebook have studios equipped with woodworking tools, a letterpress machine, and spaces for artists. A designer at one start-up said that they had weekly "crafternoons," where employees can spend an hour drawing, painting, and working on their various art projects together. Google has a company garden for gardeners, an arcade for video gamers, and a library for bookworms. Most large companies have gym facilities and fitness classes where employees can swim, do yoga, play basketball, dance salsa, practice tae kwon do, or dance Zumba.

Smaller companies that don't have gyms outsource the service by giving out gym memberships. Even companies that lack gym space usually offer regular yoga classes. Referring to the maternal care of the company, one tech professional explained, "They really want you to stretch and be less stressed, so they bring the teacher to you."

Corporate maternalism's quest to clear away distractions is so ambitious that it even touches dependents. Tech companies are not the only ones that offer on-site care for infants and preschool-aged children. But few other sectors go quite as far in trying to fit dependents into company imperatives. For example, at one large company, I observed several families coming to the company cafeteria for dinner, rather than going home. Sheba Nair, a user-experience designer, relies on her company to offer after-school child care for her seven-year-old daughter. Sheba picks her daughter up at 3 p.m. every day and brings her to work, where she can run around on the rooftop playground under the supervision of a child-care provider, while Sheba works downstairs before they have dinner at the company cafeteria at 6:30. Her company even sponsors weekend activities for the family. Only last weekend, Sheba attended the premier of a new Bollywood movie in a theater that her company had rented out. Some companies even encourage their employees to bring pets. Several companies I visited had fish tanks. At the gaming company Zynga in San Francisco, employees bring pets to work; their headquarters includes a rooftop dog park and on-site dog grooming.[24]

Corporate maternalism provides so many of the things that once occurred at home and in the community that a few companies are taking the last step toward round-the-clock integration. Some engineers have been able to avoid Silicon Valley's costly housing market by going "homeless."[25] They sleep in their cars at night because the workplace has everything else. Facebook is addressing the inconvenience of living in a place with prohibitive housing costs by developing a new housing and commercial area for employees in Menlo Park dubbed "Zucktown."[26] Now, Facebook employees never have to leave work. And when employees do leave work, the efficient care of corporate maternalism follows them home. Companies like Apple, Google, Facebook, and Genentech offer a private bus service that shuttles employees from their suburban campuses to their urban homes. With onboard wi-fi, no time is wasted, and employees can work while commuting. And if they don't have food at home, employees can pack food from work to bring back home.

Thus, companies making spirituality a part of the workplace are just offering another time-saving personal service. Many firms have meditation rooms. They host talks by religious leaders, bring meditation and mindfulness teachers to the workplace, and sponsor programs that touch on spirituality, such as Search Inside Yourself or the Well-Being Journey we saw earlier. Companies also offer prepaid memberships to mindfulness apps such as Headspace, where employees can plug in and create their own bliss whenever and wherever they want. Tech giant Salesforce invited twenty-five monks from Thich Nhat Hanh's Plum Village Monastery to attend Dreamforce, the company's massive conference that takes over all of downtown San Francisco, for two years in a row in 2016 and 2017. In their brown robes and shaved heads, the monks chanted and practiced walking meditation around the conference grounds. Speaking at the conference, one of the monks told the audience, "We're here to help people become more kind, slow, and compassionate." Thich Nhat Hanh was apparently open to Salesforce's overture. "Our teacher gave us assignments to enter into the business world and media because people are too busy to take care of themselves and their families."[27]

The monastic's quote gets at the strange irony of corporate maternalism. Employees work so hard for the company that they cannot take care of themselves, so the company steps in to provide the care. For example, one engineer at a large firm who is a single mother of two small children says she has no time to meditate unless she does it at work. Evoking Arlie Hochschild's argument that "work becomes home and home becomes work," this engineer claims that the company's weekly meditation is her sacred sanctuary. It's the only time and place that she is allowed to focus on herself, and not the needs of her family or the company. Another engineer who regularly attends the twice-weekly meditation at his firm told me that he doesn't meditate on the weekends because "I'm not at work." This man thinks of meditation as part of his job.

With the functions of home, neighborhood, and church consolidated under one roof, the workplace becomes not a merely a place to work, but a place to live. It efficiently centralizes and manages the nonproductive aspects of life so that the worker can have a "life" without sacrificing time devoted to work. The director of wellness at one firm explained that the purpose of all its personal services, clubs, and classes is to help employees "be that fulfilled person." With its endless opportunities for physical, social, and spiritual development, the tech workplace is a destination to "experience" and become "fulfilled."

And as the "life" functions of the workplace expand, so does its claim on the lives of employees. Instead of being "that fulfilled person" through a religious congregation, a neighborhood gym, or a local bar outside of work—places independent of work's claims—employees are doing it, as one human resources professional said, "at work, coding and working."

Keeping Up with Google: Spiritual Care as a Perk

When an old and established firm in Silicon Valley hired Abby Robinson for a senior human resources position, she was told to introduce perks that would "make us look like Google." She contracted with a catering service and a dry-cleaning service, brought in a fitness and diet coach, set up a spare office as a yoga/meditation room, and found a yoga and meditation instructor to offer twice-weekly classes. Abby and her boss were less concerned with how these services could "heal" employees or make them "whole" than with how these perks could make the company competitive for the best "talent" among a sea of other firms that offered similar or better perks.

That reveals another dimension of corporate maternalism: It's a way to compete for talent in Silicon Valley. Companies don't have to believe in wholeness and well-being to practice corporate maternalism. They only have to want to hire the best and brightest technologists. Corporate maternalism is now a Silicon Valley norm because of what sociologists call "institutional isomorphism": organizations in the same competitive field end up looking like one another.[28]

Google has become the industry's gold standard. Its legendary amenities are hard for most companies to match, especially smaller startups. But they need to "keep up with Google" to compete in what one human resources professional called "the war for talent" in Silicon Valley. As corporate maternalism has become the norm, personal care services have become expected perks, symbols of a desirable workplace, and markers of the industry's specialness. One human resources professional who has worked in both tech and nontech industries commented, "If you're not in high-tech, you're not competing for that same talent. You don't have to bring in a chef." Tech professionals, on the other hand, expect the company to take care of them. The head of human resources of a medium-sized start-up put it plainly: "One of my groups is recruiting, and it is hard to find the right talent. And knowing that everyone's 'at will' and they'll quit if you don't create a workplace that is satisfactory to them—you just have to be competitive."

As a result, human resources is preoccupied with monitoring employee satisfaction and boosting employee happiness. One human resources professional who had once worked at a large firm with bountiful perks described how there was no logic or systematic thought behind them. Rather, the firm had so much money that they threw it at any vendor who came through their door promising to make employees happy. Another human resources director described lavish company perks in Silicon Valley as part of a "fling" mentality. "People aren't marrying their companies anymore. They are having flings. It's a short-term relationship. And every day better be a good day!"

Even as human resources professionals listed the "data" and "science" behind the time-saving benefits and the therapeutic powers of the perks, they also emphasized their symbolic value. Rebecca Vernon, who had worked in human resources at several Silicon Valley firms, thinks that yoga and mindfulness programs don't make a difference in worker performance, but companies keep them because they signal that the company cares. Donny Hastings, the head of human resources at a start-up, waxed poetic about his company's personal services such as yoga classes, meals, and meditation sessions. But when I asked him how many of the two hundred employees at his company attended the yoga classes, he responded, "about four," and explained that the others are "too busy working." Donny claimed that offering yoga is "largely symbolic" and that "it's nice when you're recruiting to say, 'We offer perks, like yoga in the office.'" Donny isn't alone in reporting sparse participation in some wellness amenities. On the nap pods at his company, one engineer reported, "you never see anyone sleeping in them."

To be sure, some perks are more popular than others—the cafeterias are crowded, buses are full, and people eat lots of snacks and use the gyms. But the true functional value of corporate maternalism is simply that it expresses care. The care, not the particularities of the care, makes a difference. This is the pathbreaking insight of psychologists Elton Mayo and Fritz Roethlisberger's Hawthorne Studies in the 1920s. They discovered that changing the wattage of a factory's lights made no difference in worker productivity. But the employees' perception that the company cared about them did.

But corporate maternalism turns "care" into a competitive market commodity. The hot lunch that Susan Lamott started in her company years ago is now so taken for granted that it's no longer a sign of care. As expectations balloon, companies look for ways to offer bigger, better, and more personalized care.

This is most evident in the culture of food in Silicon Valley firms. Food is one of the most important ways that companies compete for talent. It is not just about nourishing the body. It's how companies tell their employees that they care about their happiness. Engineers will often casually bring up food with me, comparing their company's food to other companies, as a way to judge a company's work environment. For instance, in a conversation with a group of engineers, one person complained that Facebook offered a larger array of candy and snack options than did their company. Another engineer defended the company by saying that the healthier food options proved that their company cared more for their employees than Facebook did. After becoming accustomed to having lunch at various tech campuses, I also found myself using the quality of a company's food as a proxy for the extent of its corporate maternalism.

Along with vast profit margins, "keeping up with Google" is one reason tech companies' food offerings are so much better than what you get in public school cafeterias, military mess halls, or hospitals—other institutions that offer physical care for their members. Calling these tech venues "cafeterias" doesn't do them justice. At Google's Mountain View headquarters, employees are offered several amuse-bouches at each meal; all ingredients are 100 percent local and sustainable. Google has ten cafes, each featuring a distinct cuisine, like Indian and Japanese. The head chefs at these companies are local celebrities, like Google's former executive chef Charlie Ayers, who described his job as providing "fine food for the fast crowd."[29]

Start-ups are no less generous in feeding their employees. While they generally do not have their own cafeterias, they have well-stocked kitchens where employees can make their own breakfast, and they cater lunch. Start-ups compensate for the fewer food options by curating to employees' tastes. For instance, Margaret Chang, a twenty-six-year-old user-experience designer at a start-up, described the head of human resources as a "wonderful, nurturing woman who tries to accommodate everyone's diets." She described her start-up's food offerings with great relish. For breakfast, there are ten different cereals and eight yogurts, three of them vegan. Every morning, Margaret makes avocado toast with lemon juice, chili pepper, and fancy sea salt on multigrain bread with pumpkin seeds and flax seeds, topped with a poached egg. She often takes pictures of her breakfast for her East Coast friends to gawk at. Once a week, the company brings in professional baristas to make coffee for the employees. Lunch, served every day at 12:30, is "obscene" and "decadent." As she sketched the typical buffet lunch layout on a piece of paper for me, she said, "First you have your cutlery here, and then about four different salads, four different meat entrees, two veggies, and two desserts." Things like paella, or fish and lentils, are typical entrées. "That's like . . . normal," she said. No wonder Margaret says she feels "coddled" at work.

In this world of personalized care, spirituality is just another perk companies can offer to compete for talent. Human resources professionals told me that they convinced superiors to bring in meditation by telling them that companies like Google and LinkedIn do it. Similarly, meditation and mindfulness providers said that one of the most effective ways to drum up business is to tell the company that "Google does it." Whether meditation is considered spiritual care, a mental health practice, or a productivity technique is irrelevant. To companies, it's another "perk" that will help them compete with other firms. A human resources professional recounted that one day the CEO, who'd never shown interest in meditation before, approached her after learning about meditation at Google and asked, "Why don't we try that meditation thing?"

The trend of offering spiritual perks to keep up with Google can be seen in Claudia Schmidt's "happiness campaign" at Copernicus, an old and established firm in Silicon Valley. When she was promoted to vice president at Copernicus, the CEO charged Claudia with transforming the culture and making people "happy." The problem, Claudia explained, was that "we're not seen as a cool company. No one wants to wear our company t-shirt" the way that people in Silicon Valley wear Google and Facebook t-shirts. Not being "cool" was more than a cosmetic problem; it meant, she explained, "we can't hire anyone from UC Berkeley and Stanford." A Copernicus employee confirmed their reputation. He described work at the company as "soul crushing" and told me, "I need to get out of there." People in Silicon Valley considered Copernicus a "dinosaur." The company had been around for over thirty years and had earned the unflattering reputation of being "very traditional." The average employee was in his or her forties, not twenties, as at Google or Facebook. Claudia explained that their workforce had grown "stale"; it was composed largely of immigrants who had worked there for over ten years and could not easily find employment elsewhere. These middle-aged employees were used to a "traditional" workplace that separated work and life. Copernicus thought that was a problem. It felt it couldn't attract the new talent it needed by being a traditional workplace.

The first thing Claudia did to "make people happy" was to change the space. She hired a team of designers to give the office the "scrappy" "work as home" look. Out went the walls, cubicles, corner offices, and conference rooms. The office became a big room with moveable and adjustable desks, tables with writeable surfaces, and the obligatory Ping-Pong table in the corner. Meetings took place on three bright couches and bean bags in the middle of the room, or in the various armchairs that lined the room. They even ripped out the ceiling and exposed the ducts to give it that edgy, start-up feel. Claudia admitted that employees were still figuring out how to make private calls without rooms.

Now Claudia wanted to bring in meditation because, she said, "the research is clear that meditation makes you happy," and because if Google, LinkedIn, and Salesforce had it, then so should Copernicus. Claudia was creating a dedicated meditation space with cushions on the floor, while considering several vendors to establish a meditation program in the company. To top it off, she also wanted to give employees the option of an all-expense-paid ten-day silent Buddhist Vipassana retreat—something she wasn't sure human resources would approve. But next year it might, because other companies are catching on to the meditation-retreat trend. Indeed, Claudia had gotten that idea from another company with a similar offering. The CEO of another company eagerly told me about hoping to offer a "menu of spiritual retreats" in the future. In the "war for talent" in Silicon Valley, meditation, mindfulness, and spiritual retreats are not about healing, health, wholeness, or spirituality. They are another set of perks companies use to keep up with Google.

We Just Want You to Be Happy

On a sunny California day in April, I witnessed the postcard-perfect picture of Silicon Valley "happiness." After meditating with a group of engineers, I followed them to the company cafeteria. It was recently renovated with an earthy eco-modern look: repurposed wood walls, bamboo floors, stainless-steel counters and tables. Giant floor-to-ceiling windows looked out onto a sunny, wooden deck patio, where employees sat around tables, under cream-colored umbrellas, Van Morrison and Coldplay wafting in the background. We chose from three different main entrees: fish and lentils; pasta and tomato cream sauce; and baked chicken cacciatore. Dessert was six different flavors of homemade ice cream, all you can eat. People looked happy—very happy. They looked Instagram-vacation-photo happy. It was corporate maternalism at its best.

They were happy, not in spite of work, but because of work. They were laughing with friends and eating healthy food in the sunshine. The company gets them free theater tickets. They dance salsa at work. They meditate at work. They drink custom-made smoothies and cappuccinos at work. They play the guitar at work. They sing at work. They stretch at work. They believe they are healthier because of work. One man told me that a professional workshop on communication helped save his marriage. Another engineer told me that meditation at work helped him to be present and supportive with his teenage daughter. Several said they were living more deeply spiritual lives because of programs at work. One woman said she used to be timid, and had transformed into a confident leader because of work. Another woman told me that, because of work, "I learned to be me."

Could there be another way to be happy at work? I wondered. And whose interest does happiness serve? In his 1951 classic *White Collar*, C. Wright Mills argued that, in the absence of the Protestant ethic work compulsion, personnel departments had to make the conscious effort to "create morale."[30] During the course of my research, I asked people in human resources whether employee stress, unhappiness, and burnout could be solved in other ways: by giving employees more time off, say, or lowering expectations. What about lowering quarterly goals? Or choosing not to grow in market share? I knew that I seemed naïve asking these questions. They cut at the most basic commandment of capitalism, what historian Yuval Harari calls the "creed of growth"—that profits must always grow.[31]

Of course, no one took my suggestions seriously. They insisted that the workload was reasonable, or they ignored the question altogether. "That's just the way things are," they responded. To be sure, none of the people in human resources have the power to ease the workload or slow down work's pace. But that only compounds the irony: making employees happy and healthy is a burden that falls primarily on women confined to low status positions in a male-dominated industry, women who have no power to tackle the root causes of burnout, stress, and anxiety.

Despite their enthusiasm for promoting well-being programs and arranging healthy, gourmet meals for their employees, some in human resources told me they knew they offered merely therapeutic interventions, Band-Aids lovingly applied to deep and gaping wounds. Their programs might not be too distant from the "opiate of the masses" that Marx wrote about. Gwen, the director of learning and development whom we heard from earlier, is a staunch advocate of corporate maternalism—but also acknowledged its limits, saying, "It's not enough to put [in] a yoga room then have an implicit contract that you work fourteen to sixteen hours a day." Elizabeth Evans, a former senior leader in learning and development at a tech company, told me that she also fell victim to the work toll, even as she was trying to save others from it. Elizabeth did *everything* she could to be well. She practiced meditation and yoga regularly. She had a coach and a healer. She did regular cleanses and attended spiritual retreats. But after ten years of working ten hours a day, she says, "I walked away from my job to save my life." When she left tech, Elizabeth followed Steve Jobs's advice and did what she loved. She studied a variety of healing modalities and opened a small practice as a healer. But she didn't make enough money to raise two sons in the valley, with its exorbitant cost of living. Even though the therapeutic interventions couldn't save her from the stress of her job, she now works for a company that teaches meditation and leadership to tech firms because it pays the bills. "I don't see companies letting up on people's workload," Elizabeth observes. "Companies are running more lean and slim, and there's more competition. . . . Nobody is going to ease the workload for you. They're not going to hire somebody to help you. You're not going to get some amazing computer program that's going to suddenly make your life that much easier. I've never had a client say, 'We recognize people's workload is too much and we're going to be staffing up more people.' It's more of the opposite." The only solution to thriving in a relentless workplace is to change the worker by "renewing energy," she says. "Time is finite, but energy is expansive." Her company teaches employees how to renew their energy through meditation.

In essence, corporate maternalism aims to help employees cultivate a happy self with expansive energy. Long work hours, ambitious quarterly goals, continuous market growth—nothing needs to change so long as employees are happy. Not only do happy employees work more and better, goes the thinking, but they also don't organize into unions or challenge employers' power.[32] Tech executives aren't the first to think this. The same logic underpinned the generous wages and benefits of what was once called "welfare capitalism."[33] The rhetoric of happiness, feminist studies scholar Sara Ahmed writes, is often used to justify unequal power relations.[34]

When happiness and wholeness butt heads against productivity, productivity wins. In 2012, Facebook's yoga instructor Alice Van Ness was fired for shooting a "disapproving look" at a Facebook employee who answered her phone in the middle of class.[35] Because of this, Van Ness was also terminated from teaching yoga at Cisco, another tech company. In case anyone thought otherwise, the infamous "yoga incident" clarified that employee well-being is in service to work, and not the other way around.

Corporate maternalism cannot question capitalism's "creed of growth" because it is in service to it. Human capital "expands" when workers are pampered, massaged, fed, and ministered to. Work can maintain its relentless pace. Employees can keep overworking. And companies can continue profiting, so long as they invest in the health, spirituality, and happiness of their workers.

"Everyone's smiling, but no one's happy here," Ken Kim, an engineer in his late thirties, told me one night in the dark empty parking lot of a tech company that was known for having "happy" employees. I had joined Ken and a group of engineers for a salsa class, followed by dinner in one of the cafeterias on the company campus. After dinner, the group had dispersed. Ken, a former employee at the firm, lingered around and followed me to my car. He wanted to talk to me privately, away from the rest of his friends. "You know how when your parents come to visit you and you make it seem like your life is just great and everything is fine? Like you're eating filet mignon every night and you're really happy?" Ken asked. "That's how it is here." To him, the company was like a coddling mother who needed his assurance that he was happy. Even though

Ken had left the company over a year ago, he still came "home" for dinner, to hang out with his friends and take dance classes.

Why did Ken suggest that engineers have to feign happiness, I wondered? Why the anxiety about happiness? Were companies really making people happy, or were they teaching people how to look and act happy because it needed to advertise happy employees? Or maybe it was the other way around. Maybe Ken, who had given his whole self to work, needed the company to bring him happiness, because no one else could care for him as well as "mom."

CHAPTER 3

Managing Souls

THE SPIRITUAL CULTIVATION OF HUMAN CAPITAL

Patrick Sullivan, a young and ambitious executive at the large tech firm Euclid, noticed that his unit of one thousand engineers was flagging; they weren't as engaged as they'd been. Six months earlier, a German multinational had acquired Euclid. His high-performing team of engineers were now going through what Patrick called "change fatigue." Only one year prior, business magazines recognized Euclid, with its generous benefits and perks, as one of the best places to work. Now, the previously high rates of employee satisfaction had plummeted. He could feel a low-grade cloud of anxiety, fear, and stress in the corridors, atriums, and meeting rooms.

And so Patrick introduced a solution that might once have seemed unlikely for Silicon Valley. "Einstein said that in order to solve a problem in the second dimension, you need a solution from the third dimension," Patrick explained, quoting a possibly apocryphal line that I would hear repeatedly through my time in Silicon Valley. The "third dimension" that he and others were referring to is the spiritual dimension. Widely recognized as a management genius in the valley, Patrick told me that the typical solutions of throwing more money, perks, and status at his team wouldn't solve the longer hours, adjustment difficulties, and frustrations that inevitably come when a company is acquired. Besides, Euclid already had all the lifestyle amenities and perks—massage, meals, gyms, transportation, and so on—that Silicon Valley generally offered to make work and life seamless and easy.

Solving in the "third dimension," Patrick told me, meant understanding "change fatigue" not as an organization problem, but as a spiritual problem of the "alienated" and "fragmented" soul. He enlisted the help of Samantha Lieberman, a Buddhist dharma teacher and executive coach. Together they developed a program to "help people reconnect with themselves" and "liberate them to be fully alive." Samantha thought of it as "sneaking in spirituality" into the corporation, and creating "sanghas" at work, using the Sanskrit term for Buddhist spiritual communities. Spirituality, she said, was the heart of the program. But they gave it the corporate name "Be Your Best Self" (BBS), and dressed it up in the business lingo of efficiency, productivity, and leadership to get it past HR.

Over the course of one year, BBS facilitators coached Euclid employees in what Patrick called "connecting with their deepest selves" through contemplative practices of meditation, mindfulness, and self-examination. In addition to large group meetings and individual coaching, BBS sorted participants into "tribes" of eight to ten people that met on a monthly basis and "coached" each other. The tribes, Samantha explained, were sanctuaries in "fear-driven" corporate cultures, where people could be themselves and not feel they had to perform.

Be Your Best Self became known in the company as "the program that changes lives." Even though participants had to apply and use their own work time to participate in the program, employees at all levels of the organization signed up in droves, and there was a long waiting list to participate. Yasamin Ahmadi, an engineer in her late twenties, is one of those who said that BBS had transformed her. "Euclid has changed my life," she told me. "BBS [made] me the person who I am today right now in front of you. . . . I believe in myself more and don't doubt myself," she said, adding, "It has made me more spiritual." Another engineer, Roshan Menon, said that his spiritual practice deepened because of BBS. He was already "studying Buddhism" on his own when he joined. But with a tone of disbelief, he marveled that now "the company is paying for me to spend time on it!"

Be Your Best Self changed more than just the spiritual lives of the employees. Euclid also benefited from their "conversions." Yasamin, who once was so timid that she didn't dare speak up in meetings, is now a vocal leader of a team. Roshan went from being what he describes as a "nine-to-five guy" to a "leader type" and is now driving one of the company's newest innovations. Personal conversions like Yasamin's and Roshan's translate to higher organizational returns across the board. A third-party evaluator of the program found that Euclid was getting a two-dollar return on every one dollar they spent on the program. Patrick's unit went from having one of the lowest scores in job satisfaction in the agglomerated corporation to one of the highest.

Euclid's Be Your Best Self Program is an example of how some Silicon Valley companies are harnessing spirituality as a strategy to manage labor. To be clear, most Silicon Valley companies don't think of themselves as "spiritual." No company has a formal "Department of Spirituality." And most people do not use the word "spiritual" openly in the workplace; it is not taken seriously, I was told, and is considered "woo-woo" and "airy fairy" by analytical engineers. But behind closed doors with me, many corporate managers said that spirituality is an important—if not the most important—dimension of the work they do. And they used surprisingly spiritual language to describe their roles in the corporation: "helping people connect to self and Universe," "awakening mystery," "contributing soulfulness," and "sneaking in spirituality." In public, however, they described their programs in corporate slogans such as "unleash your potential," "be your best self," "bring your whole self to work," and "authenticity in the workplace."

This chapter focuses on these people who have institutionalized spirituality in the tech workplace—a group I call the "coaching community." They either are trained executive coaches or have been coached themselves. They bring to corporations the Bay Area coaching industry's largely Asian-inspired spiritual ideas and practices, whose roots can be traced to 1960s countercultural movements such as the "human potential" movement.[1] While they are a minority in each company, those in the coaching community are an influential lot. Some, like Patrick, hold senior positions. Others have the ear of company leaders. Companies started to hire coaches for their executives starting in the 1980s, when they began investing in the intellectual capital of their senior leaders. Executive coaches, according to a *Harvard Business Review* article are "outsourced suppliers of candor, providing individual leaders with the objective feedback needed to nourish their growth."[2] Today, executive coaching has become a standard practice in established firms across America.

The "coaching community" includes senior business leaders like Patrick Sullivan; executive coaches, most of whom used to work in tech companies and who are now independent contractors; and rising employees whose companies send them to coaching school to improve their management skills. This last group can come from any department, but many come from departments like learning and development and human resources. Collectively, the coaching community integrates spiritual concerns into tech companies through standard corporate programs such as executive coaching and professional development, as well as through individual senior leaders' spiritual approaches to management that trickle down through the company.

While some of the coaching community's concerns overlap with *corporate maternalism*, they focus on a different dimension of spiritual management: not simply caring for the spirit but *growing* the value of the spirit. Like Patrick Sullivan, members of the coaching community do this by helping people "connect" to their "authentic selves"—and thereby unleash untapped and unbound energy and creativity that can be directed toward work.

In this chapter I explore how Silicon Valley firms grow their human capital by cultivating what I call a "spirituality of authentic selfhood" in their workers. Why is "connecting to self" important to tech firms? What does "connecting to self" look like? And what does it mean for both spirituality and work in Silicon Valley that people find and define their "authentic selves" in the institution of the workplace?

Alienation and Work

To understand why Silicon Valley companies want their employees to be "connected" to their "authentic selves," we must first examine how tech executives see self-alienation not just as an existential problem but also as a problem of labor management. Workers who are alienated from their "authentic selves," according to the coaching community, are also alienated from their full working potential. Patrick Sullivan, the executive at Euclid introduced earlier, explains this principle by sharing his own story of self-alienation as a gay man living a straight life. Growing up in a devout Catholic family in Boston, Patrick considered Catholicism both a blessing and a curse. On the one hand, it filled him with a heightened awareness of God's presence in his life. "God is a part of who you are and manifests in everything that you do," he says. This awareness informs the way he manages today, even though he no longer identifies as Catholic. But his Catholicism also made him deny a fundamental part of himself: his sexuality. In his devout Catholic family, being gay "was like murder."

Patrick recounts living an alienated existence for more than half his life as a straight man. He married his best friend, a woman he loved and had an active sex life with, while maintaining close platonic relationships with men. But something wasn't quite right. His wife first pointed it out to him. One day she told Patrick, "I wish you loved me like you love Benny." It struck him deeply that she was right. He had an intense and spiritual connection with Benny that he had never had with her or any other woman. Patrick realized that the problem with his marriage was that he was not "bringing his whole self" to it. Because he was not "authentically connected" to himself, he couldn't fully give to his marriage. Instead, he used his energy to repress himself.

That alienation affected not just his marriage but also his other relationships. As he explains, "My being gay was showing up in every aspect of my life. Even though it wasn't obvious. So with my wife—it was showing up where I don't feel this true spiritual connection with her. It showed up in my relationship with my parents."

And it also showed up at work. Just as Patrick's self-alienation compromised his capacity to be "fully present" in his personal relationships, it also detracted from his capacity to give his full self to work. He couldn't be his best at work, he feels, because he was always expending emotional energy distancing himself from others and worrying about whether he appeared too feminine.

Patrick describes coming out as a painful but transformative "spiritual journey." He developed an anxiety disorder and panic attacks from the realization that he might be gay, and he sought professional help to deal with the crisis. Some therapists denied he was gay; others medicated him to manage his anxiety. What saved him, he explains, was the spiritual practice of Buddhist meditation, which made him "whole." Patrick learned to meditate by listening to tapes of Jack Kornfield, the renowned Buddhist teacher and psychotherapist. He started attending meditation retreats at local Buddhist centers such as Spirit Rock and Tassajara. After a lifetime of feeling disconnected from his body and emotions, meditation helped him "authentically connect" to himself. Patrick was finally able to come out as gay.

Patrick gained a critical managerial insight from that spiritual journey. When he is "authentically connected to oneself, others, and God," he feels "fully alive." And being "fully alive," he says, is the most optimal state to achieve the best outcomes in any area of life. "When I am fully alive at work," he says, "I produce more. I produce better." "When I am shut down, unalive, I not only produce less; I distract other people," he explains. "You know, misery loves company. And the more miserable people are, the more it has a contagious effect," one that can be disastrous to organizations.

And that's the problem with most workplaces, according to Patrick and others: People feel "shut down" and "un-alive" there. Many brought up a recent Gallup poll purporting to show that about 70 percent of workers feel disengaged from their work. They worried about the organizational consequences in quantified terms. "Companies suffer when their workers are not engaged and want merely a paycheck," Patrick says. "So if 70 percent of people are not engaged, that has a huge cost to an organization. So every day that I can have you 10 percent, 5 percent, 1 percent more engaged is a day of return."

Work and Alienation 1.0, 2.0, 3.0

Since the beginning of modern capitalism, managers like Patrick have been wondering how to get that extra 10, 5, and 1 percent more of return from workers. Patrick and the coaching community weren't the first to consider alienation to be the heart of the problem with work. In the 1867 classic text of political economy, *Capital*, Karl Marx identified alienation as one of the great casualties of modern capitalism. Workers, whose labor and worlds were controlled by the bourgeoisie, were alienated not just from the fruits of the labor but also from their very humanity in the interest of maximizing capital. Marx's prescription was, of course, quite radical: overthrow capitalism, and seize the means of production.

Alienation entered the lexicon of modern management in the 1950s with the human relations movement, a group of behavioral scientists who applied their research to industry. They turned Marx's concept of alienation on its head. In their twentieth-century iteration, or Alienation 2.0, alienation was a problem not because it diminished human freedom, but because it curtailed human productivity. The human relations movement started from a humane premise: workers are social beings who are driven by the human instinct for social belonging and acceptance.[3] They applied that insight to the aims of capitalism, arguing that when companies attend to workers' social needs, employees will be more engaged in their work and produce more and perform better. Workers who are alienated from their coworkers and the company, on the other hand, are disengaged, unmotivated, giving only just enough effort. The human relations movement underscored that managing labor involved not only the technical task of coordinating efficient production, but also understanding the human psyche. It emphasized harnessing the human need for group belonging and acceptance in order to transform it into productive labor.

The preoccupation with alienation resurfaced in popular business consciousness in the 1980s, when American corporations faced growing global competition from Japanese ones. Books such as William Ouichi's *Theory Z: How American Business Can Meet the Japanese Challenge* became best sellers.[4] Japanese firms had a competitive advantage over American firms, management experts claimed, because they emphasized unity and loyalty and were able to command deep sacrifice and commitment from their employees. American firms should learn from the Japanese and create similarly "strong cultures" that cultivated belonging, loyalty, and shared goals and values among employees and management.[5]

The "strong cultures" solution to Alienation 2.0, however, has produced a different kind of alienation in Silicon Valley, which we can call Alienation 3.0. According to Patrick and others in the coaching community, the twentieth-century corporate culture that idolizes group belonging extracts a personal cost from individual employees. People have to sacrifice individuality and authenticity—"shut down" and be "un-alive"—to fit in at work. Scholars of the late twentieth-century corporate workplace have made the same observation, portraying it as conforming and controlling. A rich academic literature details how workers internalize the values and commitments of the company by sacrificing individual freedom.[6] Sociologist C. Wright Mills called modern corporate workers "cheerful robots."[7]

The coaching community sees all this differently. It does not conceptualize alienation as the estrangement from one's labor as Marx did, or as a problem of human freedom, as scholars of the late twentieth-century workplace did. Rather, it focuses on spiritual alienation—disconnection from one's "authentic self." The problem, people in the coaching community said, is that tech workers have identified so strongly with their companies that they have lost their "true selves." And in Silicon Valley today—unlike the corporate cultures of the 1950s—that hurts rather than helps their productivity.[8]

During my time in Silicon Valley, I was struck by how frequently and fluently those in the coaching community spoke of the "authentic self" in relation to work. In the ideal workplace, they told me, people should be able express who they really are and be "authentic." Unfortunately, they lamented, the workplace too often alienates people from their "authentic selves." Consider what I heard from one man who worked in human resources in tech for twenty years before becoming an executive coach, as he described the toll that conforming to work took on him and his personal life. "So I gave a part of myself until I didn't have anything left. I shut a part of myself off." He finally left corporate life, fed up with the way work made him feel, determined "to get over feeling 'I hope the company likes me so I don't get fired.'" One engineer described work as a place where he has to "disconnect to stand being there."

Others described a fragmented life that pitted a "work self" against a "true self." One human resource professional lamented, "From nine to six I'm the LinkedIn self, and from six to ten I'm the Facebook self." Too much of the "true self" got left out at work. An engineer expressed this sentiment at a mindfulness workshop, saying, "I don't want to be David the manager, David the problem fixer, David the performer any more. I just want to be David." David sees his "work self" as fake. Another woman shared a similar feeling, claiming that after participating in her workplace mindfulness program, she realized that she had been spending all her time and energy "rehearsing" at work rather than being her "true self." In the workplace, tech workers claimed, they couldn't be "authentic." Another person said, "We don't necessarily talk about our feelings when we're at work. We don't necessarily want to be vulnerable with our colleagues at work."

People can lose their "true self," they told me, while climbing the corporate ladder. Linda Imazumi, a former tech manager who became an executive coach ten years ago, describes how the small trade-offs that people make to succeed in a corporate environment produce a "splitting of self":

> When you want to be successful, and yet, you know that you might have to . . . change because [something about yourself] isn't so accepted. Then, you start trading off, and that's where the splitting of self occurs, because then you're like, "Oh, well, shoot, you know, I really want to keep moving up, but I have to be a lot more [makes noise], you know?" And so, then pretty soon, you start kind of doing more of that and doing more of that.

Here Linda describes the incremental process of self-alienation that happens among people who want to succeed in the corporation as a "trading off" that leads to the "splitting of self," and "pretty soon," the corporate self becomes habitual and even more natural. Scholars call the work involved in this process of conforming to work culture "existential labor."[9]

Some tech workers report that they had "traded" away so much of themselves in order to succeed at work that their "real" selves got "lost" or even died. This is what happened to Taylor Epstein, an intense woman who became a start-up executive at the age of twenty-seven. She recalled "working constantly" and "losing [her]self in work." But when a much-anticipated acquisition of her company fell through, Taylor claimed, "it broke my heart and burned me out. I couldn't do it anymore, and so I left." She spent a year in deep self-reflection, practicing yoga every day, attending women's retreats, and working with a shaman who journeyed to Taylor's "underworld" with her. Through these practices she discovered how self-alienated she had become because of work: "What do I like to eat? What do I want to do in the world? Who am I? What do I value? I didn't even know these things because I gave everything to work." Taylor described leaving her job as both the "death of self" and a "resurrection" of her "real self."

Others told me stories of "losing themselves" at work to the point of becoming physically ill. Like Taylor, they attributed their illness to self-alienation and their healing to the recovery of a "true self." For instance, one woman in her late twenties who claimed that she "worked all the time" explained getting shingles as because "I was so out of touch with my body." Three people experienced temporary paralysis in the course of working in Silicon Valley. Each attributed their physical paralysis to alienation from the self. Tom Ellis was one of those unlucky people. One morning he woke up paralyzed and spent the next three months lying on his back and heavily drugged to withstand the pain. In recounting the experience, he never mentioned the medical explanation of his paralysis. Rather, he said it was his body's way of protesting his betrayal of his "true self." His work experience left him "living as someone I did not recognize."

Cultivating Human Capital by Cultivating Spirituality

To be sure, most workers have experienced some form of self-alienation in the history of modern capitalism. This comes through in popular expressions about work, such as "working for the man" or describing work as "soul crushing." It wouldn't be a stretch to say that most people in capitalism's history have *expected* work to be self-alienating. That is, after all, why work is called "work."[10] But this is where Patrick Sullivan and others in Silicon Valley depart from that norm. They think of employee self-alienation not simply as a personal problem, but as the company's problem. When a worker is alienated from him- or herself, that worker is also estranged from his or her full labor potential.

Over the past forty years, manufacturing industries got what amounts to an extra return by cutting labor costs through mechanization and outsourcing unskilled labor to developing countries where labor is cheaper. But in knowledge industries like tech, these strategies don't do much, because the most valuable assets are the knowledge and enthusiasm contained within skilled workers. So far, that intangible asset has been hard to mechanize or outsource cheaply. Instead of deskilling or outsourcing certain kinds of work, tech and other knowledge industries have turned to growing the value of their "human assets."[11] The minds and spirits of their skilled workers, after all, hold the most potential for capital development. That is why in recent years many firms have become interested in cultivating the spirituality of their workforces.[12]

The belief that interior growth translates to capital growth is a core assumption of the coaching community. Hector Gomez, a human resources professional in tech who's become an executive coach, explains the "growth" approach to labor management this way: "A human asset, if we want to use that language, is the only asset that grows. It's not fixed. An iPad gets less valuable every day, but a person can get more valuable every day." Hector points out that as "assets," humans can "grow" in value. To be sure, many companies already grow the value of their employees by training them in "hard skills," such as new programming languages, to adapt to a rapidly changing industry. But Hector points out a subjective dimension of "growth," one that has to do with employees' interior awareness: "A person becomes less valuable the less they feel valuable, and more important and significant and so on." After all, he emphasizes, "a human is not a fixed asset" like a machine; he or she is more like a plant. The leadership program that he runs is "somewhat of [a] greenhouse—a hospitable place for living things to grow." He describes the investment in daily care, vigilance, and time that interior growth entails. "Growth requires care and nurturing of a living thing. You have to water it every day, not just tons of gallons all at once and then you come back in six months. No. A little bit every day. It needs good soil and nutrition. It needs time."

If humans are like plants, then the quality and yield of their produce multiplies when they are properly nurtured and cultivated as a "whole person." It "makes economic sense to treat people as a whole person," he says, "because there is a big difference between compliance and commitment. If you treat someone like a thing, you may get them to comply, but you can't put a price on what someone will do if they are committed—that means fully alive, thriving." Like Patrick, Hector links that same interior state of being "fully alive" to an extra return on labor. The state of being "committed," Hector maintains, is something that companies "can't put a price on." Others in the coaching industry concur. Assessing the return on investment in the employees' inner development, one executive who had gone through coaching called it a "multiplier" and "a good investment." Reginald Bernstein, a seasoned executive coach, explains that the traditional approach to performance management emphasizes results, but what delivers the results is development.

Treating the soul as a source of human capital is the fullest manifestation of capitalism's ravenous appetite for growth.[13] But management does so not to exploit the soul and divest it of its value; rather, it wants to invest, develop, and grow the soul so that it can unleash its full potential in the market. Silicon Valley's solution to Alienation 3.0 is to mine what one executive calls the "spiritual need for connection to self, others, and universe," and transform it into productive labor.

A Spirituality of Authentic Selfhood

How do you grow the productive value of a soul? In the twentieth century, when companies expected to employ workers for a lifetime, management sacralized the group. In the twenty-first-century tech industry, however, where companies must get the most out of a continually changing cast of employees, management now sacralizes the "authentic self." Silicon Valley companies develop their human capital by cultivating what I call a *spirituality of authentic selfhood*. Companies ask coaches to teach employees the inner skills to "connect" to their "authentic selves." People in Silicon Valley don't typically use spiritual-sounding words like "soul," "spirituality," or "enlightenment," in the workplace. But in private, members of the coaching community make it clear that spirituality is central to their work. They translate spirituality into the corporate language of employee "engagement" and "leadership," vague, multivalent references to the intangible inner spirit. They strategically choose words such as "alive," "awake," and "centered," as well as "highest self," "best self," "true self," and "core" to describe what they perceive to be the spiritual state of being "connected" to one's "authentic self."

Taken together, these words and phrases describe a hidden, dormant "true self" that, when "awakened," "centered," or "enlivened," is a source of untapped and unbounded energy and creativity that can be directed toward work. This is evident in the way that executive coaches describe their work with tech professionals as "liberating potential," "unlocking potential," and "awakening aliveness." Explaining the importance of centering at a coaching workshop attended by tech professionals, the speaker said, "Centering is becoming more alive, more connected to what you care about! Centering means bringing to our body a shape where maximal energy and aliveness can run through it! When we're more fully alive, energy moves."

Spirituality is a competitive advantage in business. Margaret Channing, an in-house coach, puts it this way: "Mystery becomes relevant to companies when it unlocks potential, well-being, aliveness. . . . When we operate from that space, it's definitely an ROI [return on investment]." Jim Ward, a tech executive, describes spirituality as "useful." He frequently meditates and chants mantras before high-stakes meetings as a way to connect to his "highest self"—a self that is connected to divine power, he says. Filled with what he calls "divine power," Jim is his "best self," and able to negotiate the meeting with "wisdom, compassion, and resilience." Moreover, tech work is seen as so demanding that it requires drawing from deep wellsprings of the soul. "All-consuming work is not sustainable without a deep interior life that is fulfilling," a coach who works with tech executives explained.

The Tradition of the Sacred Self

The spirituality of authentic selfhood draws from a long American tradition that treats the human interior as a source of divine wisdom and energy.[14] In the 1985 classic *Habits of the Heart*, sociologist Robert Bellah and his coauthors write about Sheila, a young nurse who calls her practice of connecting to God by listening to her own "little voice" the religion of "Sheila-ism." It's an example of what Bellah and his coauthors call "expressive individualism," whose roots can be traced through the Transcendentalist thought of American writers like Henry David Thoreau to the eighteenth-century Romanticism of Jean Jacques Rousseau.[15] Romanticism, the philosopher Charles Taylor writes, is "this notion of an inner voice or impulse, the idea that we find the truth within us, and in particular in our feelings."[16]

In the United States, the art of "connecting" to one's "authentic self" has largely been the concern of the realm of religion and spirituality. It is alive and well in America's therapeutic religious and spiritual culture, from sources as varied as Rick's Warren's evangelical best seller *The Purpose Driven Life*,[17] the Buddhist psychotherapy of Jack Kornfield,[18] and the self-help spirituality of Deepak Chopra and Oprah Winfrey. Drawing from different traditions, each of these spiritual leaders promises to free an "authentic self" who is connected to a higher power from a false, broken, and limited self that is constricted by social and psychological limitations. The spirituality of the authentic self, then, is the practice of uncovering, recovering, and discovering one's "true core."

The spirituality of authentic selfhood has also spilled into the popular business genre. Self-help books on business leadership often integrate spirituality with management. Stephen Covey, Roger Merrill, and Rebecca Merrill's 1994 best seller *First Things First* counsels business leaders to attend first to their interior spirit. The book is a manual to help business leaders discern their mission in life.[19] In his later best seller *The 8th Habit*, Covey advises readers that they must connect to their mind, heart, body, and spirit to "discover" and "express" their "voice."[20]

Another business guru, former CEO of Medtronics and Harvard Business School professor Bill George, calls for a "spirituality of authentic leadership." In his popular book on business leadership *True North*, George encourages readers to examine their own lives. "Do you understand your purpose?" he asks. "Do you practice your values? Do you lead with your heart? Do you establish connected relationships?"[21] In a lecture at Harvard's Memorial Church in 2007, George asked the audience, "Can you recall a time when you felt most intensely alive and could say with confidence, 'This is the real me'? When you can, you are aligned with your True North and [are] prepared to lead others authentically."[22] True business leadership emanates from a deep interior spirituality, insist these business gurus. Great leaders who are in touch with themselves inspire others to do the same and produce from their full potential. This line of thinking is particularly evident in the "conscious capitalism" movement among companies such as Starbucks, the Container Store, and Zappos. John Mackey, author of *Conscious Capitalism: Liberating the Heroic Spirit of Business* and cofounder and CEO of the grocery chain Whole Foods, says, "The company was unable to grow until I was able to evolve—in other words I was holding the company back. My personal growth enabled the company to evolve."[23]

One of the most influential Silicon Valley advocates of the spirituality of authentic selfhood is Fred Kofman, vice president of leadership and development at Google and the former coach of Sheryl Sandberg. In his former position as a vice president at LinkedIn, Kofman called himself its "chief spiritual officer." Whereas Steven Covey, a Mormon, and Bill George, a Protestant, draw from Western religious traditions, Kofman finds inspiration in Asian religions. An Argentinean economist who once taught at MIT, Kofman underwent a profound spiritual transformation when he was a graduate student at UC Berkeley, exploring Asian religions and New Age thought in the Bay Area spiritual scene. His approach to organizational behavior marries the analytical rigor of his economics background with Asian spirituality. To Kofman, work is essentially a spiritual activity that centers on realizing the self: "The larger purpose of business—or sports, or any competitive activity, for that matter—is not to succeed, but to serve as a theater for self-knowledge, self-actualization, and self-transcendence."[24]

Where Covey and George focus primarily on the spirituality of business leaders, Kofman thinks more systematically about how spirituality can advance organizational growth. Most organizations miss out on potential capital because they fail to see the spiritual dimension of the workplace, he maintains. Kofman compares the structures of worker engagement to an iceberg, saying that we see only the 10 percent of the iceberg that is above water, the incentives that structure compliance. Accessing the other 90 percent of the worker requires "a spiritual solution," he argues, and not an economic one.[25]

Like Patrick Sullivan, the Euclid executive, Kofman ties worker engagement and organizational growth to individual spiritual growth.[26] He argues that the only way to get around the organizational problem of individuals maximizing self-interest is for companies to compensate and incentivize through "nonexclusive goods." Instead of giving employees material and status for their work and engagement, Kofman says that companies should say, "I want your enthusiasm, and I will give you the love that supports your development."[27] The typical budget constraints are removed when organizations can think beyond economic incentives and instead invest in the spiritual incentives that truly motivate individuals. "A conscious organization's goal in the personal realm is to promote the self-actualization and self-transcendence of everyone it touches," he writes.[28] When companies invest in the interior development of their workers, he maintains, they unleash the dormant powers of the "true self." According to Kofman, work ceases to be "work" when it is not merely labor exchanged for money or status but becomes the manifestation and actualization of the true and limitless self in this world. Of his own orientation toward work, he says, "I'm an infinite source of energy that's trying to manifest it in the world according to my dharma."[29] Kofman's fusing of Asian religion with American religious individualism is tech's spiritual corollary to its ethos of libertarian technological idealism.

Executive Coaching: Developing High-Potential Souls

Most companies practice a "trickle-down spirituality" by prioritizing the spiritual cultivation of their "high-pos," or high-potential employees—that is, senior leaders and employees on the way up. They do it through executive coaching. Fred Kofman says that a leader isn't the person who barks commands, but "just the person that is closer to the goal."[30] To him, that goal is not financial, but a spiritual goal that happens to confer financial and organization advantages. True leadership is a spiritual practice, Kofman maintains. He instructs business leaders to "look inside and find the truth," and do the "hard work of sitting down and noticing what's inside your heart." "When you find that infinite source of energy," he says, "then you can start running your business consciously."[31]

Even venture capitalists judge whether start-ups deserve funding by assessing the inner lives of the founders. For instance, speaking at Wisdom 2.0 in 2017, a large conference on mindfulness and tech, Tim Chang, a partner at a Silicon Valley venture capital firm, claimed that he used to use an "algorithm" to determine which start-ups to fund. Now that he has embarked on his own spiritual path of "working" on himself, however, he goes by the "energy" of the founder.[32] The boardroom pitch is "the least authentic time in the world," says Chang, so he gauges the energy of founders by taking them out on a walk so they can "take their armor off." Then he asks them questions that get at "who they really are." He wants to know, "Do they have a purpose? Do they know their core wound . . . because start-ups are an extension of their core wound."

Most large Silicon Valley companies invest in the interior development of their senior leaders by assigning them executive coaches, with whom they meet two to four times a month. With a price tag of $25,000 to $30,000 for six months of coaching, only the "high-pos" get this perk. Some companies have an in-house coaching staff, which cuts down costs. Explaining the draw of executive coaching, the director of learning and development at one firm explained, "Most companies are invested in their leaders—they are afraid of them failing." The director of engineering at one large tech firm justified the cost by comparing the leadership of an organization to the trunk of a tree. If the trunk is not strong, sustainable, and "alive" itself, how can it support the branches, he asked.

Coaching's reputation has changed in recent years. Carrie Hawthorne, an experienced coach and former human resources director at a large tech firm, explained that in the past, "they would hire a coach as a punitive thing." Management recognized your value, but you had to improve your game or leave. Nowadays, coaching is assigned not as punishment but as investment in someone's growth and development. "It's about, we need to invest in our best people," Carrie explained. "We need to help them be successful. . . . The more progressive organizations see it as an investment in human development." Having a coach is a status symbol. It shows that you are important enough for the company to invest in you. The director of in-house coaching at one large firm reported with exasperation that ambitious employees clamor to have a coach, some even demanding it in their hiring contracts.

In the past, coaching was largely "results oriented," coaches explained, focusing on "soft skills" like public speaking or effective communication. Coaching today is different. "It used to be about results and performance," one coach observed. "Now it's about healing the whole person." Coaches used this kind of holistic and therapeutic language to describe their roles in the corporation. Healing, wholeness, and quarterly performance are all connected, they said. Firms cannot afford senior leaders whose personal and inner lives are broken and in turmoil. Unhappy marriages, strained relationships with children, midlife crises, not knowing one's true purpose, living an unfulfilling life—these problems can distract executives from being their "best selves" in the firm. Being a business executive is tough and lonely, they told me. "It's hard to be at the top, all alone," one coach explained, and so coaching is "basically therapy without the stigma." Gwen Kowalski, a matter-of-fact director of learning and development who hires coaches for her company's senior leaders, calls them "spiritual guides."

Ostensibly, coaching's purpose is to develop senior employees' leadership skills. Yet coaches think they have more impact: Clients "start off with a smallish problem, like 'how do I be an effective, or whatever, leader in this company?'" says one coach. "Then it evolves to something much bigger." To this coach, becoming an "effective, or whatever, leader" is "a smallish problem." The "something much bigger" that she refers to is helping leaders reconnect to their "authentic selves." Tom Sanders, an established Silicon Valley coach, articulates this theme of work and alienation. He asks a room full of coaching students, including some employed in tech: "What's most meaningful to us?" Here's how he answers the question, complete with scare quotes: "We know what that is as children, but we lose sight of it once we get a 'real job' in the 'real world.'" He concludes by saying, "Coaching is a chance to return to ourselves. In our day-to-day lives we separate ourselves from ourselves."

Coaches described the results of their interventions as inner transformation, a way to answer the question "Who am I at my core?" One coach contrasted coaching with consulting by saying, "It's not like consulting; it's about deep change." Similarly, another coach told me, "With everyone I work with I'm always really clear that we're going to do inner work and then that will show up in your outer work." Joseph Stark, a former Catholic priest who is an executive coach, claims there is no difference between the spiritual direction that he did as a priest and the work he does now as a coach. "Both are about getting right with yourself," he says.

Joseph may be right that both spiritual direction and executive coaching are about "getting right with yourself," but he overlooks something important: the meaning of spiritual cultivation is different in a religious context from what it is in a business context. In the first, Joseph is a priest who has vowed his life's labor to the Catholic faith; his spiritual direction is intended to help parishioners "get right" with God. In the second, Joseph is an executive coach hired by a company to help his client, a senior leader, "get right" with the company. In both cases, spiritual cultivation is the means, but with very different ends.

The example of executive coach Linda Imazumi and client Susan Marshall illustrates how companies reap the fruits of the inner work that business leaders do with their coaches. Susan was a powerful executive at a large tech firm in the valley. She was a brilliant business strategist but struggled as a leader. According to Linda, she had trouble "connecting with people." The company needed Susan to succeed and arranged for her to work with Linda to "improve her communication skills." Linda, a petite and no-nonsense woman in her sixties, was a former sales manager in a Silicon Valley firm who transitioned to coaching ten years ago—and was familiar with the pressures of being a woman in a male-dominated corporate world. While it appeared that Susan's problems were with communication, the "real" issues, Linda explained, were deeper, and had to do with her "core." "I try to see them at their core and help them see that." Linda said, "My work is about awakening and reconnecting to self, other, planet, and greater mystery."

Over the course of the next eighteen months, Linda met with Susan for an hour and a half every other week to figure out "Susan's life narrative." To evaluate Susan, Linda conducted a "360 assessment," in which she shadowed Susan and interviewed a dozen people who work closely with her. In addition to work colleagues, she also interviewed Susan's close friends, people who Linda claimed could give her insight into the "real Susan" outside of work. Linda had Susan take an Enneagram test, a personality test that is used in both business and spiritual settings, integrating psychotherapeutic and spiritual insights. The Enneagram, she says, helps her to see the "core essence and shadow" of her clients. It's what Linda calls a "doorway to spirituality," which opens her clients to work with her on a deeper spiritual level.

The 360 revealed that Susan's coworkers regarded her as a manipulative, political, ambitious woman that they could not trust. People were afraid of her. Linda explained that as a woman in a man's world, Susan had learned to play the game by developing a hard shell around her, staying impervious to vulnerability or emotion. But according to Linda, the "work Susan" was the opposite of the generous and kind "real Susan" that her friends adored. As an example, Linda shared a story about Susan that, Linda claimed, represented Susan's "core." Before coming to tech, Susan had worked as a camp counselor during her summers as a graduate student. Her favorite camper was Ashley, an eight-year-old who was in a wheelchair. She could not run around, swim, and climb trees like the other kids in camp. But Susan always found a way for her to be a part of the fun. When the other kids went swimming, Susan strapped Ashley to a paddle board and shepherded her through the waters. Instead of traditional tag, Susan devised a version where the other kids hopped around with their legs bound together while Susan pushed Ashley in her wheelchair. Together, they became known in the camp as the "dynamic duo." According to Linda, this generous, compassionate, and loving Susan, was the "real Susan."

When Linda reported her findings from the 360, Susan was devastated. She couldn't believe that after everything she gave to the company, people didn't trust her. The first part of Linda's work involved helping Susan accept how her coworkers could interpret her behavior in such an unflattering way. Linda said that Susan slowly recognized that she had built her outer self in a certain way to succeed in the firm, and that it wasn't making her happy.

To Linda, the root of Susan's "communication problem" was that she wasn't in touch with her real self—the generous and loving Susan who would do anything to bring joy and happiness to a girl confined to a wheelchair. Instead of being authentic at work, Susan tried to prove herself by conforming to the model of the strong male executive. But in doing so, she lost her coworkers' trust. Even more tragic, according to Linda, Susan lost touch with her "true self."

Linda's plan was to help Susan become more aware of her emotions and her body—to reconnect with herself. Linda asked Susan to come up with a tangible reminder of her relationship with Ashley. Susan chose a picture of Ashley, and put it on her desk to remind herself of the "real Susan." Linda taught Susan to meditate and assigned her daily "homework": practicing yoga to cultivate awareness of her body, and writing in her journal to get in touch with her emotions. Susan attended a weekend retreat on feminine spirituality at Esalen, a well-known New Age retreat center on the central California coast, at Linda's urging. These practices helped Susan "get in touch with what makes her heart sing," Linda explained. "She was in touch with her inner self and not just about how she showed up for the world."

According to Linda, the company's investment in Susan's spiritual development paid off. Susan started to allow the "real Susan" to come out at work. Connected to her "authentic self," Susan communicated and interacted with others with more honesty, vulnerability, and empathy. People started to feel safe with her, Linda claimed. By learning to connect with herself, Linda said, Susan tapped into a set of inner resources that empowered her as a leader to connect with others. Reflecting on her work with Susan, Linda told me, "You can only be a responsive leader if you have a strong interior life."

The Spiritual Exercises of the Tech Company

AWARENESS OF SELF

The basic premise of executive coaching—that the potential of the spirit can be cultivated and coached into being—is also the foundation of all religious practices. The first executive coaches were not business gurus, but religious gurus. One of the earliest practices of coaching was formulated in the sixteenth century by Saint Ignatius of Loyola, the Spanish Catholic priest and founder of the Jesuit order. In his classic guide to spiritual direction, which is still widely read today, *The Spiritual Exercises*, Saint Ignatius outlines a set of contemplative practices to follow under the guidance of a spiritual director. Through them, the practitioner discerns the will of God. The similarities between the "spiritual exercises" of today and those of five centuries ago are striking. Both are done under a director's guidance. Both include meditations, prayers, and reflections to cultivate attentiveness, openness, and responsiveness in the practitioner. But in tech's religion of work today, spiritual exercises are directed to a different goal. In the Ignatian Spiritual Exercises, the objective is to become more attentive and responsive to God in order to serve God. In coaching, however, the objective is to become more attentive, open, and responsive to the desire and passions of the "authentic self" in order to serve the company.

The first step in the "spiritual exercises of authentic selfhood" involves cultivating awareness of "body, mind, and spirit." In group workshops and individual coaching sessions, coaches and facilitators often introduce meditation and mindfulness practices to develop employees' physical and emotional self-awareness. Meditation and mindfulness are Buddhist spiritual practices that have been adapted to the corporate, secular context, a point that I will discuss in later chapters.

Here's an example of such an exercise from one off-site professional development workshop. Nicole, a coach in her fifties who is also a dharma teacher, leads the audience of one hundred in the following simple guided meditation:

> Just sit and settle in. [pause] Gently close your eyes. Take several deep breaths and settle into your chair and fully arrive. . . . Feel the soles of your feet on the floor. Feel your thighs and sit-bones against the chair. Notice your shoulders. Are they tensed up to your ears? Are they hunched towards your chest? Gently pull them down and open them. Notice your eyes. Soften them. Let the corners of your mouth melt down. Notice what it's like to be here in this room. . . . Are you tired? Anxious? Distracted? Happy? No need to judge; just notice. [long pause] When you are ready, please open your eyes and bring your attention back to the room.

In the meditation, Nicole takes us on a tour of our bodies, minds, and spirits. She invites us to "feel" and "notice" thoughts, emotions, and bodily sensations—parts of ourselves that, like Susan, we may have "shut down," repressed, or ignored in order to fit in the work environment. "No need to judge; just notice," Nicole reassures us.

These meditation practices instill a nonjudgmental and detached state that allows participants to develop what coaches call a "third-person" gaze of the self. Through these practices, meditators bring to consciousness emotions and sensations that usually go unnoticed. Afterward, participants respond with self-discoveries: "I didn't know my shoulders were so hunched over," or "I didn't realize that I'm feeling anxious."

Coaches often describe their engineering tech clients as being "in their heads" and out of touch with their bodies. Because of this, coaches try to cultivate embodied awareness in their tech clients. They ask questions like "where do you feel it in your body?" to help people get in touch with how emotions like stress and anxiety are experienced physically. For example, in one workshop the facilitator asked us all to recall a painful experience, and then to notice where we felt it in our bodies, then a joyful experience, and again notice where we felt it in our bodies. Some coaches bring in meditative practices like yoga to help tech professionals gain awareness and control over their bodies. Others use mental imagery, such as relaxing and tensing certain muscles, or breathing in and out certain colors associated with calming and energizing emotional states. In several workshops we assumed psychologist Amy Cuddy's "victory pose"—arms stretched out above the shoulders in a V—to activate testosterone and put us in a state of confidence and success.[33] And in a few workshops, we danced to "get into our bodies." In all these practices, the goal is to get engineers out of "their heads" so that they can attend to their bodies and emotions.

LISTENING TO THE SELF

Moving from the body, thoughts, and emotions, coaches lead clients to go deeper into the interior self through practices such as meditation, journaling, and, when appropriate, small-group discussions. These practices help clients do what coaches call "listening to what wants to emerge" from the self. The following meditation at a leadership workshop, led by Nick, a former engineer, is an example of such a practice:

> Find a comfortable position and just take a deep breath. . . . Let it out. Close your eyes. Just allow yourself to be fully present. Whatever happened before you came here, just let it be. Allow yourself to fully arrive. . . . And maybe go inside to that deepest part of yourself, that true part of yourself, the highest, infinite part of yourself. I think of it as soul. You think of it as however you like. And get in touch with

> that. . . . The real you. And as you breathe in, breathe in that gratitude that the world has to offer, and as you breathe out, breathe out anything that is not the real you. . . . And from that deep seed of knowing, let it emerge. . . . What wants to arise in you?

The meditation puts the practitioner in a state to "listen." In it, Nick invites us to "be fully present" and to "fully arrive" by letting the past "be." He leads us to "go inside" into the "deepest part" of ourselves, the "soul," which is "true" and "infinite." We can cleanse the self of "anything that is not the real you" by breathing. Once we've "fully arrived" and gone "deep" into the "soul," we are ready to listen to it.

The Ignatian Spiritual Exercises of self-examination are supposed to help practitioners discern the voice of God amid the clamor of others. Similarly, coaches teach clients to quiet the voices of the "false self" in order to listen to the "true self." In several workshops that I attended, we practiced what I call the "really really" exercise. It's the practice of continually asking ourselves questions of purpose, going deeper each time and asking what's "really" the root of our motivation. For example, at one leadership workshop we reflected and wrote on a series of questions: "what brought me here is . . ."; and the second question, "what really brought me here is . . ."; and the third question "what really really brought me here is. . . ." Each iteration is supposed to peel off layers of the performed self to reach the core self. At another workshop geared toward entrepreneurs, the speaker encouraged the participants to engage in a "spiritual practice" of asking three questions of themselves: "Who are you really? And keep double-clicking. . . . What do you really want? And double-click. . . . And what are you in service to? And double-click. Is it your ego . . . validation?" Through this practice of reflection, practitioners go deeper into discovering the "real self" with each spiritual "double click."

ALIGNING THE SELF TO PRODUCTIVE LABOR

In the last part of the Ignatian Spiritual Exercises, practitioners are directed to respond to God's voice through action, to "love and serve the Lord" in the world.[34] In tech's spiritual exercises, the disciplines of awareness and listening are also directed toward action in the world, not to "love and serve the Lord," but to produce. According to the coaching community, someone who is "aligned" is living out his or her "authentic self" through his or her work. No longer encumbered by false distractions and attachments, the authentic self is liberated to draw from this deep wellspring of inner energy, and to channel it to the world *through work*.

When someone is "aligned" with his or her work, work *feels* different. It becomes energizing. Work ceases to be "work." This is evident in a quote by Zen teacher Allan Watts that I heard repeatedly in Silicon Valley: "This is the real secret of life—to be completely engaged in what you are doing in the here and now. And instead of calling it work, realize it is play." When one is "completely engaged" rather than "alienated" from work, as Watt suggests, work becomes joyful, lighthearted, and fun, "play."

Companies get more out of alignment than "play." Their bottom line increases. But they insist this is a happy by-product, not the goal. Here Carrie Hawthorne, an executive coach, reflects on her earlier days as the human resources director of a successful start-up that became public:

> I'm thinking back to the early days of the company, the people who joined in the early years; it was a lot of work. Nobody knew if it was going to lead to anything. . . . The reason they came was because it's so connected with who they are . . . what their whole life has been about for whatever reason. Because of that alignment and everyone cared so deeply about this thing, they ended up creating something amazing which made a lot of money for everyone. . . . When you put your heart and soul into it, you can't help but make something awesome. Do you know what I mean? It takes, I think, a risk, and because there are many years where people are working and they're not making any money, it's not about the money.

Carrie attributes the wild success of the start-up to "alignment." "For people to do their best work, they need to personally care about it," she explains. "Not only like their job; it needs to be aligned with who they are."

Like Carrie, who says working at the start-up was "not about the money," many in the coaching community ignore the material function of work and emphasize its spiritual function. Work, they claim, is a sacred calling. They sanctify the meaning of work by referring to it using language such as "calling," "vocation," and "service." They quote sayings that beatify work, such as Kahlil Gibran's "work is love made visible," or Gandhi's "work is worship." (They carefully avoided the much more famous saying about work on the Auschwitz gates, "work sets you free.") Some tech professionals also adopt this language, describing their work as a form of "love" and "service." One person described his job as "bringing the gifts that I have to the world and sharing them with others."

Another way that coaches elevate the meaning of work is through the telling of "the cathedral story," which I heard repeatedly in Silicon Valley. It's a story about two men cutting stone blocks for the town cathedral. One begrudgingly says that he is a stonecutter. The other jubilantly describes his work as "building a cathedral." The lesson of the "cathedral story," an earnest director of leadership and development tells an audience of engineers, is that "we feel most alive when our activity is in connection with our highest purpose. We need to connect to our cathedral story."

Coaches help their clients create their own "cathedral stories." That's what Glenn Brooks, a coach who "helps people find their purpose in life," says he did with Tina Baker. Her boss, the vice president of a small start-up who had been coached by Glenn, hired Glenn to "work his magic" on Tina, a talented rising employee in the company who had not been performing to her usual high standards. Tina explained to Glenn that she was burnt out from maintaining the company website. But Glenn didn't tell her to take a vacation or rest. Instead, he told her to shift her focus to what brings her energy and joy in her life, by journaling about it every day. In one coaching session, Tina talked about how much fun she had hosting a dinner party the night before. "What did you enjoy about it?" Glenn asked. Tina loved making the dinner table beautiful with her careful attention to the candles, flowers, seating cards, and table setting—all so remote from her life at work. After more sessions, it became clear that creating beauty energized Tina. Glenn helped her realize her purpose in life: bringing beauty into the world. He instructed her to spend more time cultivating the artist within by devoting time each day to beautifying the world. Glenn shared that this changed how Tina oriented herself to work. She asked to be more involved in the aesthetic design of the website, rather than its technical aspects. She saw her job—designing beautiful websites—as aligned with her calling to bring beauty into the world. According to Glenn, work no longer burned her out and depleted her; it energized her. Connecting Tina to her purpose in life, her "cathedral story," was like discovering a wellspring of energy and inspiration right under her feet.

Tina was lucky that she was able to find a way to align her job with her calling. But what happens when people discover through their coaches that they can't be aligned with their jobs, or, to put it differently, that their job isn't their calling? I asked these questions to many coaches and got the same reply: the employee should find another position. An employee who is not "aligned" to his or her job is serving the interests of neither the company nor him- or herself.

In an industry where people change jobs every three to five years, tech workers must be vigilant about discerning their calling. For instance, one workshop, Discovering Your Real Work, promised to help participants "examine whether your current living aligns to your calling." In it, the facilitator, an executive coach, asked a series of questions: "What brings you joy in life?" "What makes you alive?" "Where do you feel that in your body?" She had us close our eyes and guided us to "listen" to ourselves: "Let your body sense this question," she told us; "listen without resistance." The meditation culminated with the question "How can you change your work to reflect your aliveness?" "Your real work," the exercise taught us, manifests through productive labor.

In the spiritual exercises of tech, listening and reflection are regular practices, like prayer for the religious. Coaches encourage people to make time in their schedules and space in their minds and hearts to regularly reflect on their calling. One coach gave the example of a busy executive who created a daily ritual "to remember his vocation." Once a day he'd leave his phone in the office and walk to the company garden and take three deep breaths to remind him of his "call" in life.

The language of "calling" and "vocation" suggests the presence of a higher power that communicates with each person. A phrase that I heard often, "the work I am called to do," conveys that something outside of and larger than the human person or the company "calls" him or her to behave in a certain way. Similarly, when coaches refer to "your life" in the third person—as in the question "what does your life want to say?"—they treat "your life" as an entity that is separate from the individual and immanent self, a repository of undiscovered wisdom. Some people give that higher power a name. But they never call it God. At the 2018 Wisdom 2.0 Leadership Summit, the founder of Wisdom 2.0, Soren Gordhamer, declared, "The Universe is on our side," then asked, "How do we partner with it more? How do we listen and let what wants to emerge from us?" Evoking Buddhist language, one coach, a former engineer described her coaching as getting companies "one step closer to their own organizational enlightenment . . . so that they realize their true purpose in the world and what it means to truly serve society." When the worker is "aligned," productive labor becomes a sacred way to "partner" with the Universe and to achieve "organizational enlightenment."

Thinking of work as a form of "calling," "love," and "service" might get workers closer to their own enlightenment, but it also fulfills management's desire to get an extra return on labor, a point that writer Miya Tokumitsu and historian Bethany Moreton also make.[35] The best-selling business writer Daniel Pink tells business leaders that managers can tap into the deep wellspring of interior motivation if they connect organization goals to transcendent and "soul-stirring ideas." Pink quotes the business writer Gary Hamel: "The goals of management are usually described in words like 'efficiency,' 'advantage,' 'value,' 'superiority,' 'focus,' and 'differentiation.' Important as these objectives are, they lack the power to rouse human hearts." Business leaders "must find ways to infuse mundane business activities with deeper soul-stirring ideas, such as honor, truth, love, justice, and beauty."[36] By harnessing "soul-stirring ideas" and practices, tech's spiritual exercises ultimately "awaken" the full potential of the tech professional to serve not God, but the company.

From Managing to "Coaching"

A spirituality of authentic selfhood trickles down through firms, as enlightened business leaders who've been coached, in turn, coach their employees. As a result of coaching, managers claim that they shifted their management styles from commanders to guides and inspirers. Managing labor, they say, is not just about organizing efficient production, but also about getting employees to that soulful state of being "alive" and "connected" to their "authentic selves." Instead of "managing" employees, leaders talk about "supporting" and "coaching" them. For example, Benjamín Vejar, the director of engineering at one large firm claims, "I never say that I manage people. I always say that I support people." Sujeet Menon, a marketing executive at another large tech firm, says that managing is not telling people what to do, but "bringing out the best in others." He claims that he is a "coach" who "supports the personal and professional lives of his team." Doug Robinson, the founder and CEO of a small start-up, even goes so far to call himself "head pastor" of his company, whose role is to "help people be who they want to be."

Being the "head pastor" and "supporting" the interior development of employees requires managers to know their employees more personally. For instance, Benjamín Vejar credits Buddhist teacher Jack Kornfield for his management mantra: "people need to be met, seen, and heard." To Vejar, supporting people means that he needs to understand their lives, so he takes extra time to get to know his employees. Similarly, Jeff Weiner, the CEO of LinkedIn, speaks of his first principle of leadership as practicing "compassionate management." He invests in getting to know his team and makes them feel heard and valued so that he can support them in being the best in their position. Weiner, who was mentored by Fred Kofman, credits his management style to inspiration from the book *The Art of Happiness*, based on the teachings of the Dalai Lama.[37]

When marketing executive Sujeet Menon conducts job interviews, he always begins, "Tell me about your life journey." A deeply spiritual person, Sujeet believes that "everything is spiritual" and that "we bring our spirituality to our work." So as a manager, he says that he wants to understand what moves each person to his or her core. When Sujeet assembles a new team, they do an exercise called "the river of life." Each person shares the major events and people in their lives that have formed them. That meeting sets the tone for openness and authenticity, making work a place where they can be their "true selves." People go deep, he says, and many cry. Sujeet told me about how one person shared his sense of inferiority, after growing up with an older brother who became an Olympic gold-medal skier. Another revealed being physically abused by his father. And another spoke of the deep betrayal he felt at the age of sixteen when his father left his mother for another woman. As a manager, Sujeet's mantra is to "coach and support, not judge." And Sujeet says it's worked for him. Two years ago, he was voted the best manager at his ten-thousand-plus-person firm.

Doug Robinson, the "head pastor" of his company, engages in even more personal mentoring. To illustrate how he "help[s] people be who they want to be," he gives the example of Allison, a member of his executive team who, when they first met, was full of "self-doubt" and "self-destructive tendencies," struggling with depression and anxiety. Yet Doug felt she could be "a very powerful leader and a strong woman, and somebody who has a big voice and can do all these amazing things." Allison, he says, was meant "for the big leagues"—but lived like she was "small potatoes." The work of "pastoring" Allison was an intense labor of love for Doug. He sent her on a weekend retreat to Esalen and paid for Allison to undergo regular therapy and coaching so that she could let go of the destructive messages of unworthiness that had filled her life. He even tripled her salary to reflect the leader that he knew that she had the potential to become. Doug says that his "pastoring" has paid off—and that Allison's now the "powerful leader" she was always meant to be.

Work as a Spiritual Journey

In Silicon Valley, work is seen neither as soul crushing nor as a place where people "sell their souls." Rather, work is where people "find" themselves and "connect" with the deepest parts of themselves. Many told me that work is part of their "spiritual journey." "People are thinking about work as an opportunity to grow and learn," the director of human resources at a well-known tech firm told an audience at one tech and mindfulness conference. "People aren't showing up to work asking, 'how do I become a great manager,' but 'how do I become a great person?' How do we use the [work] environment as the journey?" She illustrated the "journey" depicting a lotus, a common Buddhist symbol: four stones set in a stream as a walking path leading to a lotus.

Many tech workers, especially those who've worked with coaches, embrace this idea of work as spiritual journey. They describe their work careers in the language of sacred pilgrimage. Career changes, disappointments, and successes are part of a larger "journey" or "path" toward self-discovery and self-actualization. "I am working on myself," they say about work. Alex Stockton, an entrepreneur in his mid-thirties, says, "The work of founding a company is finding yourself." After several unsuccessful attempts to fund his start-up, he hired a coach to help him with his self-presentation. The coach guided him in looking deep inside himself to ask who he was and what really drove him to start the company. As a result, Alex radically changed the way he presented himself and the company. That interior work was necessary, he claims; it's why his start-up successfully secured funding.

During my time in Silicon Valley, I was struck by how easily and clearly people articulated their calling in life. Many had a personal mission statement that they could whip out at any time: "my job is to bring animating force into everyday interactions," "help people find their North Star," "connect people to their core," "help humanity thrive by making it easier for teams to collaborate," "connect people to their friends and family." People equated themselves with their callings. In one workshop, we introduced ourselves by our calling, by using the phrase "I am a commitment to . . ." For example, "I'm John, and I'm a commitment to democratizing digital knowledge." In Silicon Valley, people identified the deepest parts of themselves by their work.

In most venerable religious, spiritual, and cultural traditions, however, the journey toward the "true self" is usually a solitary one; it happens apart from the distractions of social institutions such as work and family. Take Henry David Thoreau's experiment at Walden Pond. To "connect" to his "authentic self," he left his family and his work behind. So too, many religions teach that "connecting" to the divine begins with renouncing things of "this world." The Buddha's journey to enlightenment began only after leaving home, family, and the "job" of being a prince. In the Gospel of Matthew, Christ learns who he "really" is during his forty days in the desert alone, away from his family, community, and work.

What does it mean, then, when we define the deepest and truest part of ourselves in and through our work? My visit to a large tech firm one afternoon gave me clear insight into the answer. An employee in the wellness department gave me a tour of the company's wellness facilities. The company had lavished millions of dollars on employee well-being. The campus had a ten-thousand-square-foot gym, an outdoor track, a swimming pool, tennis courts, and private rooms for dance classes, Pilates, yoga, Zumba, meditation, and more. At the end of the tour, we walked out of the air-conditioned gym onto a stone-set circular patio. Here we found a wellness "amenity" that surprised me: a walking labyrinth of a kind typically found in cathedrals and other sacred spaces.

Walking a labyrinth is a practice that symbolizes a sacred pilgrimage, a spiritual journey of three parts: "Releasing" attachments as you walk to the center of the labyrinth; "receiving" from the divine at the center; and then "returning" to the world as a transformed being. Who and what is at the center depends on the religious tradition. But the meaning of the center was unequivocal in this tech company. Etched in the stones at the center of the labyrinth was not a crescent moon, a cross, or a lotus. Rather, it was another religious symbol: the company logo.

The walking labyrinth centered around the company logo perfectly represents the spiritual journey of so many in Silicon Valley: "releasing" attachments that are distractions from work; "receiving" the divinity that comes from work; and "returning" by manifesting it into the world through technological innovation. The labyrinth proclaims Silicon Valley's truth, one that is both prophetic *and profitable*: we become divine through work.

CHAPTER 4

The Dharma according to Google

Nathan Thompson, a sixty-two-year-old human resources professional, has witnessed a lot of change during his forty-five years in the Bay Area. Sitting underneath a rambling oak tree on the grounds of a Buddhist retreat center where he volunteers, Nathan remembers: "Back then, it was about drugs, sex, and rock and roll." He pauses and then continues with a plaintive smile, "Now it's about productivity." Clad in an orange-and-red-striped shirt with a Tibetan print, Nathan is reflective and soft-spoken. In 1973, when he moved to San Francisco from his small hometown in the Midwest, the Bay Area was "abounding with opportunities to learn about Asian religions." Nathan says that his "spiritual path" began his first week after arriving in San Francisco, when he found a copy of *The Autobiography of a Yogi* at a café. After devouring the book, he filled out the form for the self-realization correspondence course, mailed it in an envelope with $12, and waited for Paramanhansa Yogananda's "lessons on meditation and spiritual living" to arrive. Nathan lived in a community with other hippies who spent much of their time getting high, meditating, chanting, and learning at the feet of every Asian guru who came through town. Now, as a human resources consultant, Nathan sees tech companies taking the same spiritual practices that animated his youthful quest and using them to make workers more productive. He's also noticed a change at the Buddhist retreat center where he volunteers. Spiritual seekers like him are giving way to tech professionals, who come to the center in their Teslas, determined to optimize their work performance.

So far, I've argued that work replaces religion in Silicon Valley. Tech workers find meaning, belonging, identity, and their "true selves" through work. For their part, tech companies enthusiastically embrace the pastoral role of religion, offering spiritual care and spiritual cultivation as vehicles to make their workers more engaged and productive. Nathan's observations, however, raise another question about tech's colonization of life and spirit in Silicon Valley: how does the meaning of religious traditions change when they become a part of work? Tech workers today are rushing to learn meditation, but not as a spiritual practice like in Nathan's day, rather, as a productivity practice. When work replaces religion, I argue, *religion takes on the instrumental logic of work.* This chapter explores how changes in work and the economy in the last forty years have shaped the spiritual ethos of Silicon Valley today. I focus especially on Buddhism and the practice of meditation or mindfulness—terms that my respondents used interchangeably—both of which are at the center of tech culture. Silicon Valley's religion of work illustrates how the new economy, and neoliberalism more broadly, is changing the way tech workers understand and practice religious traditions.

A Tale of Two Generations: From the Mystics to the Users

The Mystics

To understand how the tech industry has changed the practice of Asian religious and spiritual traditions, we need to go back fifty years and look at the spiritual lives of another cohort of young adults: those who migrated en masse to Northern California in the 1960s and 1970s. They also left their homes, families, and communities from small towns and big cities in the Midwest, the East, and the South to seek out "innovative technology" and to create "start-ups" out West. They too engaged in a movement that transformed America and "disrupted" the establishment. Their migrations, however, weren't journeys to develop work and career, but journeys to expand the spirit and consciousness. These migrants wanted to disrupt the social, political, and religious systems of their day, not an industry. They also explored technologies, but through spiritual practices, and not through silicon. And instead of forming new communities through capitalist enterprise, their start-ups were communes and new religious movements. This cohort of migrants was the counterculture movement of the 1960s and 1970s, and now some of them are executive coaches for tech companies.

Those of my research participants who were a part of this countercultural cohort shared a distinct orientation toward religion and spirituality. They are what the sociologist Max Weber calls "mystics," and they have an "otherworldly" orientation toward life. The Buddha and Saint Teresa of Avila are archetypal mystics. They've renounced the economic, political, and social institutions of "the world" to seek mystical union with the divine. I refer to the 1960s and 1970s countercultural inheritors of the tradition as "the Mystics." Although the Mystics I studied participated in "the world," they prioritized spiritual quest over advancement within these worldly institutions.

Melissa Brady is one of these Mystics. A sixty-seven-year-old executive coach with a mass of curly white hair, she explains escaping her patrician East Coast roots and moving to the Bay Area at the age of twenty-four: "It was 1968. I basically turned on, tuned in, dropped out, and never left," she says, quoting Timothy Leary's famous countercultural mantra. Back then, the phrase meant "turning on" through psychedelics, "tuning in" to one's conscious, and "dropping out" of conventional society, she says. Melissa completely "dropped out" after she came to the Bay Area: she lived in a commune with other musicians and never got a paycheck, paid bills, or even voted. Her life, she says, was so "far out" that she had her first child in a mountain cabin that lacked running water and electricity. Melissa's life revolved around music and getting high. Acid trips, Melissa explains, proved to her that the spiritual realm was real. But drugs gave her only momentary access to the spiritual realm. She'd have these amazing spiritual experiences when she was high, but then she'd come down from it. Longing for something more permanent and sustainable then a temporary hit, she became a "student of Asian religions"—studying Tibetan Buddhism; transcendental meditation; and aikido, a Japanese martial art with a strong spiritual emphasis. Like other members of the counterculture, Melissa rejected what she perceived as the legalism and hypocrisy of her own Christian heritage, turning instead to Asian mysticism for more authentic spiritual experience. These traditions gave her access to powerful, mystical experiences *all the time*, states that she compares to her childhood love of horseback riding: "It's like riding an awesome and beautiful power so much bigger than you."

Al Hoffman is another one of the Mystics. In 1970, he was a twenty-one-year-old "New York Jewish kid" who moved to San Francisco and underwent a "profound spiritual awakening" in Asian religions. He wasn't drawn by economic opportunity like the tech migrants today, but by *spiritual* opportunity. San Francisco was at the forefront of the counterculture's love affair with Asian mysticism. Every well-known Asian spiritual teacher stopped in San Francisco, he says, because "they were looking for Westerners as students." With great relish, Al describes San Francisco in the 1970s as a "vortex of Asian gurus, yogis, and roshis . . . a wonderful banquet of spirituality." He had no career aims, no angel investors, no venture capital, and no marketable skills. He didn't need any of that because he'd committed his life to spiritual quest. For three and a half years, he worked in odd jobs, making just enough money to live so that he could devote his life to "doing kind of postgraduate work—if you want to put it that way—of studying with whatever Buddhist teacher or Hindu teacher that appealed to me." He learned intensively from the circuit of well-known Asian spiritual teachers who made their way to San Francisco: people like the Karmapa, the head of the Kagyu lineage of Tibetan Buddhism; Baba Muktananda, the founder of Siddha Yoga; and Yogi Bhajan. One of his most memorable experiences was lying on the floor of the grand Drake Hotel in downtown San Francisco in a trance with three hundred other Mystics.

Mystics like Melissa and Al participated in one of the greatest American spiritual awakenings of the twentieth century.[1] Rebelling against the authoritative moralism of their parents' Christianity and Judaism, the

Mystics flocked to the Bay Area to seek an otherworldly experiential spirituality in the wisdom and practices of Buddhist and Hindu sages. Instead of the ascetic rationalism of their middle-class Judeo-Christian religions, Asian spiritualities opened them to mystical experiences that they described as "expanded consciousness," "connecting with God," "connecting to the Universe," "feeling love," and "feeling high." The Mystics accessed transcendent experiences through "technologies" of Asian spiritual practices such as meditation and chanting, as well as psychedelic drugs. Spirituality wasn't just a personal practice, but something they shared together in their new experimental communities—their communes, religious movements, and monasteries. For instance, some Mystics, like Melissa, created informal communities where Buddhism and other Asian spiritual traditions were a part of the culture of "drugs, sex, and rock-n-roll." Others converted to Zen Buddhism and lived lives of strict religious practice in Zen communes such as the San Francisco Zen Center. Some, like Al, did not live in intentional spiritual communities but saw themselves as part of a larger Asian spiritual awakening taking hold in the Bay Area.

Many of the Mystics I spoke to maintained their otherworldly and mystical orientation as they grew older, became parents, and built successful careers. They continued to critique the establishment, even as they became a part of it. And they pursued spiritual experience as the world around them changed with the tech industry.

"You're On!" Tech and the Ethos of Self-Optimization

In 1971, at the height of the countercultural movement, Coca-Cola produced one of the most famous ads of the twentieth century. Hippies and youth from all around the world gathered on an Italian mountaintop and sang, "I'd like to buy the world a home and furnish it with love. Grow apple trees and honey bees and snow-white turtle doves. I'd like to teach the world to sing in perfect harmony. I'd like to buy the world a Coke and keep it company." Love, apples trees, and honey bees captured the spirit of the Bay Area counterculture in the 1970s. But fast-forward fifty years, and apple trees, honey bees, and snow-white turtle doves are nothing but a memory. Instead of selling a peaceful world singing in perfect harmony, Coca-Cola's 2015 ads in downtown San Francisco sold the city's young tech workers an edge in the tech hustle: "You moved to San Francisco with an engineering degree, an app idea, and an investor named Nana. You're on, Diet Coke." The two Coca-Cola ads underline a fundamental difference between the Mystics and the current generation of tech workers in the Bay Area. Today's tech workers aren't searching for mystical experiences. They're looking to optimize themselves to compete in the tech industry.

Reminiscing on his childhood in 1960s San Jose, tech veteran Hector Martinez explains that people used to call his hometown "Garden City." San Jose was a farming town with acres and acres of lemon and orange orchards. The pace of life was "slow" and "organic." "There is a way of relating to other things when you grow things," Hector observes. The main preoccupation of the region, he says, was "nurturing life." In fact, tech was already an established presence by the 1960s; IBM had set up its western headquarters in San Jose in 1943. But people like Hector didn't feel tech take over until later in the 1980s and 1990s. Hector's description of Silicon Valley resonates with Melissa Brady's memories from fifty years ago of walking through the rolling hills of Marin and never running into another human being. Her life also had that "slow" and "organic" quality of agrarian time. Melissa describes spending her days "playing music" and "getting high." The Bay Area was the perfect place to "drop out" of society.

Since 1960, the population of San Jose has quadrupled, largely from the influx of young tech workers, making Santa Clara County, where San Jose is located, the fastest-growing county in California.[2] Sprawling citrus orchards have been replaced with rambling company campuses, housing developments for incoming tech workers, and busy roads swarming with nondescript white double-decker buses shuttling tech workers to and from work. The once-quirky university town of Palo Alto—where hippies flocked to attend writer Ken Kesey's famous "Acid Tests," a series of LSD parties where they could "turn on, tune in, and drop out"—is now one of the most desirable places to live among those who've dropped in most deeply to twenty-first-century capitalism.

During these years, the conditions of work changed. The Mystics who worked in tech described a different orientation toward work from the Coca-Cola "you're on" work ethic of today. The earlier cohort of tech migrants were recruited to Silicon Valley in the 1970s and early 1980s by companies like Hewlett Packard and IBM that promised lifetime employment. Employees had pensions, and companies took care of their employees in retirement. The Mystics imagined working in one company for their entire lives, trusting that the company would provide a pathway for mobility and seniority. Companies, they believed, valued and rewarded loyalty. For most, that bubble burst in the dot-com bust of the 1990s when masses of tech workers got laid off by the very companies that had seemed to promise lifetime employment. Many among these earlier cohort of tech workers got laid off at middle age and faced dismal job prospects in an industry that is aggressively ageist. Today, no one expects their company to take care of them and their careers for the rest of their lives.

This earlier cohort of tech workers experienced fundamental changes in work that hit many American workers in the late twentieth century: a shift to what sociologists call "precarious working conditions," where jobs have become short term and less secure, and the worker, rather than the company or the government, bears the risks associated with employment.[3] One veteran tech worker put it this way: In the past people had stable "marriages" to the company; now they have passionate "flings," where there is mutual agreement that "any day you can walk, or we can say we don't need you." (Indeed, corporate maternalism assures that "flings" are fun and exciting.) Corporations think they benefit financially from the "passionate fling" model of employment. Human resources professionals say that a cyclical workforce keeps the workforce vibrant and innovative, as opposed to a "marriage," where things can grow stale. They fail, however, to mention that "flings" also relieve companies of the burdensome financial costs of being "married" to workers whose bodies, minds, and skills are aging.

While middle-aged workers bemoan the insecurity in employment these days, most millennials know of no other reality and embrace the "fling" mentality. "When I do not have passion for work, I leave," one engineer told me.[4] Silicon Valley slogans such as "do what you love," and the use of words such as "passion" and "authenticity" to describe work, paint it as fun, exciting, and empowering but obscure the less attractive thing about flings—you can get dumped any day. While short-term jobs are an increasing feature of all industries in the new economy, the "flings" in tech are especially brief. Tech workers told me that they usually change jobs every three to five years.

The "fling" orientation has shifted the employment contract, according to Gwen Kowalski, the director of learning and development at a medium-sized firm. "Companies can't take care of employees like they used to," she and so many others in human resources claimed. Instead of trading security for loyalty, Gwen told me that tech companies help employees "develop skills" so that they can "build their personal brand" and be competitive for their next job. Companies, according to her, aren't providing a clear career path anymore. "You're not growing your career on the company's dime anymore," Gwen explained, pointing out that now, "it's on you."

This new orientation to employment, where "it's on you" and "you're on" all the time, creates a particular kind of subjectivity that anthropologist Ilana Gershon calls the "self as business." "When you are a business," Gershon writes, "you see yourself as a bundle of skills, assets, qualities, experiences and relationships."[5] Thinking of the "self as business" is natural in Silicon Valley today. One veteran engineer who moved to Silicon Valley in the late 1970s to work with humungous supercomputers said that with the relative ease and speed in developing software products today, every person in Silicon Valley is a "walking company of one." LinkedIn founder Reed Hoffman titled his popular business book *The Start-Up of You.*

Living in a world where secure employment is no longer an option, and where people are "businesses" that sell their skills, creates what I call an *ethos of self-optimization*, where tech professionals are vigilant for ways to optimize their marketability.[6] The pressure to stay relevant and competitive is amplified in tech's rapidly changing industry, where workers are painfully aware of their growing obsolescence. Silicon Valley's ethos of self-optimization is an extreme version of the West's general shift in the last fifty years toward what political theorist Wendy Brown calls the "governing rationality of neoliberalism." That rationality construes the person as an item of "human capital [that] is concerned with enhancing its portfolio value in all domains of life."[7]

The ethos of self-optimization marks a generational shift from the spirit of the counterculture, and it is especially prevalent among younger tech workers. Work and the optimization of work-related skills are now constant preoccupations. Many engineers told me that they spend their free time "upgrading skills" by learning new programming languages and watching videos of how to build new systems. Peter Kim, an engineer who has had many "flings" in his professional career, explained how he used to spend his Sundays at his company learning Hadoop, a collection of open-source software utilities, to stay competitive on the market. Another engineer self-consciously laughed at himself as he confessed to reading tech journal articles and watching videos on building systems in his scarce free time after working twelve-hour days at his start-up. On top of keeping up with the latest programming languages, engineers in Silicon Valley are expected to have "passion projects," projects that engineers build in their free time that can become marketable products. Facebook, for instance, is an oft-lauded example of a "passion project." Older tech workers, on the other hand, were more likely to report involvement in community organizations and engaging in hobbies that had nothing to do with work in their free time.

To be sure, the Mystics started their careers in a different economic climate, during the United States' postwar years of economic opportunity and expansion. The spirit of opportunity and abundance matched the idyllic memories of the untouched Bay Area landscape fifty years ago. Tech was still the wild frontier where college dropouts like Larry Ellison and Bill Gates could succeed. The industry had room for people like my study participant Peter Lucas, who disappeared from established society to live in a Buddhist monastery for a decade and then returned in the mid-1980s to work as a software developer.

But that's not the Silicon Valley of today, where most engineers come from the top fifteen universities and had summer internships in tech. Many feel insecure about working in a place that's filled with the brightest engineers in the world. One person described all the engineers at his start-up, who come from top universities like Cal Tech, MIT, and Stanford, as vying to be the company "alpha geek." Young engineers feel that they need to prove themselves, the wellness director at one large firm explained: they used to be the smartest guys in their elementary schools, high schools, and colleges and now they are just "average."

The constant pressure to upgrade one's skills, compounded by feelings of personal inadequacy, creates an environment where the ethos of self-optimization extends beyond technical skill to personal habits. This ethos lauds self-improvement or personal development, or what some people call "self-hacking," the belief that all facets of the self can be manipulated and optimized for cognitive performance.[8] Jack Dorsey, a cofounder of Twitter, is famously known for his habits of taking daily ice baths and eating one meal a day.[9] I talked with several people who fasted, claiming that it gave them more energy and mental clarity. A start-up entrepreneur who regularly fasts for two to eight days calls it "biohacking" and explains: "Instead of hacking computer chips, they can hack their own bodies."[10] Another engineer who is concerned about the "shrinkage in brain tissue" that results from dehydration religiously lines up eight glasses of water on the side of his desk the first thing every morning. Others optimized their performance through the use of chemical stimulants, a perverse update of 1960s counterculture. One engineer confided that he used psychedelics to improve his capacity to innovate, an activity that programmers in the 1970s also engaged in.[11] Some turn to Ritalin, and a whole host of other "performance-enhancing drugs," which are reportedly on the rise in Silicon Valley.[12] Still others experiment with wearable mind-altering devices such as Thync Vibe, a thin, white metal piece attached to the forehead that sends electronic waves to the brain to improve cognitive functioning.

It is with this same ethos of self-optimization that many tech workers adopt the practice of meditation. Meditation has evolved from a countercultural spiritual practice to a "science," a form of "neural self-hacking," and one of the most revered practices in Silicon Valley's cult of self-optimization. Many tech icons—Steve Jobs, Larry Ellison, Mark Benioff—are dedicated meditators. Jobs made meditation not only cool, but a necessary practice in the tech entrepreneur's playbook. Tech firms are training their employees in meditation. Venture capital firms and angel investors are hiring meditation coaches for the young and inexperienced founders they hope will make them richer. And young tech workers flock to places like the San Francisco Zen Center, the Insight Meditation Center, and Spirit Rock to learn meditation. "Scientific" claims abound that there's a clear cognitive advantage to meditation: improved focus, clarity, efficiency, confidence, and creativity, as well as reduced blood pressure and stress levels. Who doesn't want a competitive edge?

The Users of Religious Technology

Meditation, fasting, physical deprivation, and the chemical alteration of consciousness are among some of the oldest "technologies" of the world's religious traditions. Monastics, sadhus, yogis, and other holy men and women were the original "self-hackers." They devised sophisticated ascetic exercises of "self-hacking" to master, perfect, and transcend the human condition. Today's tech workers are also taking up these ancient technologies to transcend their human limitations, but they are directing them to the religion of work.

Silicon Valley tech meditators are what I call "the Users" of religious technology. The Users aren't interested in mystical experiences, like the counterculture Mystics were. Instead, they treat religious traditions—their practices, rituals, and teachings—as tools or technologies to optimize their work performance, like problem-solving apps. The Users use religion, but they aren't "religious." That is, they don't identify with or belong to religious traditions or communities like the Mystics did. Instead, the Users belong to "faith communities" of work. And it is the concerns of work that define the practice of meditation for them.

Steve Mitchell, a tech entrepreneur in his early thirties, is a good example of a User who has taken up meditation. "Growing up in Iowa, I'd heard of meditation," he reflects, "but I just thought that it was this Eastern art, like if you do it good enough, you'll levitate off the ground. I thought of meditation the same way I thought of voodoo. It was so foreign." After moving to Silicon Valley to work in a large tech firm, Steve started to hear more about meditating and mindfulness. In fact, it felt as though "everybody's smoking pot or meditating." A lot of the guys at work were into meditation, including his good friend Mark, a recent convert who liked to preach about the gospel of meditation and its productivity benefits. Some of Steve's coworkers attended the company's weekly meditation session.

With hesitation, Steve attended one of the company meditation classes. He expected the teacher to be a guru with a shaved head in robes. Instead the teacher, who was called a "trainer," was a "cool-looking guy" in his early thirties who had "an aura of stillness and confidence." The trainer led them in "attention-training exercises" to help them focus their attention. This would help them with problem solving and decision making, the trainer said, especially at times when they felt anxious, stressed, or distracted. Steve describes that first sitting as a conversion moment: "When I opened my eyes after it was over, I was taken aback because there were thirty other people in the room. I totally forgot about that. . . . For the first time, I had some stillness that I don't think I had experienced before." He realized that meditation wasn't "voodoo." "It's just about me being here and breathing and relaxing," Steve explained. He started meditating after that class. Meditation, he said, "absolutely changed my life for the better." He did it to calm himself when he felt stressed, tired, and anxious so that he could stay focused at work.

A year later, Mark and Steve left the company and founded a start-up. Having experienced the productive benefits of meditation, they decided to incorporate it into the company culture. Steve called meditation a "skill" that increases focus and awareness and minimizes mistakes. He added that the science is clear that people who meditate can process information with more efficiency and precision.

Steve and Mark hired an executive coach to train members of the executive management to meditate. The executive coach introduced what he called "Buddhist-inspired" practices and vocabulary such as "compassionate management" and "mindful communication." All meetings began with a two-minute meditation, so that participants could be "fully present." The company also hired a meditation trainer to hold thirty-minute meditation sittings twice a week.

Steve acknowledged that devoting thirty minutes twice a week to meditation bore a "high productivity cost" but insisted "that taking thirty minutes to slow down and breathe and be present will probably give us a better return on our investment than if we just had people crank all the time." The positive results were obvious to Steve. "A lot of engineers who understand the kind of work we do, they're like 'Man, you guys are operating at such a high level consistently. Your design is killer. Your technology is amazing. You're pioneering all this stuff. We never hear about drama at your company.' . . . I attribute almost all of it to [us] reinforcing and fostering a place where mindfulness is celebrated." Steve's story illustrates how work defines the meaning and experience of meditation for the Users today. Steve experiences meditation as a "skill" that makes him more productive and less prone to mistakes. He considers the time devoted to meditation to be "investments" that produce "killer design" and "amazing technology."

The Users like Steve think about work differently from how earlier Mystics did. The Mystics moved to the Bay Area to "drop out" of society. They considered work ancillary to spiritual quest, something that gave them the financial means to support their spiritual journeys. In a survey conducted among members of new religious movements in 1973, sociologist Robert Wuthnow found that people who frequently experience religious "peaks," such as the Mystics, value material or social status less than those who do not experience them.[13] This was true for Al Hoffman, who says that he went back to work after three and a half years of "studying with whatever Buddhist teacher or Hindu teacher" was available because he "ran out of money." Al didn't have a career; he had a job working at a children's camp in order to support his spiritual quest. Work, for Al, was something he *had* to do when he wasn't studying with an Asian spiritual teacher.

The Mystics treated work not only as secondary to spirituality, but as separate from, and even oppositional to, the world of work, business, and career. For instance, Gil Goldman, a convert to Zen Buddhism, worked as an engineer while studying to be Zen monk. He did not meditate at work like tech workers do today. Instead, he practiced with his Zen community at his local zendo, apart from work. Gil separated his religious and work life to such an extreme that none of his work colleagues even knew that he was studying to be a Zen monk. Moreover, Gil recognized that Buddhism could be at odds with the world of business. Gil claims that Zen made him *less* ambitious rather than more.

Peter Lucas is another of the Mystics who is a Buddhist convert. He lived in a Zen monastery for a decade. When he returned to the secular world, he became a software engineer. Like Gil, Peter did not meditate at work and was involved in a Zen faith community apart from work. Even Steve Jobs, who credits meditation for giving him intuition and focus, never tried to bring meditation to Apple employees.

The Users, on the one hand, organize their lives around work. Having moved to the Bay Area to build their careers, religion and spirituality are not only secondary but ancillary to work. The Users use spiritual practices like meditation to help them become better workers. For instance, Patrick, a tech executive in his early forties, turned to Buddhism to deal with his depression, which compromised his professional and personal life. When his attention deficit disorder hindered his capacity to lead his company, Doug, an entrepreneur in his late twenties, turned to Buddhist mindfulness and meditation, preferring to "meditate rather than medicate." Tony, the founder of a new start-up, turned to Buddhist meditation to "enhance" his "cognitive performance." Cecelia, a rare User who became religious and converted to Buddhism, criticizes her earlier User orientation: "I had this very acquisitive relationship to meditation practice. Like, it's going to solve my stress, it's going to do this for me. . . . I was so attached to this idea of what meditation could do for me."

To be sure, the instrumental attitude toward Buddhist meditation is not just a tech thing. The fields of psychotherapy, mental health, and medicine have also framed meditation and mindfulness as useful tools. But those fields use it for therapeutic healing and mental health.[14] The

Users are different, because they use Buddhist practices to improve work performance. And this trend is spreading beyond Silicon Valley.

For some of the Users, meditation is more than just a productivity tool. Many are drawn to it as a form of therapy and healing. Still others, albeit a minority, are drawn to meditation and other Asian spiritual practices for the same reasons the Mystics were: as tools to access mystical, spiritual experiences. And instead of living in communes and monasteries, the Users participate in spiritual community through the consumption of spiritual products like meditation retreats. But even among the Users who have mystical tendencies, work continues to be central to their spiritual journeys. Meditation, they claim, supports their work performance, even if its function is only to provide a mental respite to refresh them for work.[15]

But even though some of the Mystics teach meditation in corporations, a topic that I turn to in the next chapter, none of them rationalized their personal meditation practice as a productivity practice. As one of them, Peter Lucas, says dismissively, "If all you want is stress relief and to be calm, you can take Xanax." For him, meditation is supposed to be "transformational"; or as Samantha Lieberman puts it, "mindfulness is about freedom."

Meditation and Its Virtues: How Wholesome States Become Work Skills

How does the meaning of Buddhist meditation change when it becomes a part of work? In Buddhism, meditation is a spiritual practice that cultivates "wholesome states," or virtuous states, that are ends in themselves. But in the workplace, meditation becomes a practice that cultivates professional skills that raise productivity. When work replaces religion, religion takes on the utilitarian logic of work. The Users develop Buddhist virtues of equanimity, compassion, and a clear mind, not because they are Buddhist or want to be virtuous, but because they want to optimize their performance. And they value Buddhist virtues of focus, equanimity, and compassion because they produce economic value.

Focus: Transcending Distraction

Alex Stockton, the founder of a small start-up, started meditating two years ago "purely for job performance." He's an affable thirty-five-year-old man who grew up atheist in San Mateo, just south of San Francisco. Alex was a programmer for many years, spending the majority of his time doing just one thing: writing code. Back then, he says it was easy to get into a "flow" state, a term coined by psychologist Mihaly Csikszentmihályi that describes a mental state of intense focus that many also call "the zone."[16] Alex told me about one extraordinary time when he was in flow and coded for seventeen hours a day, three days straight, forgetting to shower and barely remembering to eat. It's hard for him to get into flow state now that he is the CEO of a start-up. "I've a different problem every hour," Alex says. In his small start-up of ten employees, he wears many hats, and his attention is always divided. He's constantly multitasking, and it's much harder to focus.

Alex started meditating when his angel investor, a serious meditator, learned of his struggles and hired a meditation coach to meet with him weekly to "train" his brain. Now, Alex is a vocal proponent of the cognitive benefits of meditation. He describes it as "practicing controlling your focus." Focus, Alex says, is a "core competence." For him, meditation is a work skill. Knowing the cognitive benefits of meditation, Alex now encourages his employees to meditate for "performance reasons" and has made membership in Headspace, a meditation app, an employee benefit.

Like Alex, many tech professionals meditate for "performance reasons" to sharpen their mental focus at work. For example, when asked what they wanted to learn at one company's mindfulness retreat, one young man raised his hand and answered, "to learn tactical techniques to get to flow state." Others in the room nodded in agreement. One engineer told me that he practices *hakalau* meditation, what he calls an "ancient Hawaiian practice of centering on the third eye," to help him concentrate. And another tech worker said that she uses meditation to "calm and focus the mind to be more productive."

Even for those who aren't start-up CEOS like Alex, the fast-paced tech workplace is full of distractions, I'm told. One senior leader said that his day is so packed with back-to-back meetings that he often feels like "my body and my head are not in the same place." Another compared her mental state at work to a snow globe that is constantly being shaken. The smart phone, which some call a "weapon of mass distraction," is a big reason for the lack of focus. One tech worker told me that she's so distracted by the phone that she can never feel fully present to either her work or her family. Many complained that people aren't really there in meetings because they are checking their phones underneath the table.

The tech industry thinks mindfulness can solve the problem of distraction for their employees. For example, Bernie Lewis, the director of learning and development at a firm who initiated a mindfulness program, reflected, "I think it's a practice that's needed because of this bombardment and this philosophy of multitasking. We're a data organization. Being overwhelmed with data, being overwhelmed with two hundred emails, three hundred emails a day, being overwhelmed with the amount of work you got to do and dealing with people and the list goes on. It's like, 'how can I have some time to myself and not go crazy.'"

The idea that the brain can be tamed and disciplined has been an accepted truth in Buddhism for centuries. Only in the last fifty years has science provided evidence for the plasticity of the brain. Buddhists call the untamed mind the "monkey mind," a state of restlessness, distraction, confusion, and indecision.[17] In Buddhism, the problem with the monkey mind is not lack of productivity, but that it produces suffering. In a state of delusion, distraction, and unsettledness, humans "grasp," as Buddhists say, at solutions that are untethered to the reality of impermanence. Suffering arises from the gap between illusion and the true nature of things. In Buddhism, a distracted state of mind is in fact a moral problem because it is an obstacle to acting virtuously.[18] The solution is to train the mind to perceive reality clearly. Meditation does this by building awareness of the fleeting and illusory nature of thoughts and emotions. Various meditation practices, such as repetitive chanting and concentration on images and breathing, help practitioners to shift their state of consciousness from one of monkey mind to one that is disciplined, calm, and focused, ultimately leading toward liberation or enlightenment.

But in the religion of work, the distracted mind is an obstacle to optimal performance. If corporations "suffer" from distraction, it is as a loss of efficient production. In mindfulness workshops, tech professionals learn that meditation reduces corporate "suffering" by improving employee cognitive functioning as measured along dimensions such as focus, insight, innovation, memory, perception, and decision making, to name only a few. Mindfulness teachers quote scientific studies correlating meditation with improved cognitive skills. Meditators have a thicker cortex in brain regions associated with attention and sensory processing, they claim. Meditators have a better capacity to focus, and they score higher on the verbal GRE than nonmeditators.[19] One mindfulness teacher promised, "Meditating for twenty minutes a day for four days results in improvements in cognitive skills."

The Users treat meditation as a system update for the mind, a tool to adapt to the frenetic pace of work. They have turned the Buddhist practice of disciplining the "monkey mind" into a strategy for market advantage.

Emotional Mastery: Taming Counterproductive Emotions

Alex Stockton initially picked up meditation as a tool to help him focus. But as he delved in further, meditation has helped him with more than that. Alex now thinks of meditation as a "skill set" that deepens his awareness of his emotions. This awareness in turn detaches him from his emotions, giving him greater rational control over them. Alex found this particularly useful in dealing with his problem of procrastination. Mindfulness meditation helped him to name the emotion of avoidance, which leads to procrastination, and then meditation "lets your prefrontal cortex, like your conscious mind operate on it." Alex shared a self-awareness exercise that his mindfulness coach taught him. The coach had him

> pair up with someone, stare into each other's eyes, and tell the other person what thoughts are going through your head [but] with one caveat. You had to start each sentence with, "I am aware that." "I'm aware that I'm looking at your glasses, right? I'm aware that you are looking back at me." These are like the actual thoughts that are coming through my head, right? And it was that um, that realization that once you are aware of something, you can work with it. Gives me power to act rationally. I use that for procrastination now. I say, "I'm aware that I don't want to do this. I'm aware that I'm afraid that I . . . I'm aware that I don't know the answer." It's something that comes up for me a lot. That's like a whole other realm that meditation opened up for me, but it's still performance based.

Here, Alex demonstrates the User mentality of using mindfulness as a "performance-based" tool to solve a productivity problem by detaching from and objectifying his emotions. This awareness gives him the "power to act rationally" and master unproductive emotions and thoughts. Even as the benefits of meditation progressed from cognitive focus to emotional mastery for Alex, he was quick to reassure me that "it's still performance based."

The emotional mastery that Alex describes is what Buddhists call the state of equanimity, characterized by tranquility and a lack of bias in one's perceptions and interactions with others and oneself.[20] According to the Kāyagatāsati Sutta (Mindfulness of the Body Sutta), mindfulness practice is a form of "purification." It eliminates mental defilements such as "discontent, delight, fear, and dread." Equanimity is considered a wholesome state because it liberates people from attachments that blur their perception of reality. Buddhist practices then, are disciplines that cultivate a fine-tuned awareness of the mind, body, and spirit (mental processes, bodily sensations, and states of consciousness) to undo the forms of cognitive bias that imprison sentient beings in the cycle of death and rebirth.

But in Silicon Valley the wholesome state of equanimity has become the "skill set" of calm and collected tech professionals, people who master their emotions so they do not get in the way of their work performance.

In Silicon Valley, equanimity goes by terms such as "emotional intelligence," "emotional mastery," and "self-regulation," thanks to an army of organizational psychologists, neuroscientists, and productivity gurus. At one company mindfulness workshop, the presenter told his audience of engineers, "Self-regulation is the process of managing one's internal states, impulses, and resources for the purpose of performing optimally." In Alex's case, emotions like fear and dread made him procrastinate and prevented him from attending to certain tasks. But by cultivating his awareness of his emotions, and recognizing the fleeting nature of them, Alex was able to exercise rational control, overcome the emotional block, and power through. Emotions like anxiety, anger, and fear are no longer what Buddhists call "mental defilements" that are obstacles to *wholesome* action, but hindrances to *productive* action.

Corporate meditation teachers describe the lack of emotional mastery using words such as "reactive," "enslaved to unconscious reactions," "being on autopilot," and "operating from the amygdala." Mindfulness, on the other hand, "makes people less reactive. They're not so quick to fly off the handle, [not so] quick to judge. . . . They can actually take a few minutes and be with their feelings of frustration, angst, anxiety, disappointment, anger, whatever it is—rather than just immediately react to it," one meditator explained to me.

Corporate mindfulness instructors teach employees to master their emotions by cultivating what Buddhists call "nonattachment." Blending Buddhist wisdom with modern psychology, trainers assert that the key to nonattachment is understanding emotions as trainable physiological reactions. Famed Google engineer and mindfulness teacher Chade-Meng Tan calls mindfulness the practice of moving "emotions from existential to experiential."[21] Doing it requires the practice of "third-person objectivity,"[22] a shift from equating the self with emotions, to acknowledging emotions as a physical sensation. For instance, instead of saying "I am angry," practitioners say, "I experience anger in my body."

Meditation instructors teach tech workers that they can master their emotions through awareness and choosing to be in a different state. They offer pithy phrases and acronyms to workers to help them remember to "respond and not react" in the moment of being triggered. Or to "recognize, reframe, and resolve." Or to "stop, breathe, notice, reflect, and respond." They have the same effect of halting instinct by cultivating self-awareness.

Like Alex, many tech workers consider meditation an effective tool to tame counterproductive emotions in the workplace. In fact, they mention the benefits of mindfulness in regulating emotions more than the benefits of mental focus. One example of this is Don Bruno, a former director at a large tech firm and now a strategy consultant who approaches his emotions with "third-person objectivity." He says, "I meditate daily, and it's a way that keeps me centered so that when somebody does something that drives me a little nuts, I kind of step back from it. 'Oh, that's an emotion coming out of me, and I have a choice.'" Don links this state of detachment to his professional performance: "By being centered, and not letting emotions get in the way of the results, I raise the results of the organization." Don's stance toward undisciplined emotions is similar to Alex's attitude toward procrastination: unexamined emotions are counterproductive and can "get in the way of the results."

Sonya Sharma participated in the mindfulness program at her company during a tough time when her father was battling cancer and she had just been promoted to manager. She describes the program as giving her the tools to "self-manage and regulate myself to go through these experiences with strength and not get triggered." Mindfulness helped her work performance. "I was happier and had the clarity to handle the complex problems of the company," Sonya says. The benefits of mindfulness that she learned at work flowed into her personal life. When later her daughter was diagnosed with a chronic illness, Sonya claims that she had the inner resilience to be "fully present" for her family and her company.

Steve Lansing explains how mindfulness helps him, especially when interacting with colleagues that he's "not crazy about."

> This really is about when you're in the middle of a meeting and so and so walks in that you just dread and you become aware of the fact that, "Oh, no, there they are." And you start projecting about them. Then your body starts to get triggered, and it affects your skill.

The problem with getting "triggered" is that "it affects your skill." Mindfulness, Steve claims, gives him the tools to be aware of and differentiate his reactive body from his rational self so that his emotions don't compromise his "skill."

EMOTIONAL MASTERY AND "RAISING THE RESULTS OF ORGANIZATIONS"

Emotional mastery is a valuable skill because it creates efficient work cultures, according to tech managers and executives. As Don puts it, "not letting emotions get in the way raises the results of organizations." Managers and executives promote mindfulness in employees to remove the inefficiencies of poor communication, emotional baggage, and hurt feelings—the invisible things that can paralyze organizations. That's one of the main reasons that Patrick Sullivan, the vice president at Euclid we met in chapter 3, trained his unit of over one thousand employees in mindfulness. Like others, he sees mindfulness as a practice to train what he calls "human hardware" to act more consciously and rationally. Unregulated emotions have serious organizational costs that hurt the bottom line. One example is the problem that Patrick calls "mood contagion." He explains:

> So mood contagion is a big problem. You know, misery loves company. And the more miserable people are, the more it has a contagious effect. And mood contagion can happen for an infinite number of reasons. Like it's not preventable. Somebody is going to shit on you, and you are going to have a reaction to it. And so when you come to work it is going to affect your work, and it is going to affect your coworkers. Well if I helped give you skills that helped you access your limbic brain and manage it more effectively, that would be hugely valuable. It would be hugely valuable to you because a bad experience wouldn't ruin your whole day, right? It might prevent you from making it worse. You as an individual will go, I am so glad that I just got out of this meeting with a customer who pissed me off royally and who would have ruined my whole day. But instead of ruining

> my whole day, she only ruined an hour. And I am now back on track. Right? So this is a major problem within an organization. So if I can do something—let's call it mindfulness—that will help you get off that roller coaster, it would be good for you because nobody's having fun—you're not having a good time bitching about what happened five years ago. And it is not helping the company.

Here, Patrick considers the cost of mood contagion and unregulated emotions to the firm. Mood contagion, he claims, lowers overall productivity. Companies can mitigate mood contagion by teaching employees the skill of emotional regulation. Through mindfulness, employees can "get off that roller coaster" and "get back on track" by limiting the productivity costs of untamed emotions to "an hour" instead of a "whole day," and contain mood contagion from spreading throughout the company.

According to Patrick, the mindfulness program at his company more than paid itself off. The prior year his unit was facing five pending lawsuits over job terminations. This year there were none, which he attributes to the emotional skills that employees gained through the mindfulness program. Some people who were fired had participated in the mindfulness program. Because the program had "increased their capacity for dealing with difficulty," Patrick says that they left the company "gracefully," even thanking the company for the mindfulness program. "Well I can tell you right there—just that—paid for the program," he claims.

David Stein, the head of learning and development at a 120-person start-up, also talks about the organizational advantages of mindfulness. People don't let problems escalate at a mindful company, David says. They don't let their emotions get in the way of communicating smoothly. He draws a short, thick zigzag on the whiteboard to illustrate progress in a typical company where communication may be full of triggering conversations. People are reactive. Some people avoid difficult conversations, and tensions escalate. Progress is slow and flat because it is encumbered by emotional boulders. Drawing a narrow, tall spiral, David explains that in a company where people are trained to communicate mindfully, progress is fast and looks more like a narrow spiral. David believes that mindfulness offers direct value to the company. When people aren't "wasting energy on judgment and poor communication" and instead "having fun and being creative," he argues, "they will be more productive."

The company offers twenty-minute guided meditation sessions three times a week, and David actively coaches the executive team in mindfulness so that employees "act from their prefrontal cortex rather than the amygdala." Under David's leadership, Buddhism has become a part of the company culture. David leads employees through "a kind of Buddhist" mental exercise where they explain a tense scenario in five different ways. This exercise gets people to what David calls—borrowing another Buddhist religious term—"beginner's mind,"[23] a state where people can "ask a question out of curiosity rather than judgment." Buddhist terms like "grasping," "nonattachment," and "beginner's mind" are now part of the company vocabulary.

The examples of David and Patrick illustrate how the meaning of Buddhist traditions shifts when applied in the work context. Mindfulness is no longer a religious practice to cultivate the wholesome state of equanimity, which is an end in itself in Buddhism. Instead, in the religion of work, mindfulness is a tool to develop the skill of emotional regulation, which is a means toward creating efficient work cultures. "Mindfulness," David says, "is a competitive advantage."

Compassion and Empathy: Designing Human-Friendly Products

To Iris Yen, the forty-two-year-old head of user design at a large firm in the valley, the biggest problem in product design is neither lack of focus nor impulsive emotions among tech workers, but the lack of a critical emotional "skill"—empathy—the skill of connecting with other human beings. With a doctorate in engineering herself, Iris admits that engineers are too much in their heads. They create technologically sophisticated systems that fail as products on the market because they are neither useful to, nor useable by, ordinary people. Steve Jobs was a genius not because of his technical skill, she observes, but because he got how people lived with technology. To design a product that is natural in the hands of the user, Iris maintains, the product designer must have the skill of empathy.

Iris discovered that she herself lacked this skill during a painful divorce. At first she didn't feel any pain. She explains that, having been in the tech industry for so long, she'd overdeveloped her left, analytical brain, but lost touch with her emotions. She didn't realize how much she had repressed her emotions from the divorce until she started taking yoga classes. Three months later, she found herself crying uncontrollably in her yoga class one day. Since that moment, Iris has been on a quest for healing through Asian spiritual practices such as yoga and meditation. These practices helped her to have "self-compassion" and to "connect" with herself, she says.

The problem in tech, according to Iris, is that empathy is scarce. Tech workers, she points out, "interface" more with screens than with humans. Tech companies are run by engineers and business people who reward designers for their ability to rationalize based on data and reason rather than on intuition and empathy. Unfortunately, she claims, science has shown that the human capacity for empathy is inversely related to analytical skill. "There's a neurological divide in the brain that represents these modes of understanding." The lack of empathy does not bode well for creating what designers call "human-friendly" technology.

The emotionally disconnected engineer is a common stereotype among the non-engineering "support staff" in tech—people in human resources and in learning and development, executive coaches, and meditation instructors. They characterize engineers with euphemisms such as "right brain people," and descriptions like "trained in the technical stuff but less able to deal with the messy, mysterious world of human beings." Or, engineers "can deal with data but they can't hold the room" and they "don't want to deal with feelings."

The engineers' lack of empathy has put a sharp edge on tech companies' already notorious gender imbalance. Women engineers complained about their mostly male colleagues. For example, engineer

Susan Kim describes the behavior of her colleagues who've "forgotten how to be with other human beings":

> They're practically like . . . Asperger's. They get so snarky and rude because they're so entrenched in the computers that they forget how to interact with people. You see this firsthand in the meetings every week, the questions that they ask the leaders. It's like, I can't believe that people feel so entitled to be . . . really demanding about what happened to the bagels on Monday. It's like they've forgotten how to be with other human beings.

The specter of Asperger's looms large in the valley. It's common to hear "He's being 'asby'" and jokes about "being on the spectrum."[24] Teachers at the local schools voice the challenges of teaching the undiagnosed children of undiagnosed parents who are unaware of the problem. Asperger's is believed to be so common in the tech industry that some companies have programs to support their employees who are on the spectrum.

But the costs of emotional disconnection are more than social for the tech industry; they are also financial. Engineers who lack the skills of empathy and compassion, according to people like Iris, create products that fail on the market because they are not "user friendly."

This is where mindfulness comes in. In Buddhism, compassion and empathy can be cultivated through meditation. Compassion, according to the Dalai Lama, is the "wish for another being to be free of suffering."[25] It is fundamentally empathetic, "based not on our own projections and expectations, but rather on the needs of the other."[26] In Buddhism, a compassionate state is considered an important "wholesome state." It is a virtue, an end in itself.

But in Silicon Valley, compassion is a means to more user-friendly product design. This is why Iris brings mindfulness and yoga to her design team: so they can connect with product users. Product development requires more than focus groups, she maintains. Product designers need to *feel* what users feel. "True empathy," Iris says, "is about getting out of your head and feeling what they're experiencing in your bones." To get to that state of "true empathy," she leads her team in "heart opening" exercises that counteract the "defensive poses" of hunching over phones and computers that most people assume "to protect the ego." Heart-opening poses, Iris claims, open the chest and shoulders, and emotionally open our hearts to others. By assuming a physical posture of openness, she says, we also assume an emotional posture of openness. "We can exploit the mind-body connection to help us relate to other people!"

According to Amber Tate, a boisterous and free-spirited woman with computer science degrees from Stanford, the problem with many tech companies is that they have no idea how users use their products in real life. "Ninety-nine percent of start-ups in Silicon Valley were built to scratch someone's own itch," she says. They are "solution[s] without a problem." Amber helps companies find the best problems. She trains programmers to interview users to learn how they use their products by "feeling into those people's pain, articulating their core problems, and thinking how you're going to make their pain go away." She guides them in the Buddhist practice of *metta* meditation, also known as "loving-kindness meditation," where they meditate on "reducing suffering by knowing user needs."

John Ashton, a tech entrepreneur in his early thirties, also sees empathy as the key to the success of his social-media start-up. Like Amber, he maintains that most engineers are in their own bubble, creating products that are disconnected from the needs of the world. "We want to build a platform to change the world," he says. "In order to do that, we really need to understand the people whose problems we're trying to solve. And that's an empathic thing to do."

In the world of tech, the "suffering" and "pain" of modern sentient beings are the inconvenience and frustration generated by poorly designed products. Designers and engineers are bodhisattvas who alleviate user "suffering" by weaving compassion and empathy into the "mindful" design of products. Meditation and mindfulness are "tools" to "train" tech workers in the "skills" of compassion and empathy so that they can enter the heads and hearts of users to design products that they "need." Silicon Valley injects a utilitarian logic into the Buddhist notion of compassion. No longer a wholesome, virtuous state that is an end in itself, it is a "skill," a means to better product design.

Creativity: Accessing Inner Wisdom

The tech industry thrives on creativity, one of the most challenging skills to develop. Unlike focus, emotional mastery, or even compassion, Americans tend to believe that creativity is innate, that some people are creative, and some are not. Moreover, even creative people aren't creative all the time. Creativity is difficult to contain and pin down. According to Western mythology, creativity is inspired by a mythical muse, dependent on the caprices of the gods. The assumption that creativity is elusive has spawned a culture of innovation anxiety in Silicon Valley, one that goes back to the 1970s, when some engineers dropped acid to achieve an altered state of productive creativity.[27]

During my time in Silicon Valley, I met many people who sought out mindfulness as a tool to address their innovation anxiety. One example is Abby Robinson, who was looking for something "new" to energize her company's older workforce in order to compete with newer firms with fresh, young employees. With a manic energy, she relayed to me her firm's predicament: Bitcoin, Apple Pay, and other financial products were making its product obsolete. "If we don't innovate we will die," Abby pronounced with alarmed and fearful eyes. "We *need* mindfulness," she said. Tech executives and HR professionals felt anxious "to infuse mindfulness into" their companies, to give their "stagnant," middle-aged workforce a creative competitive advantage.

Although the Buddha did not identify creativity as one of the outcomes of mindfulness meditation, he did list access to supernatural forms of intelligence as one of the secondary benefits of mindfulness. According to the Kāyagatāsati Sutta, these include memory of past lives, mind reading, and miraculous powers of hearing and sight, all considered valuable forms of knowledge in the Buddha's time.[28] In Silicon Valley today, the Users practice meditation to access the "supernatural" skill of creativity.

Melissa Brady, the Mystic we met earlier, is now a leadership consultant who teaches tech executives "how to access the part of their brains that govern[s] creativity, innovation, big-picture thinking" through meditation. Asian spiritual practices counter the "very narrow Western view that leads you to believe that we are limited," she says. "There's also a whole other truth, [which] is that we have tremendous resources." She cites examples of the extraordinary feats of Asian spiritual masters: "monks who go to sleep at eighteen thousand feet in a light shirt and don't get hypothermia, and people in India who are lying on nails and having bricks broken over them." These Asian monks can achieve these superhuman feats, she maintains, because they enter a state of "flow," a near-spiritual experience that "suddenly" makes work "feel effortless."

Melissa coaches her clients to access flow through the body. Drawing from her expertise in martial arts and her own spiritual work with shamans and Tibetan Buddhist lamas, she leads her clients in embodied mindfulness practices to "activate a different energetic pattern" in their systems. Melissa explains that she works with the body because our limbic system, which governs our physical instincts, is evolutionarily millions of years older than the neocortex, which controls our rational thought. According to Melissa, "the body always wins." Exemplifying the dominance of the limbic system, her clients, many of whom have multiple PhDs, "become stupid when they're stressed."

Melissa teaches clients how to release testosterone and oxytocin in their bodies, the hormones they need to fully access the power of the neocortex and connect with others, a critical skill in leadership. Flexing extensor muscles releases testosterone, "which gives you that confidence, big picture thinking, and creativity," she explains. The combination of breathing exercises with "thinking of someone [who] makes you smile" releases oxytocin, "the chemical that makes you feel connected, want[ing] to help others and receive help from others." By intentionally modifying the chemical reactions in the body through embodied mindfulness practices, Melissa and others claim that we can activate a state of consciousness that is conducive to creative problem solving. You just have to "know where to look" inside yourself.

Iris Yen, the user-experience design executive whom we met earlier, also uses Asian spiritual practices to unleash creativity in her team. As Iris sees it, the mind is its own obstacle to creativity. The "natural human tendencies to be judgmental and attached to ego" hinder the design process, she says. "Everybody at some level doesn't want to be judged, doesn't want to look stupid. When designers are brainstorming, [that fear of judgment is] detrimental because if you're holding back ideas and editing yourself, you're not going to be as creative. You're not going to come up with as many ideas as possible." "Mindfulness helps us let go of fear that stifles creativity," she says, and "access a creative state more readily and efficiently."

Iris prefers embodied mindfulness practices, like yoga, that "exploit the mind-body connection." Certain physical postures activate a more open and less judgmental mind. She makes a point of leading teams in hip openers during brainstorming sessions. "The psoas [hip muscle] is connected to the reptilian brain," she explains. "It tightens up when we are stressed, an instinct that we inherit from our evolutionary past to spring forward or curl up when threated. When we relax the psoas, we put ourselves in a 'position of play and creativity.'" She tells her team, "We're opening up the body to open up the mind to let your ideas flow freely and be playful." Yoga and mindfulness help her team "let go of fear" and "open" to creativity.

Regina Ligouri is a strategy consultant in Silicon Valley who teaches what she calls "neurobiological short cuts" to access creative states of consciousness. A neurobiologist and a shaman, Regina combines her formal training in science and spirituality, "merging the East and the West." Although Regina doesn't advertise her credentials as a shaman, she uses her spiritual expertise to train clients how to access their "intuitive gifts."

According to Regina, most people are well trained in using their analytical minds, or "left brains," but creative problem solving requires people to use a different part of their minds—what some people call "the right brain," and others may call "the unconscious" or "inner wisdom," and still others call "God." Regina works with clients to "access a different emotional state to be creative" through meditation. She believes that meditation is "a tool to access the unconscious." She has clients visualize a "power spot," a physical place where they feel safe, comfortable, and loved. From the "power spot," she urges them to address practical problems in their companies. For example, one of her clients is the founder of a start-up who "needed to get over limiting thoughts" that were undermining his ability to fundraise. Regina led him in a meditation where he imagined himself in his "power spot" and then invited his investors into it, asking each of them what they wanted to see happen in the company. When another client had to make a difficult decision, Regina guided him into a meditation to induce a state where he felt "immense love." Once resting in that state, Regina asked him, "What does your inner wisdom say?"

Iris, Melissa, and Regina are examples of people in Silicon Valley who use Asian spiritual practices to enhance creativity. They offer the "spiritual," "intuitive," and "open" "right brain" of "the East" as an antidote to the "analytical," "data-driven" "left brain" of the West. Creativity is a supernatural power that resides in every person, they maintain, yet is often hidden from Westerners. According to them, Asian spiritual practices help tech workers override their limbic systems and "let go of fear" in order to activate a "different energetic pattern" that releases the "right chemical balance" to "get into flow" and access "inner wisdom"—giving them a competitive advantage in the workplace.

Alex Stockton, the start-up entrepreneur we met earlier, had a "weird" experience at a mindfulness retreat for technologists in the spring of 2015. The retreat took place at Esalen, the well-known New Age retreat center that was founded by Mystics in the 1970s on the central California coast. Late one night, Alex and the others from the retreat went to soak in Esalen's famous hot tubs, perched on a cliff overlooking the Pacific Ocean. It was a warm, spring weekend, and people from around the Bay Area had come to Esalen to enjoy the views and the clothing-optional tubs. Many of them were Mystics who had been regulars at Esalen since the 1970s.

"Yeah, it was weird," Alex reflected, referring not only to their physical nakedness, but also to the nakedness of his group's ambition and wealth against the countercultural vibe of the Mystics. Some among Alex's group were high on weed, laughing and talking shop loudly about raising tens of millions of dollars, when he noticed the uncomfortable silence and stares from the Mystics who shared their hot tub. Soon after, the Mystics quietly left, leaving the hot tub to Alex and his group from Silicon Valley. When he brought up the incident to me, Alex was still processing it, rambling on without a clear point. But the experience clearly left an impression on him. Alex didn't know what to make of it, except that it felt "weird."

Asian religions in the Bay Area have come a long way from the 1970s, when countercultural youth borrowed them in order to access mystical experiences. The awkward hot tub incident measures the distance between the new and old spiritual culture of the Bay Area. Just as Alex and his tech colleagues took over the hot tub at Esalen, a onetime haven for the Mystics, the tech industry and its religion of work have colonized the Mystics' creative borrowings from Asian religions. They have turned Asian spiritual practices into tools to optimize work performance, and Buddhist virtues into the "skill set" of the level-headed business leader. Now, when renowned Buddhist leaders like Thich Nhat Han and Venerable Pomnyun Sunim visit the Bay Area, they don't go to the Haight-Ashbury, but to Google headquarters. The instrumental logic of work has so thoroughly penetrated and transformed the practice of meditation that its earlier mystical and countercultural roots are unrecognizable and feel "weird" to Users like Alex today. His "weird" feeling suggests that there is nothing natural or inevitable about a religious practice morphing into a productivity tool. How meditation teachers alter Asian religions to conform to the tech workplace is the topic of the next chapter.

CHAPTER 5

Killing the Buddha

When Gil Goldman, a Zen priest in Silicon Valley, noticed that attendance at his zendo (temple) was flagging, he came up with an entrepreneurial solution. Tech professionals, who are a sizeable proportion of the members of his zendo, were so busy with work that they didn't have time to attend services, he realized. What if, instead of asking people to come to the zendo, he brought meditation practice to them at the workplace? Gil, who had been an engineer for over thirty years, was familiar with tech culture. He knew that he couldn't bring incense, robes, and chanting into the company offices. Instead, Gil made meditation practice that is "based on Buddhism . . . appropriate for work." He pitched meditation as a tool for "high performance," "productivity," and "resilience," all words that, he knew, tech companies liked to hear. Instead of wearing robes to teach, he wore khakis and a button-down shirt and never mentioned that he was a Zen priest.

Helen Sommers, a middle-aged Buddhist meditation teacher, faced a different dilemma from Gil's but reached the same solution. She'd taught meditation and yoga for years. Her passion was teaching meditation and yoga to people in prison and to kids in inner-city schools, who she felt would really benefit from it. But Helen couldn't afford to limit her teaching to community centers, prisoners, and inner-city students now that the influx of well-paid tech workers was driving up the cost of living in the Bay Area. Helen realized that she needed to market meditation to a more affluent population to survive. Taking a tip from a fellow meditation teacher, Helen rebranded herself as a "mindfulness leadership coach" and learned all the science on meditation that she had previously dismissed. She avoided words like "consciousness," "dharma," and "liberation." Teaching mindfulness to tech employees, she says, "pays the bills," so that she can live out her true calling of bringing meditation to prisoners and students.

Gil's and Helen's experiences show how tech "disrupts" Buddhism. To survive in Silicon Valley, religion must conform to the logic and culture of the tech industry. This is true for religious organizations, whose members are working too hard to attend the zendo. It's also true for individual religious and spiritual teachers, who must learn new ways to monetize their teachings or be priced out of the Bay Area. But not everyone sees Buddhism's adaptation to tech as a means for survival. Others, such as Google engineer and best-selling author Chade-Meng Tan, are trying to spread the dharma to new "users" by linking the benefits of Buddhist practice to productivity and success.

Gil, Helen, and Meng teach Buddhist meditation in companies for different reasons, but they share the same challenge: how to sell a religious product in a professedly secular workplace. They are what I call *meditation entrepreneurs*. They include three groups: contractors who teach meditation for a fee, such as meditation teachers, executive coaches, and companies producing meditation products; company administrators, such as human resources professionals and executives who develop or teach meditation within their companies; and company employees who are starting grassroots meditation groups. They are "entrepreneurs" because they are selling an old religious practice repurposed as a new workplace productivity tool. While some of my research participants strategically refer to meditation as "mindfulness," a point I will discuss, others just call it "meditation." I use both terms, *meditation* and *mindfulness*, interchangeably, as they did with me.

In order to sell meditation, entrepreneurs feel they must remove its religious qualities and replace them with nonreligious ones that align with the company's goals. I call this process "killing the Buddha." This startling phrase comes from the well-known Buddhist koan or puzzle posed by the prominent Chan (Zen) master Linji Yixuan in ninth-century China: "If you meet the Buddha, kill him." There have been various Buddhist interpretations of this teaching, including the virtue of stamping out religious fetishism, and the importance of removing the illusion of a separate self. Here, I mean the "killing" of religious trappings in the practice of Buddhist meditation in Silicon Valley.

"Killing the Buddha" isn't something that's happening only in Silicon Valley. Even though mindfulness is a Buddhist practice, Buddhism is hardly mentioned in the current explosion of secular self-help mindfulness that promises to improve nearly every aspect of life, from parenting to eating, from losing weight to grieving and having sex.[1] According to one study, 22 percent of businesses in the United States offer mindfulness training.[2] There is no consensus over exactly what "mindfulness" is, but the parading of this astounding number in business magazines suggests it is very popular in corporate America.[3]

The term "secular mindfulness" is a source of deep tension among both practitioners and scholars of Buddhism. Buddhists have vigorously debated whether secular mindfulness is a departure from, or the radical embrace of, authentic Buddhist teaching.[4] Scholars have disputed whether Asian spiritual practices like yoga and meditation are religious or secular when practiced in settings such as schools and gyms.[5] My concern is not to adjudicate whether corporate meditation is "true" Buddhism, or whether it is secular or religious, but rather to unearth the assumptions about the religious and the secular that become clear when meditation crosses the threshold between them. When someone enters religious life as a monastic, he or she must renounce the ways of secular life and replace them with those of religious life. The monastic leaves family and job, marking the crossing of boundaries by putting on robes, shaving the hair, and living in a religious community. When a religious practice enters the secular world of work, it too must "renounce" parts of itself and take up new secular habits. What does Buddhism have to give up, what does it have to take on, and what does it become in order to be a part of the tech company?

There is nothing natural or inevitable about tech companies taking up meditation. This chapter shows how meditation entrepreneurs use five strategic frames to transform a religious practice into a secular business practice: Hidden Buddhism, Whitened Buddhism, Scientific

Buddhism, Bottom-Line Buddhism, and On-the-Go Buddhism. It examines how meditation entrepreneurs—some of whom are Buddhist and some of whom are not—make Buddhist meditation "appropriate for work," and, in the process, are producing a new kind of Buddhism that "works" for the tech industry.

Hidden Buddhism

When Natalia Bernstein, a young Buddhist mindfulness teacher, first started teaching meditation in companies, she made a big mistake by using "the B-word." The company kept her on but warned that she could not refer to Buddhism or the Buddha in her instruction. Natalia, who was already struggling to make ends meet as a mindfulness and wellness consultant, felt she had no choice but to agree. She says that in the corporate setting the "B-word" makes people "alienated and scared," so she "takes out Buddha" and "strips the Buddhist language" from her teaching.

Natalia's experience is an example of *Hidden Buddhism*—where meditation entrepreneurs hide meditation's religious dimensions in their teaching. Many resort to euphemisms, such as "wisdom tradition," "contemplative tradition," or "ancient tradition." One business article calls mindfulness "a centuries-old idea that has been reinvented to address the challenges of our digital age."[6] The popular meditation app Headspace describes meditation as "rooted in ancient history and a topic of modern science."[7] Others hide Buddhism by replacing religious references with ethnic ones. For example, Gil Goldman says that when he shares Buddhist teachings in a corporate setting he identifies the author as "a Chinese poet in the ninth century," and not "the third Chinese Chan (Zen) patriarch." And others evasively refer to meditation as an "ancient practice."

To be sure, meditation is not an exclusively Buddhist practice. It is not inaccurate to describe meditation as "ancient," "contemplative," or "Chinese," or as a "wisdom" tradition. But most meditation entrepreneurs hide its Buddhist origins because they, and the companies that hire them, fear the liability of bringing religion to the workplace. Under Title VII of the Civil Rights Act of 1964, companies may not discriminate against employees on the basis of religion. This means not only that companies must make reasonable accommodations to the religious beliefs and practices of its employees, but also that companies cannot coerce employees to adopt or abandon a religious tradition as a condition of employment. Title VII does not ban religion from the workplace. But many of the people I spoke with do not understand the nuances of Title VII. They are so intimidated by the possibility of a lawsuit that they remove anything that is associated with religion. I found this to be true even among people in human resources, who should know better. For instance, I asked one senior human resources director for an example of her firm complying with Title VII. She told a story of asking a secretary to remove her "big Bible" from her desk. A Bible is a religious object, but its presence does not in itself constitute employee coercion, especially when it sits on the desk of a low-level secretary. Yet for even this seasoned human resources professional, the sight of a Bible in the office set off such fear of legal liability that she had it removed.

To be sure, meditation's legal liability is a legitimate concern. In recent years, public schools offering mindfulness have come under legal scrutiny.[8] Given the confusion surrounding Title VII and the ambiguity of meditation's status, most meditation entrepreneurs figure that they had better avoid Buddhism. For example, Ted Johnson, an engineer who started a meditation program at his company, said that he originally wanted to bring Buddhist priests to the company to teach. His company, however, told him that to comply with Title VII he'd have to bring in meditation teachers from multiple religious traditions so it didn't seem like he was favoring any one religion. Ted dropped the idea of bringing priests to teach and volunteered to lead the group himself. The work of finding multiple teachers was too much on top of his existing job. Bringing priests in would make the program seem "too religious," he said, and his sponsors in HR would "roll their eyes" and he'd "be in trouble." "Religion is a minefield," he concluded, and he keeps anything that seems "religious" away from work.

Ted's example illustrates how Buddhist meditation must conform to the secular norm of universality in the workplace. So long as meditation is "universal" and rooted in many traditions, it's not "religious" and is welcome in the corporation.[9] Sven Olsen, the director of the mindfulness program at a large tech firm, agrees, pointing out that it was a problem when employees in the program got "too religious" about meditation. I asked him what "too religious" means. Sven explained that it's when people insist on a particular way of practicing and interpreting meditation and back it up by quoting Buddhist texts. He is referring to how religious groups are bound by particular rites, rituals, and traditions, which function, according to anthropologist Mary Douglas, to delineate the boundaries and identities of a particular religious community.[10] But the boundary-drawing nature of religion violates the secular norm of universalism. Sven explained that since the mindfulness program is under the Wellness Department, it is a benefit for all employees. The employees who are "too religious" don't belong in the mindfulness program, Sven said, but in one of the employee-sponsored groups under the Division of Diversity and Inclusion. Meditation practitioners who are "too religious" transgress the universalism of the secular corporation and rightfully belong to a minority group.

To make meditation secular, meditation teachers downplay the Buddhist origins of their particular form of meditation and frame it as a universal practice. For instance, one engineer who started a meditation group at his company "avoid[s] religion" by "saying 'many contemplative traditions practice this.'" Another meditation teacher tells me that he will bring up a Buddhist text only if he can also "balance it with one from the New Testament." At one company's mindfulness retreat, the teacher explains that the practices are based on "ancient traditions" and practiced by people as varied as Hindus, Sufis, and Quakers. Although the teacher is referring to religious traditions when he mentioned "Hindus, Sufis, and Quakers," he uses the term "ancient traditions." Furthermore, he evokes the universality by listing multiple religious groups other than Buddhists. It's true that Hindus, Sufis, and Quakers have contemplative practices, but the meditation practice the teacher taught the group is specifically from the Theravāda Buddhist tradition. The Buddhist origins of mindfulness were obscured in another instance at the popular tech and mindfulness conference Wisdom 2.0 in 2019, when the speaker on a panel was asked whether corporate mindfulness "watered down the tradition." She responded obliquely by listing various traditions of mindfulness around the globe, concluding to loud applause that "mindfulness doesn't belong to anyone!"

The idea that meditation belongs to multiple traditions skips over the fact that most teachers teach *Buddhist* traditions of meditation. They are not instructing tech workers to recite the rosary by meditating on the mysteries of Christ's passion, a contemplative Christian tradition. Nor are they teaching them to perform salat, the Muslim postural ritual that is sometimes called a form of meditation. Instead, meditation instructors teach Buddhist meditation practices, such as counting breath, a method outlined by the Gautama Buddha in the Ānāpānasati Sutta; or observing thoughts and sensations as they arise, also known as Vipassanā, a practice in Theravāda Buddhism; or metta, also known as loving-kindness meditation, another Theravāda Buddhist practice. Because most meditation entrepreneurs assume that acknowledging the Buddhist origins of meditation practice violates the norms of the secular workplace, they "renounce" meditation's association with Buddhism.

Connecting meditation with Buddhism presents another liability to entrepreneurs, one that goes beyond violating secular norms—it reduces market share. Religion, entrepreneurs told me, "makes people feel uncomfortable." It is "alienating" and "divisive." Their fear is not baseless. Countless bloody wars have been waged over religion. Meditation entrepreneurs, however, are mostly concerned that associating meditation with Buddhism will make people assume that only Buddhists can practice it, and thus scare off potential clients. Teachers therefore must find creative ways to assure consumers that meditation is not religious. For example, the website of meditation app Headspace claims: "Meditation is not necessarily spiritual or religious. It shares a very long history with religion and offers an important spiritual component for many practitioners. But anyone can meditate, regardless of creed."[11]

Jacob Simon, who has practiced Buddhist meditation for over twenty years and is a branding and executive coach who brings mindfulness to clients, says that the only difference between teaching meditation in a Buddhist organization and a corporation are the "overt references to the dharma and the teachings of the Buddha." He claims that "Buddhism is baked into the content" of mindfulness and is "based completely on the teachings." Yet one of the first things that he does when he teaches corporate mindfulness is to tell the audience that "this is not religious." "You might be Catholic, you might be Protestant, you might be Hindu," he tells them. "Whatever religion you are, this is not going to get in the way of what you're doing. This is not religious. This is about waking up. This is about being more present to your life. And so it can complement any practice, any discipline, any religion that you have." By telling clients that meditation "is not religious" and framing it in universal terms ("this is about being more present to your life"), Jacob defuses any potential conflicts of loyalty to other religions and is able to cast his net to a wider market of clients.

The same concern about reaching the largest possible audience motivates many meditation entrepreneurs to downplay their Buddhist identities, a tendency among many in the mindfulness movement, according to sociologist Jaime Kucinskas.[12] For example, Gil Goldman, the engineer who is a Buddhist priest that we met earlier, doesn't reveal that he's a priest when he teaches at companies. "I don't say that I'm a Zen person. Might turn people off," he reasons. Gil says that he's concerned that people will find religion "divisive." In most settings, professional credentialing is an asset. But when it comes to religion and the workplace, many teachers see their religious credentials as a liability. Several meditation entrepreneurs mentioned the example of the meditation app Headspace as a cautionary tale. Many tech companies had been offering Headspace subscriptions to their employees as a wellness benefit. Yet several firms dropped their subscriptions after discovering that its founder and teacher, Andy Puddicombe, is an ordained Buddhist monk. Meditation entrepreneurs watching Headspace's travails concluded that if they wanted to keep their jobs, it was best to keep the "B-word" to themselves.

Not all meditation entrepreneurs conceal Buddhism to the same degree. Ordinary meditation teachers and lower-ranking employees, who fear losing their jobs, do it most thoroughly. Celebrity meditation teachers and high-ranking corporate executives, on the other hand, freely incorporate Buddhism into their teaching. Well-known Buddhist meditation teachers such as Jack Kornfield, Jon Kabat-Zinn, and Chade-Meng Tan frequently toss around terms like "the Buddha" and "dharma" and openly refer to Buddhist texts in their teachings. Status and rank also make a difference among employees who are trying to start meditation programs in their firms. Low- to midranking engineers say things like "religion is a minefield." Executives, who have the authority to float above the tedious rules of human resources, freely integrate Buddhism into the company however they see it.[13] Jim Ward, a vice president at a large firm, was "in the closet" about his religion and meditation practice until he became an executive. Safe in his status, he's "come out" and uses religious language like "soul," "God," and "spirituality" with impunity.

The organizational culture of the firm also affects whether meditation entrepreneurs bring Buddhism into their teaching. In general, I found that they are more likely to avoid religion when teaching in large firms with human resources departments. In smaller start-ups, however, where there may be no human resources personnel, and where the culture is more informal and homogeneous, teachers more openly incorporate Buddhism into their teaching.

The patronage of senior leadership plays an important role in determining how liberally meditation entrepreneurs can bring in Buddhism. At one start-up that was exceptionally open to Buddhist teaching, the meditation teacher gave what he called a "dharma talk" about the Buddha that was no different from a talk one might hear at a temple. I soon learned that the meditation class had the strong backing of the founder-CEO and was part of his vision to create a mindful company. The meditation teacher, who was hand chosen by the CEO to teach in the company, wasn't concerned about using the "B-word." In fact, the teacher had said that he would not come to the company unless he could teach the dharma alongside meditation. He told me that he had turned down other meditation jobs in companies that lacked the support of the CEO. Executive support and company culture made all the difference for Gan Saetang, a midlevel employee and Buddhist meditation teacher. When he tried teaching meditation at his own company, a traditional computer hardware firm, human resources told Gan to stop because meditation was "religious" and therefore illegal. However, when a top executive invited Gan to teach meditation at his hip social networking tech firm, human resources said nothing.

Hidden Buddhism reflects the popular idea that religion has no place in the workplace, least of all in a tech company. So meditation entrepreneurs try to obscure meditation's association with Buddhism. To sell a Buddhist product in tech's secular territories, they must pay a tariff: they must renounce meditation's association with Buddhism. The rules of the secular workplace, however, don't apply equally to everyone. Business executives, celebrity meditation teachers, and ordinary teachers who are protected by the patronage of executives use their high status to openly bring Buddhism into workplace meditation.

Whitened Buddhism

Why do some meditation entrepreneurs feel that it is acceptable to bring Buddhist teachings and practice into the secular workplace? One reason has to do with the high status of some meditation entrepreneurs. Another reason, however, is that some meditation entrepreneurs don't think that Buddhism is a religion at all.[14] This form of "nonreligious" Buddhism is what I call *Whitened Buddhism*. It erases the "ethnic" and "religious" Buddhism of Asians and Asian Americans in favor of the thinking and experience of White Westerners.[15] "Whitened" also refers to the process that has so thoroughly domesticated and normalized Buddhism for White, urban, and educated populations that Buddhism feels universal and "nonreligious," a process that Jeff Wilson discusses in his book *Mindful America*. Unlike hiding Buddhism, most meditation teachers do not strategically Whiten Buddhism to make it fit in the tech workplace. Rather, Whitened Buddhism describes the *prerequisite state* that a foreign religion like Buddhism needs before it can cross into any mainstream American secular institution. Renouncing its Asian heritage is a precondition for Buddhism's entry into the tech company.

Teachers who subscribe to Whitened Buddhism use the "B-word," quote Buddhist teachings, and integrate Buddhist practices and artifacts, such as using a Japanese prayer bell, or pressing palms together in prayer by the forehead as a gesture of greeting or thanksgiving, and keeping ritual silences. Those who are Buddhists tend to openly identify and share religious credentials if they are monks and priests.

Tim Breen, a corporate mindfulness teacher and Buddhist priest, is an example of someone who embraces Whitened Buddhism and liberally incorporates Buddhist elements into his corporate mindfulness teaching. After participating in one of his seminars, I asked Tim about this. "In the Bay Area, Buddhism is in the air," Tim explained. "Buddhism has not become a religion, but a decoration. . . . People have Buddhas around who have no religious interest whatsoever," he said with a bemused smile. "And I think that's good." A prosperous Silicon Valley firm holds its executive retreats at a Buddhist monastery, because the Buddha is a "decoration," he said, but it would never imagine holding a company retreat at a "religious" place like a church because of its "religious iconography." Tim doesn't have to hide or downplay Buddhism, because to him and others in the Bay Area, Buddhism isn't a religion.

What Tim describes is the *ambient Buddhism* of the Bay Area. When Buddhism becomes "part of the air," it's so thoroughly integrated into the mainstream secular, cultural, and social landscape that it has lost the "religious" qualities that make it distinct. Tim is right that the image of the Buddha is no longer a sacred devotional object but a "decoration," one that evokes a feeling of calm, or projects a sense of the mystical and exotic. In the Bay Area, "Zen" describes a feeling of peace, not a sectarian Buddhist tradition. Mala beads, or prayer beads, are trendy pieces of jewelry, not devotional objects. Meditation is not a religious practice but a self-help exercise that people do at health clubs, therapists' offices, schools, and at work. Buddhist monasteries such as Tassajara and Green Gulch and the meditation center Spirit Rock are popular leisure and self-care destinations for the well-heeled.

Whitened Buddhism is a part of the Bay Area's legacy as the center of two White youth movements enthralled with Asian religions. The Beats of the 1950s and the counterculture of the 1960s and 1970s set themselves apart from Asian American Buddhists. Japanese Zen teacher Shunryu Suzuki and his White students founded the San Francisco Zen Center in 1962 separate from the Japanese American Soto Zen temple in Japantown, in order to focus on *zazen*, or sitting meditation, a practice of little interest to most of Suzuki's Japanese American parishioners.[16]

Many of the youth in the Zen scene came from elite backgrounds. With their social capital, and the visionary leadership of Shunryu Suzuki and his successor, Richard Baker Roshi, Zen Buddhism's influence in the Bay Area swelled in the late twentieth century. The San Francisco Zen Center established Tassajara Monastery, the first Zen monastery outside of Asia; zendos in nearby Santa Cruz and Los Gatos; Green Gulch Farm; Tassajara Bakery; and Greens Restaurant, one of the premier gourmet vegetarian restaurants in the United States.[17] Other White Buddhist groups were also drawn to the Bay Area. For example, Insight Meditation West established Spirit Rock, one of the premier Buddhist retreat centers in the United States, in 1990. In these largely White spaces, Buddhists have cultivated a distinct Whitened Buddhism, one that religion scholar Joseph Cheah describes as meditation centered, that downplays ritual and is psychologized.[18] This "Buddhism without beliefs," as some call it, is a product of a White racial legacy whose essence, according to Buddhist teacher Jack Kornfield, lies in its meditative practices.[19] These Buddhist organizations have attracted powerful patrons—people such as Steve Jobs, former California governor Jerry Brown, poet Gary Snyder, writer Ken Kesey, Laurence Rockefeller, and Xerox inventor Chester Carlson.[20] Their brand of Whitened Buddhism has seeped into the "air" of Bay Area cultural, social, and political institutions.

The Bay Area's ambient Buddhism demonstrates how regional context affects what is considered "religious" versus "nonreligious." People like Tim Breen include many Buddhist elements in their corporate meditation teaching, concepts such as karma, monkey mind, and the dharma, as well as some ceremonial elements such as ringing bells. But they don't include other practices—incense, ceremonial robes, prostration, bowing, chanting—things that feel "religious," "divisive," and "alienating" to most Bay Area professionals. Adapting meditation for the workplace does not mean removing *all* religion, only certain religious symbols and rituals that mark distinction and difference. Pressing of palms to the forehead as a gesture of thanksgiving, Tibetan singing bowls, sayings of the Dalai Lama—these are all associated with Buddhism but they no longer feel "religious" to White people because they are part of the ambient Buddhism that has been domesticated and normalized into the sociocultural landscape of the Bay Area.

It's easy for Americans to believe that Buddhism is not a religion because the popular Buddhism that is propagated in the West does not fit the Judeo-Christian definition of religion. There are no deities, no requirement of faith, no supernatural claims, and no need for formal affiliation. Instead, many Americans consider Buddhism a "philosophy" or "science" whose teachings are self-evident and universal.[21] For instance, explaining the attraction of Buddhism to many White Americans, one meditation entrepreneur said, "I think the thing that attracts American people to Buddhism and to Zen practice is there's no belief system. . . . You're not required to swallow something whole. You can figure it out as you go along." He added, "Because there's no belief system, people don't consider it a religion like they would the other major religions." Another meditation entrepreneur who is an executive coach sees no problem in sending a Christian client to a Buddhist temple because Buddhism is a "philosophy."

Not only is there nothing to believe in Buddhism, but it's also "natural," simple, and self-evident, and therefore free for the taking. The editor of *Mindful Magazine*, Barry Boyce, told the audience at a work and mindfulness conference that "mindfulness is not based in Buddhism. It's an innate natural ability." "What I like about Zen is the stark simplicity," said a former tech executive. "There's nothing to believe. Just sit."

Many Western practitioners of Buddhist meditation point to certain famous Buddhist teachers who have also eschewed the religious label. "The Dalai Lama and Jack Kornfield both say that 'Buddhism is not a religion. It's a science of the mind,'" one person asserted triumphantly. (In fact, the Dalai Lama said, "Buddhism is *more than* religion.")

But most White Westerners don't realize that the Buddhism they know is a *particular brand of Buddhism* that has repeatedly been altered and adapted to appeal to them. According to historian Anne Harrington, Asian religious leaders such as the Maharishi Mahesh Yogi and the Dalai Lama have decoupled meditation from the category of religion precisely in order to establish the credibility of their foreign traditions to the modern White West,[22] a tactic White Buddhists have unwittingly continued. In establishing Insight Meditation in the West, Jack Kornfield explains, he and his team culled the "complications" of "religious tradition" from meditation: "We wanted to offer the powerful practices of insight meditation, as many of our teachers did, as simply as possible *without the complications of rituals, robes, chanting and the whole religious tradition*."[23]

Other groups have also employed rhetorical claims of nonreligion to appeal to new and different audiences. For instance, some evangelical Christians also claim that Christianity is not a religion. Both Buddhist and evangelical claims of nonreligion are less about secularity than about setting themselves in opposition to the antiquated traditionalism that is associated with "religion."

This brand of "nonreligious" Buddhism, however, has racial implications. It associates Asian Buddhism's "rituals, robes, and chanting" with the "complications of religious tradition." It dismisses the religious reality of most Buddhists who are Asian and is therefore a form of White supremacy, according to scholar Joseph Cheah.[24] For the vast majority of Buddhists who reside in Asia, Buddhism is a devotional faith that involves the veneration of deities and beliefs in the supernatural. For example, in Chinese, the phrase that describes practicing Buddhism, "bai Buddha" translates to "worship Buddha." Most lay Buddhists in Asia orient their devotional practices—offerings of incense and fruit, ritual chanting, praying, bowing, donating money to temples and monasteries—to the attainment of merit for a favorable rebirth. Most lay Buddhists in Asia do not meditate. For them, Buddhism doesn't mean "just sit." "Nonreligious" Buddhism is the Buddhism of a very small and circumscribed group of people who are largely White and affluent and live in the West.

Whitened Buddhism tends to portray the "religious" Buddhism of Asians and Asian Americans as burdened by unnecessary accoutrements—"complications," "culture," "folklore," "ethnicity," "baggage"—that distract from the essence of the Buddha's teaching.[25] For example, Mandy Stephens, whose company runs a meditation app for corporate clients, explains that they distill meditation to "the fundamentals," "the part that isn't religious or spiritual." Her company gets to "the fundamentals" by getting rid of teachers who are "zany gurus" and replacing them with "strait-laced trainers" in business-casual clothes. The chanting at the local Asian temple is "folklore," says former tech executive Pierre Beaumont, irrelevant to "what's good for me in meditation." Mandy and Pierre dismiss the very elements of Buddhism that tens of millions of Asians hold most dear.

Indeed, Asian people are curiously missing in tech's Buddhism. Most meditation entrepreneurs are White. Participants in corporate meditation programs also tend to be White. In my observations, I saw only a few Asian Americans, even though they make up 47.3 percent of the professionals in the Bay Area's manufacturing and information sectors and two-thirds of the Buddhist population in the United States.[26]

The absence of Asians in corporate meditation is particularly glaring at the popular mindfulness and tech conference Wisdom 2.0, where White celebrities like Goldie Hawn and Twitter founder Evan Williams have been given the main stage, but never an Asian monk who's dedicated his or her life to the practice. The Wisdom 2.0 meeting in 2015 invited about a dozen Tibetan monks to create a sand mandala. Over the course of three days, the monks, who stood out with their shaved heads and crimson robes, created a stunning sand mandala while Wisdom 2.0 attendees looked on. The Tibetan monks functioned much like images of the Buddha in Whitened Buddhism. They were invited to be "decorations" in the meeting, to be seen but not be heard. More recently, Wisdom 2.0 has addressed issues of race. The discussions, however, have been led largely by African Americans and are centered around including non-Whites in their practice of a "nonreligious" Buddhism, rather than critically engaging with the "religious" Buddhism of Asians and Asian Americans. Asian Americans have voiced their criticism of the "White supremacy" and "White privilege" of the mindfulness movement, including the late blogger Aaron Lee of the popular website Angry Asian Buddhist. Except for one Asian American Buddhist, none of my respondents acknowledged this racial dimension of corporate meditation.[27]

Whitened Buddhism renounces the ethnic dimensions of Buddhism that make it appear foreign and religious in the United States. It "liberates" the "fundamentals" of Buddhism from the "religious baggage" that is encrusted in the traditions, histories, and cultures of Asian Buddhists. This unencumbered Buddhism becomes a universal "philosophy" and "science." It becomes "White"—floating above context, invisible, and normal—as if "part of the air." So that when a meditation teacher quotes the Buddha at work, it doesn't scare anyone. Instead, tech workers can take in Whitened Buddhism as the practical wisdom of a safe and familiar "ancient philosopher."

Scientific Buddhism

Is religion still "religion" if it's scientifically verifiable? Most people in Silicon Valley don't seem to think so. Hiding Buddhism and Whitening Buddhism go only so far in convincing the tech industry of the value of Buddhist meditation. To truly "kill the Buddha" in Silicon Valley, you need the modern arsenal of scientific facts. This is the lesson that Miranda Smith learned in her twenty years as a strategy and mindfulness coach. A self-assured redhead in her sixties who practices Buddhism, Miranda is a business consultant who teaches meditation as a strategic business practice. She's been doing this for years, even before the latest meditation and mindfulness fad began. Miranda learned the hard way that you can't bring Buddhism into the sales pitch. When she talked about Buddhism, companies didn't hire her. So Miranda left out the Buddha and kept everything else. But she still struggled to get the attention of corporations. People in tech thought of meditation as "airy fairy," too "woo woo" for hard data crunchers like them, she explained. They associated it with long-haired hippies and Asian gurus. Everything changed with the advent of popular neuroscience, according to Miranda. She calls it a "revolution in secular Buddhism." Now, according to her, "you don't need to quote the Buddha; you just quote the scientific facts." Miranda's experience is an example of *Scientific Buddhism*—meditation entrepreneurs appealing to the authority of science to establish meditation's value and credibility in the workplace.

The curious alliance between modern neuroscience and Buddhism began in the late twentieth century, according to historian Anne Harrington.[28] The science of meditation first entered the popular consciousness in 1975, when Harvard Medical School cardiologist Herbert Benson argued that people could reverse the autonomic response to stress through their thought patterns, in his best seller *The Relaxation Response*.[29] Benson used science to vigorously dissociate meditation from religion, and he medicalized it by calling it a "relaxation response." You don't have to be Buddhist, Hindu, religious, or believe in anything to reap the physical benefits of meditation, Benson reassured readers. Anyone can do it. Buddhist teacher Jon Kabat-Zinn further institutionalized medicalized meditation when he established a program in 1979 at the University of Massachusetts Medical Center in Worcester to help patients deal with pain, stress, and illness. The program, which he subsequently named Mindfulness-Based Stress Reduction (MBSR), taught patients "moment-to-moment awareness" based on a secular adaptation of Buddhist teachings of mindfulness. Since the mid-1990s, MBSR's medicalized version of meditation has been widely adopted in clinics and hospitals around the world.

While medicine was interested in meditation as a therapeutic intervention, religious leaders like the Dalai Lama were looking for scientists to legitimate Buddhism in the West. Meeting with the Dalai Lama during his first visit to the United States in 1979, Herbert Benson persuaded him to allow his monks to participate in physiological experiments. Reluctant at first, the exiled leader soon agreed, hoping that cooperation between Buddhism and science could burnish Tibetan Buddhism's image in the West and make Buddhism relevant to the modern world. Although inconclusive, Benson's work on Tibetan Buddhist monks opened the doors to a robust relationship between the Dalai Lama and Western scientists.

Included in that impressive roster of Western scientists is Richard Davidson, a leading neuroscientist and founder of the Center of Healthy Minds at the University of Wisconsin, Madison. Davidson had long been interested in Buddhism and meditation. In the 1960s he traveled to India with the best-selling science writer and meditation advocate

Daniel Goleman. Davidson says that he'd been a "closet meditator" for forty years.[30] He had dabbled in research on meditation earlier in his career, but it had not gotten much traction.[31] All that changed when he met the Dalai Lama in 1992, a meeting that Davidson describes as "a total wake-up call for me" and "a pivotal catalyst" for changing his research trajectory. "He challenged me," Davidson recalls, "saying 'You've been using the tools of modern neuroscience to mostly study anxiety, depression and fear, all these negative feelings. Why can't you use these same tools to study qualities like kindness and compassion and equanimity?' And I didn't have a very good answer for him."[32] According to Davidson, the Dalai Lama was interested in what modern neuroscience could discover about the minds of people who spent years "cultivating qualities of mind which promote a positive outlook."[33] Soon after their meeting, Davidson brought Tibetan monks to his Wisconsin lab and studied their brains by attaching electrodes to them and scanning their brains with MRI and FMRI machines. What he found was that these advanced meditators had minds that were more resilient and conducive toward compassion and other "prosocial" behaviors. Davidson's research established the theory of neuroplasticity, and the proposition that, with practices like meditation, ordinary people could optimize their mental and emotional functioning. His research catapulted mindfulness out of the medicalized treatment of pathology—depression, stress, anxiety—to the betterment of healthy, already high-functioning people. Davidson's work opened the floodgates of academic research. In the year 1990, not one academic article was published on mindfulness or meditation. In 2000, there were twenty-one, and by 2013, the number had reached a staggering 549 articles on mindfulness published that year.

Science is so fundamental to the Dalai Lama's vision of modern Buddhism that he elevates its authority even above Buddhist tradition. "If scientific analysis were conclusively to demonstrate certain claims in Buddhism to be false, then we must accept the findings of science and abandon those claims," His Holiness wrote in 2006.[34] Moreover, at a gathering of Buddhist monks and priests from Asia in 2006, the Dalai Lama said that Buddhism "is more than a religion. It is a science of the mind."[35]

By calling Buddhism a "science," the Dalai Lama has let the genie out of the Buddhist bottle, liberating Buddhist practices like meditation from the circumscribed world of "the religious" to shape and to be shaped by "the secular." Buddhism has migrated from the fuzzy world of wisdom, virtue, and ethics to the empirical scientific world of data, metrics, and facts. Moreover, as a "science," Buddhist practices such as meditation no longer belong to any one tradition but are "natural," "universal," and protean "tools" whose functions alter depending on whose hands it is in. As religion scholar Jeff Wilson has written, meditation can be all things to all people—a practice to improve health, focus, productivity, eating, relationships, testing, athletics, and so much more. It's in this light that the earlier observation that neuroscience "revolutionized" secular Buddhism makes sense. It might be more accurate to say that *Buddhism used neuroscience to revolutionize itself.*[36]

The Dalai Lama is right that aligning Buddhism with science makes it legible to the secular tech industry. Science has erased meditation's lingering association with religion and thrown tech's doors wide open to the practice. Teachers in Silicon Valley especially feel the need to use science because their audience of engineers is "turned off by airy-fairy talk," as one teacher put it. Jacob Simon presents meditation differently depending on the audience. "The engineers want to hear the language in their terms—[terms that] can resonate with them—and the science substantiates that this works."

I found this generalization regarding the authority of science to be mostly true. One programmer who attended a meditation training told me that he was willing to try it because the teacher offered "enough science to deal with skepticism." During presentations on meditation, I noticed that the predominantly engineering audience seemed more attentive when it came to the science portion, and many nodded in agreement, taking notes. Furthermore, when tech leaders rationalized why they used meditation in their companies, they always mentioned the science. When Evan Williams, a cofounder of Twitter, explained at Wisdom 2.0 in 2013 why they meditate at his new company, Medium, he explained, "We believe in the science. It's not just something fluffy."

Ready for skeptics, meditation entrepreneurs armor their PowerPoint slides with tables, graphs, and figures quoting the latest neuroscience research. As one meditation teacher explained, "We spend a lot of time on neuroscience. This opens [engineers'] minds to do the practice." A common topic at meditation and work conferences is how to convince management that meditation works. The answer is always "science." For instance, at a mindfulness workshop in San Francisco, one engineer-turned-human-resources-professional who was establishing a mindfulness program in his company schooled the audience in how to sell mindfulness to skeptical executives: "first present the science," and show that "it's proven by science and brings business results."

In many of the corporate mindfulness classes that I observed, teachers presented the science early on. Their presentations followed a predictable format. First, there was a short anatomy lesson of the brain highlighting the amygdala, and then came the scientific evidence proving the benefits of meditation. The lecture at one workplace meditation workshop provides a good example. Shelley, a gentle and knowledgeable White psychotherapist in her sixties, began by showing the class several anatomical slides of the human brain. She focused on the amygdala, two almond-shaped nuclei located deep in the temporal lobe that control the autonomic responses associated with fear, arousal, and emotional stimulation. When we are fearful or stressed, Shelley explained, the amygdala activates the "flight or fight mode" in our bodies, signaling the hypothalamus to activate the pituitary gland, which stimulates the adrenal gland to release cortisol, the "stress hormone." We experience "amygdala hijack"—a term coined by the popular science journalist Daniel Goleman—when our amygdala takes over and we lose control of our rational and executive thinking functions.[37] Meditation, Shelley tells us, is the solution to "amygdala hijack."

Meditation entrepreneurs fill their presentations with references to the swelling body of scientific research linking meditation to enhanced mental functioning. They cite studies showing that meditation produces a thicker frontal cortex and reduces activation of the amygdala, which is linked to emotional regulation, compassion, and empathy;[38] studies demonstrating that mindfulness practitioners can utilize more of their brain circuitry, making them more effective at regulating emotions;[39] the findings of Richard Davidson and Jon Kabat-Zinn that employees trained in mindfulness had lower anxiety, increased activity in the parts of their brains associated with positive emotions, and stronger immune systems;[40] and studies suggesting that research subjects trained in mindfulness can process stimuli more efficiently.[41]

Meditation entrepreneurs are making science a "selling point" that widens their pool of potential customers. Executive coach and strategy consultant Daniel Perlman says, "I never give a business pitch and say, 'We're going to bring in meditation.' Instead, I say, 'Do you want to leverage state-of-the-art knowledge on neuroscience and system theory?'" Daniel doesn't even mention the word "meditation." Instead, he scientizes it, calling meditation "state-of-the-art knowledge on neuroscience and system theory." Similarly, Matt Stevens, a mindfulness and strategy consultant and longtime meditator, always starts with the science because it is a "doorway into the room." Organizations offering corporate mindfulness carefully position science in their publicity literature. For example, the Search Inside Yourself program describes itself as "the original mindfulness and emotional intelligence training program developed at Google, based on *neuroscience*" (emphasis added). Its literature frequently reminds the consumer that its product is "evidence based." Wisdom Labs, a mindfulness-based consulting group, advertises that "science is at the forefront and heart of our approach."[42] The meditation app Headspace has an entire tab on its website devoted to "the science," publicizing the scientific studies it is a part of, and claiming that "science has been an integral part of the Headspace business since day one."[43] Similarly, a consulting group in corporate leadership boasts: "We use neuroscience, social psychology, and contemplative practice to teach leaders to connect," preferring to use the more ambiguous term "contemplative practice" instead of "meditation."

The declining interest in yoga, the less lucrative cousin of mindfulness, suggests that if mindfulness entrepreneurs want to stay in business, they are wise to use the science. One entrepreneur reflected, "Everyone wants to see scientific evidence. That's why mindfulness has been more successful than yoga or other modalities." Companies may have yoga classes to reduce stress, but they devote far more time and resources to meditation practices that have been "proven" to improve cognitive functioning. That's why we read about "billionaires who meditate," and not those who practice yoga.[44]

Scientific Buddhism has made Buddhist meditation more accessible outside of religious circles, but it's come with certain trade-offs. Meditation entrepreneurs frame meditation in scientific terms on the job, but in private, most said that the science is of no personal value to them, and that they thought of meditation as a spiritual practice. Many of them described science as a way to "sneak in spirituality" into the data-driven world of tech. An example of this is Samantha Lieberman, who "couldn't care less about the neuroscience" and says mindfulness is "about liberation." Ethan Horowitz was also dismissive about the science and defines meditation as "connecting with something deep inside themselves." The scientific discoveries of meditation changed nothing for Jim Ward. Meditation, he says, is about connecting to his soul. But many meditation entrepreneurs hide the spiritual dimensions of meditation in the workplace because concepts such as liberation and soul have no "scientific" basis.

Violet Lee's experience shows how meditation entrepreneurs wrestle with integrating the spiritual dimension of meditation with science. When her company, a wellness application, considered adding meditation to its menu of features, the process of defining the product with her colleagues, she says, was "a perpetual struggle." Violet says that her colleagues would ignore her if she spoke about the "spiritual side of meditation," so she "tried to toe the line by explaining it in very outcome-oriented terms." "I found myself referencing these scientific studies quite a bit," she says, "because those were very outcome based. That was the language that the people I was with could understand and resonate with." Notice how Violet describes herself as *unconsciously* resorting to science: "I found myself referencing these scientific studies." Similarly, Regina Ligori, a shaman who is a corporate strategy consultant, also exhibits this compulsive reliance on science when she tells me adamantly, "We need the science to support the budgets!"

Because meditation entrepreneurs feel they must "toe the line" even if they don't care about the science, their parading of scientific facts about meditation can seem perfunctory and performative. I witnessed more than one meditation entrepreneur speak in a presentation passionately about his or her journey to meditation, but then mechanically recite the scientific studies supporting meditation.

Scientific Buddhism, however, does not remove magic and myth from corporate meditation. It simply replaces it with its own version of magical and mythical claims. Many of the so-called scientific claims about the benefits of mindfulness in the workplace are inflated and based on circumstantial evidence. Most studies on meditation are controlled lab studies whose results may not translate outside the lab. Scientists warn the public to "mind the hype" because the science is still in its infancy and riddled with "misinformation and poor methodology."[45] Yet these warnings are rarely heeded by industry journalists or by meditation entrepreneurs like Regina who "need the science" to sell meditation. Over and over, I observed meditation entrepreneurs performing science without seriously engaging the data. They backed "scientific"-sounding claims with spurious precision: meditation lowers cortisol by 23 percent, or increases IQ by ten points, or increases focus by 10 percent. These statements might be true in a controlled lab, but no one has proven them in a workplace.

Entrepreneurs pay a competitive price when they take the science seriously and "mind the hype." The story of Violet Lee's company is a telling example. When Violet researched competing meditation apps, she says that she was "horrified at the kind of claims that the apps were making." Commonplace claims such as meditation curing depression or making people happier were based on "circumstantial evidence," she thought, and would expose her company to lawsuits. Because the company CEO had encountered legal issues regarding false claims in his previous company, he took extra care to make this company's claims conform to FTC regulations, a fastidiousness that Violet says is unusual in the mindfulness industry. Instead of stating a relationship of direct causation, the company lawyer made them use language to suggest correlation, such as "mindfulness has been linked to . . ." But being rigorous about the science handicapped them. "We argued with our general counsel about how much leeway to give us in terms of marketing language, especially since we would see firsthand how customers unfamiliar with mindfulness and meditation were often unconvinced by the 'value' or 'benefit' of these practices," Violet says. "Our claims were essentially nonclaims compared to the statements made by our competitors." Honoring rigorous science cost them their market share.

Violet's story illuminates the pressure meditation entrepreneurs feel to scientize meditation, even if the science is based on circumstantial evidence or faulty methodology. Ironically, the pressure to conform to the secular scientific imperative creates sloppy science, by rewarding inflated claims and punishing those who make more rigorous but modest ones. The result is that Scientific Buddhism swaps the "woo woo" and "airy fairy" claims of religion for the "woo woo" numbers and data of pop "science."

To become a part of the tech company, Buddhism must renounce its own systematic knowledge that is based on centuries of Buddhist tradition—a knowledge base that still eludes the data, metrics, and analytics of modern science. Instead, Scientific Buddhism trades its rich repertoire of wisdom for the thin veneer of modern scientific legitimacy. Scientific Buddhism may improve people's cognitive functioning, but it lacks the wisdom to tell them what to use it for, except to produce more, and produce better.

Bottom-Line Buddhism

When George Troy, the founder of a start-up, wanted his employees to meditate, he thought long and hard about the language. Despite scientific evidence on the benefits of meditation to brain functioning, he knew that people still associated it with religion, gurus, and hippies, none of which he thought belonged in his company. George came up with a different way to talk about meditation. "We didn't say, 'We want you to meditate,'" he explained. "Instead we say, 'We're bringing in a productivity expert,' or 'a better way to project manage.'" George's rhetorical appeal to meditation's usefulness to worker performance is an example of *Bottom-Line Buddhism* and illustrates how Buddhist meditation must change its currency from religious utility to economic utility in order to circulate in Silicon Valley's tech companies.

As I've discussed, religion in the workplace is seen as divisive, unscientific, and illegal. Strategies of hiding, Whitening, and scientizing Buddhism make meditation more palatable, but they don't necessarily convince management of its economic value. Science and the medicalization of meditation have elevated meditation's reputation from the countercultural margins to the mainstream spaces of the hospital and therapist's office, but meditation is still associated mostly with relaxation and stress relief. The name of one of the most well-known secular meditation programs, Jon Kabat-Zinn's Mindfulness-Based Stress Reduction, suggests this very purpose. As a result, meditation entrepreneurs feel that they need to rebrand meditation as a productivity tool and disassociate it not only from "divisive" religion and hippie counterculture, but also from the secular medicalized discourse of relaxation. For instance, when Gil Goldman first started approaching companies with meditation, he said, they'd respond, "Oh no, it will cause my people to zone out. They will lose their ambition." Similarly, when user-experience designer Cecelia Lau tried to start a meditation program in her start-up, people objected, claiming they'd "lose their edge" and "chill out too much." Such objections made Cecelia "very keen to refute these beliefs."

The meditation app Headspace goes out of its way to counter the image of meditation as a nonproductive activity. "Meditation is not 'checking out' or escaping our problems or duties," its website reminds users.[46] But throughout history, that is exactly what meditation has been about. In the 1960s, many in the counterculture lived by Timothy Leary's mantra "turn on, tune in, and drop out" and used meditation to "tune in" to their inner consciousnesses and to "drop out" from productive society. Buddhist meditation originated from a monastic lifestyle, which typically involved the renunciation of, or "checking out" from, social institutions such as the family and the formal economy.

This historic link between meditation and economic withdrawal sets up hurdles for meditation entrepreneurs, who want to monetize it.

Meditation was traditionally the practice of monastics who renounced participation in the market economy, and relied on charity for their livelihood. The economic benefits of meditation are therefore neither natural nor self-evident. Meditation entrepreneurs have to invent them and then market them carefully. This is what the Google engineer Chade-Meng Tan did when he developed the idea for the popular Google mindfulness course Search Inside Yourself. "Contemplative practices can be made beneficial both to people's careers and to business bottom lines," he proclaimed.[47]

Emphasizing the bottom line is especially important for people like coaches, meditation teachers, and people in human resources who make a living selling meditation. David Stein, the head of learning and development at a start-up, put it frankly: "We have to do this because people are going to come after us. I mean I'm always framing things that way, of course, because otherwise, how do you justify the expense of having somebody like me around. It's a business. I'm expensive. If I'm not contributing to the bottom line, then why are we paying me?" Other meditation entrepreneurs said the same thing: "You have to appeal to the bottom line." Appealing to the bottom line is also important to tech employees who want to start meditation programs within their companies. Engineer Ted Johnson started teaching meditation at his firm informally among friends and acquaintances. But after his classes started attracting more people and he needed company support, he had to change the rhetoric to make it "official." He told human resources that "getting engineers to meditate fifteen minutes a day" would yield "better code, lower stress levels . . . all the stuff the executives like to hear."

Most people don't associate meditation with productivity, so most meditation entrepreneurs do not use the word "meditate." As one entrepreneur told me, "you have to disguise it for management." A few get around the dilemma by not calling it anything, like Jacob Simon, an executive coach, who says, "I really just don't even label it." But most of them resort to euphemisms: "high-resolution attention," "attention training," "mental training practices," "evidence-based mental conditioning," "technology to explore and train the mind," "mental fitness," "direct attention network," and "high-resolution self-awareness on demand." The masculine language of discipline, training, and results disassociates meditation from the soft, spiritual, feminine world of religious and therapeutic practice in a way that jibes with the tech industry's image of itself as cerebral and "data driven." Labels matter. Mental-health monikers for meditation, such as "quiet sitting" and "mindfulness-based stress reduction," just don't work in tech corporations. One meditation entrepreneur put it this way: "Jon Kabat-Zinn's definition of mindfulness—paying attention in the present moment, on purpose, without judgment, as if your life depended on it—that might be too poetic for most engineers."

To counter its image as relaxation, teachers present meditation as a form of athletic discipline. Tech meditators are not patients in need of therapy, or hippies who want to escape reality, but elite mental athletes who engage in the productive practice of "training" their mental "muscles." And when meditation providers do make therapeutic claims of reducing stress or increasing well-being, they present it as a form of self-mastery—"governing stress" or "developing resilience"[48] rather than "letting go" and "relaxing." Meditation teachers are "trainers," not "gurus," "dharma teachers," or "therapists." The "mental workout" metaphor was vividly evident in one meditation entrepreneur's presentation when he showed a slide of a man lifting weights under the title "Mindfulness Training Is Fitness for the Mind." We can develop highly desirable skills of mental focus, attention, clarity, and self-awareness, the presenter told the audience, by training the "muscle" of the mind.

Layered atop these tropes of science and athleticism are themes of "progress" and "optimization."[49] Mindfulness is "an evolutionary development that maximizes our potential," well-known Buddhist teacher Tara Brach proclaimed to a crowded auditorium of tech workers at Salesforce's annual conference, Dreamforce.[50] Author and Google "Chief Evangelist" Gopi Kallayil compares humans to machines that need to "reset" their connections and "optimize" their "systems" through meditation and mindfulness practices.[51] And in *Search Inside Yourself*, Chade-Meng Tan, yet another Google employee, tells readers that mindfulness helps you "optimize yourself and function at an even higher level than what you are already capable of."[52]

Choosing the right language to frame meditation can make or break a corporate contract, so meditation advocates devote a great deal of attention to it. One person explained, "We work on messaging about mindfulness because how we talk about it matters. It's the difference between opening and closing a door." This often leads to what sociologist Jaime Kucinskas calls "the vague multivalent language," and what business scholar Ronald Purser calls the "language game," of the mindfulness movement.[53] For example, when an audience member from one mindfulness conference asked the speaker, a seasoned meditation vendor, how he could bring mindfulness to his company when his CEO doesn't believe in meditation, he replied, "Fiddle with the languaging." The speaker gave his own example, "We don't say meditation; we say 'mindfulness.' The languaging is very important. At one company when we started, we didn't call it mindfulness; we called it 'neuro-self-hacking.' But at another company, they talk about code refactoring, so I told them, 'It's a way to refactor your mental capabilities.'" The speaker's response highlights how important it is for meditation entrepreneurs to "fiddle with the languaging."

Others capitalized on mindfulness's more favorable image over meditation. "Of course we believe that everyone would be better off if we all meditated ten minutes a day," the head of wellness at one large firm said, "but we can't tell people that meditation is mindfulness." When one engineer started a meditation program at her company, she deliberately called it "mindfulness meditation" so that it would be more acceptable. Similarly, meditation teacher Natalia Bernstein says that calling meditation "mindfulness" is less controversial.

Disguising meditation is a common theme among meditation entrepreneurs. For example, one engineer who was trying to establish an official mindfulness program in his company said, "For many people, 'mindfulness or meditation' causes allergies, so we have to find the right Trojan horse." At another workshop on the benefits of "attention training," the presenter turned to the audience and cupped his hands around his mouth as if telling a secret and stage-whispered into the microphone, "We are really teaching meditation." The audience loved it. At the same workshop, another presenter shared what he thought was a funny story about how he had led several executives on a meditation that he called "mental conditioning." At the end of the meditation he said, "Congratulations on your first meditation," to which one of the executives responded, "Did you mislead us?" The audience laughed. The presenter reassured us that even though he'd blown his cover, no damage was done, and that he and the executive became good friends.

There's a reason meditation entrepreneurs work so hard to frame meditation as productivity *and not* wellness. Stress reduction and employee wellness are now bona fide concerns of tech companies, as we saw in chapter 2. But wellness is also a low priority for most firms. Meditation entrepreneurs don't want to associate meditation with yoga, sleep pods, gym memberships, and massages, mere perks that will be cut in leaner economic times. When mindfulness is framed as "wellness," it is the first thing to go, warned one presenter at a meeting for meditation entrepreneurs.

Meditation entrepreneurs make meditation seem indispensable by tying it to the performance of the most important members of the company, the senior leaders. They call it a "leadership" skill. For instance, one conference speaker ticked off a list of what mindfulness is not—"religion, New Age, emptying the mind, relaxation." Arguably, mindfulness is all those things. Indeed, at the very same conference, clothing designer Eileen Fisher identified herself as a "New Age, self-help junkie." The problem with "religion, New Age, emptying the mind, [and] relaxation" is that none of these contribute to the bottom line. Instead, the speaker defined mindfulness as training "leadership excellence"—qualities of "focus, clarity, creativity, and compassion." Other meditation entrepreneurs also gravitate toward marketing mindfulness as "leadership," a catch-all term positively associated with business acumen, by catering programs to upper-level management. Making mindfulness about the higher-priority performance of senior leaders rather than the wellness of the masses makes a lot of sense for meditation entrepreneurs. As I've discussed earlier, Silicon Valley firms spare no expense in enhancing the peak performances of their "high-potential" employees. Meditation entrepreneurs can charge more when their services are perceived as indispensable to senior leadership.

One of the problems with Bottom-Line Buddhism is that it's very difficult to measure or prove meditation's ROI, or return on investment, in the workplace. As I discussed, most studies of meditation are controlled lab studies whose results may not translate outside the lab. The vast majority of studies on meditation focus on health measures, such as cortisol production, blood pressure, depression, and inflammation—all of which may be indirectly related to productivity, but are not direct measures of productivity. Furthermore, clinical studies on meditation and work performance are often based on self-reports, which can be biased.[54]

Recognizing the dearth of evidence linking meditation with workplace productivity, some mindfulness entrepreneurs have conducted their own studies to prove the case for mindfulness. For instance, the website of the mindfulness program that started at Google, the Search Inside Yourself Leadership Institute (SIYLI), reports a study that employees who participated in the SIYLI program were less stressed and more engaged and had a higher sense of well-being and better communication. Participation in SIYLI, the study concluded, yielded a 200 percent return on investment.[55] Yet the results of another study showed that participation in SIYLI was associated with *increased* work exhaustion and disengagement.[56] This study, however, is not on the SIYLI website. At another tech company, an employee who started a grassroots meditation group devised a study measuring before and after stress levels, employee satisfaction, and well-being among workplace meditators in order to receive human resources funding. According to him, their findings proved the benefits of meditation to be "through the roof," and HR approved its funding because of this.

Most meditation teachers and vendors do not conduct such studies.[57] Moreover, because the studies are vendor-specific, it's not clear whether the results can be generalized. And since they do not compare participants to a control group, or alternative workplace interventions,[58] it's difficult to say whether meditation's benefits are superior to exercise, gardening, playing video games, or napping—all activities that also can boast of scientifically proven mental benefits.[59]

Hence, claims of productivity often serve more as rhetorical strategies to win over corporate supporters and "data-driven" engineers than a reality grounded in "evidenced-based facts." An example of this is how John Olsen, an engineer turned meditation teacher, used numbers to paint his claims about meditation's ROI with the sheen of scientific data, even though he didn't actually have any evidence. In his marketing spiel, he'd ask companies, "What if I could make your workforce 1 percent more productive?" When I asked John how he came up with the number, he said that he made it up. None of the people in human resources ever asked him where he got the numbers. Statistics give the illusion of data and science. John wasn't trying to be duplicitous. He believed that meditation would make employees more productive, even more than 1 percent. But he couldn't back up the claim, so he resorted to the next best thing, making it appear scientific by using numbers.

Despite (or perhaps because of) such tactics, the scientific and instrumental framing has been effective in "killing the Buddha" and increasing meditation's market share. I didn't find anyone who objected to meditation on religious grounds, not even conservative Christians. David Jacob, an Indian American evangelical Christian who's worked in large tech firms for the last thirty-five years, observes that in the past, "I had some weird meditation stuff like visualizations that I had to go through in the old days," but says, "now it's very clinical."

I discovered that when meditation can prove its utility to the bottom line, it eases worries about whether it is religious. David Stein, the head of talent and development at a start-up, has instituted a culture of mindfulness at his company, a culture he describes as "kind of Buddhist." But he says that this "kind of Buddhist" approach to mindfulness is neither religious nor spiritual, because it's a "practical tool" that is "rooted in pragmatic business-oriented outcomes." Alice Martinez, the director of human resources at a large tech firm, had a similar attitude regarding profits and Buddhism. After we attended an off-site mindfulness training session together, she seemed unsure about whether to hire the vendor. At times the vendor seemed "too religious," she observed. But then she turned around and said, "It can work if we tie it back to business goals and profits." Meditation entrepreneurs have so successfully removed religion from Buddhist meditation that one human resources professional, after watching a presentation on the science and productivity benefits of meditation, turned to me and asked, "Wait . . . is Buddhism a religion?"

But there are trade-offs to Bottom-Line Buddhism. To win over Silicon Valley companies, Buddhism has to renounce some of its religious dimensions that run counter to corporate goals, such as its otherworldly focus and ethical teachings. This may be why meditation entrepreneurs expressed more reservations about Bottom-Line Buddhism than about any of their other marketing strategies. One person who manages a popular Buddhist retreat center told me that most influential Buddhist teachers "have no appetite" for bringing meditation to a secular audience. "They don't want the tradition to be bastardized," he explained. The tension between company goals and meditation entrepreneurs' idea of Buddhism comes out in in emphatic statements, such as "meditation is not about productivity" and "meditation is not about stress relief."

A few said they worried that Bottom-Line Buddhism is completely divorced from Buddhist ethical teaching. This is the critique of Peter Lucas, a Zen priest who has chosen not to teach in companies:

> In Buddhism, the technical term mindfulness refers to a wholesome mental state where the underlying intention is ethically positive. . . . Focused attention is ethically neutral, and there's actually a term in Buddhist technical literature called wrong concentration. . . . Wrong attention, wrong concentration is that faculty which allows the murderer's knife not to miss. In other words, criminals are very focused. . . . Just because you're paying attention doesn't mean what you're doing is good. It doesn't mean that it is wholesome. . . . There is a danger in "mindfulness" being so divorced from a larger ethical context. Buddhism is after all, at root, just like any great religion and ethical teaching. It's a teaching about how to live, how to live in the light of compassion and wisdom. It's not a technique for training your mind.

Peter rejects the instrumental framing of mindfulness when he says, "It's not a technique for training your mind," and emphasizes that Buddhism is "just like any great religion" that offers an ethical teaching. To Peter and others, separating mindfulness from the Buddhist ethical context is "a danger" and an example of "wrong concentration."

Buddhists have raised concerns about the absence of ethical teaching in secular mindfulness, a development religion scholar Ann Gleig calls the "mindfulness wars."[60] One of the most searing critiques is a *Huffington Post* essay gone viral, "Beyond McMindfulness."[61] In it, management professor Ron Purser and Zen teacher David Loy argue that erasing ethical teachings from secular mindfulness is a "Faustian bargain."[62] "Rather than applying mindfulness as a means to awaken individuals and organizations from the unwholesome roots of greed, ill will and delusion," they write, "it is usually being refashioned into a banal, therapeutic, self-help technique that can actually reinforce those roots."[63] The mindfulness movement leaves the structural injustice of capitalism intact, they maintain. Purser and Loy are not alone. A host of critics have accused secular mindfulness of being coopted by capitalism.[64] At least for the tech industry, their characterization of mindfulness seems hard to dispute. Consider what happened in 2014, when a group of activists protesting against San Francisco's housing crisis stormed onto the stage during Google's presentation at Wisdom 2.0. Security officials immediately hustled them off the stage. Amid the ensuing hubbub, a Google mindfulness leader invited the audience to "check in with your body." Once tensions had been eased, order restored, he went back to his presentation. The issue of housing insecurity went unaddressed.[65]

Yet most meditation entrepreneurs, who are struggling to find a foot in the door of companies, cannot afford to introduce ethical teachings that challenge the principles of capitalist enterprise.[66] Meditation entrepreneurs, after all, are hired to raise worker productivity, not advise on business ethics. Al Hoffman is a corporate meditation teacher who is aware of the "Faustian bargain" he has struck. He thinks that the dharma can transform corporations, if it is truly practiced. But this would require dramatic changes, such as an across-the-board living wage and reducing the vast pay gaps between tech companies' highest- and lowest-paid employees, not to mention reducing their reliance on subcontracted nonemployee workers. But Al, who's worked in the tech industry for a long time, knows that's not going to happen. Even if he talked about it, companies won't hear it or do anything about it, he says.

So he does the next best thing, using mindfulness to help employees cope with the "toxic environments" that they work in.

Others feel that Bottom-Line Buddhism goes against the Buddhist teaching of letting go of attachments. When Cecelia Lau wanted to convince her start-up to establish a meditation program, she says, she circulated studies "showing how meditation is good for productivity." But she "had very mixed feelings about it. I didn't like having to do that. I felt it kind of corrupted the teaching, because I was reifying this idea of meditation being a means to some sort of end."

But most meditation entrepreneurs cannot afford to give up selling meditation as a productivity tool. Cecelia described being "shocked and horrified" when she discovered that a highly respected dharma teacher at her zendo was teaching on a "cheesy meditation app," only to learn that he, like most meditation teachers, was getting next to nothing to teach at dharma and retreat centers. To survive in the Bay Area, meditation teachers have no choice but to monetize meditation and gloss over the ethical teachings of the dharma. One Buddhist engineer who started a grassroots meditation group at his company insisted that teachers be volunteers, because, he said, "Weird things happen when you pay for meditation." Meditation teachers who got paid, he was convinced, couldn't be trusted to teach it the right way. His position as a salaried employee allowed him to insist on a "purer" message than most meditation teachers can afford.

To get around this ethical dilemma, some teachers emphasize that meditation is *more than* just a productivity tool. When asked how he responded to the "McMindfulness" critique, the chief mindfulness officer of the tech company SAP replied that although sometimes corporate mindfulness can be guilty of watering down the teaching, mindfulness instructors can counter that by teaching empathy and compassion along with concentration.[67] But as I've discussed in chapter 4, Silicon Valley's interpretations of those qualities are also driven by the bottom line. Even Chade-Meng Tan has backpedaled from earlier hyperbolic claims that mindfulness can make practitioners rich and successful, urging practitioners to preserve the "depth of the dharma" in mindfulness and warning that "it's not just stress reduction or leadership; it's freedom from suffering."[68] Tan doesn't deny that mindfulness is "stress reduction or leadership," only that it's "not just" that.

Others defend the instrumental framing of meditation as the Buddhist practice of *upaya*, or skillful means to enlightenment: meeting business people where they are, and using the language of productivity as a doorway to explore the dharma deeper.[69] This is how Cecelia Lau justifies marketing meditation as a productivity tool even though it "kind of corrupted the teaching." She herself is an example of how the practice can deepen with time. Cecelia started meditation for an instrumental reason: to reduce her stress. But as she practiced more seriously and immersed herself in Buddhist teaching and community, its meaning shifted for her, from a mental-health practice to a religious practice. For Al Hoffman, "it's about creating access to the dharma without the religious or spiritual obstacles that people face." He agrees with the criticism that the emphasis on productivity somehow reduces the practice of mindfulness, but he doesn't see it as an affront to Buddhism. Instead, he laughs it off as merely a missed opportunity for those whose heart's desire is merely to "work an extra hour at Google."

Most of the meditation entrepreneurs I spoke to are like Al and Cecelia. They have to accept the trade-offs of teaching meditation as a productivity enhancer, even if they have mixed feelings about it. If they don't make the productivity pitch, they don't get hired. This is what happened to Gil Goldman when he tried to teach meditation at one tech company. He had filled out all his employment papers and was set to start teaching meditation at a large tech firm when he stopped hearing from his contact at the company. Through inside channels, Gil discovered that the company had instead hired what he called "a professional meditation company" with "professionally trained meditators" offering "meditation [a]s a product that's sold."

I understood better why the company dropped Gil when I asked him how his program was different from the "professional mediation company." He pulled out his brochure. "Look at all these topics I cover," he said. Gil proceeded to list the topics that he teaches in his corporate meditation class. They were the same basic teachings of the dharma that he regularly covered at his zendo: letting go of attachments; mitigating the desire for control through meditation; understanding how discouragement can be helpful; giving up self-image; and recognizing, accepting, and dissolving habitual tendencies. "These other folks don't do that," he said proudly. But nowhere did Gil mention things like mental training, leadership, or focus—skills that can translate to the bottom line. Gil's problem is that tech companies don't want workers who let go of control and accept discouragement. They want a meditation that gets people to produce and perform. The message is loud and clear: if Buddhism wants to swim in tech's secular waters, it must contribute to the bottom line. And that means renouncing anything that yields no ROI (return on investment).

On-the-Go Buddhism

On-the-Go Buddhism is a close cousin of Bottom-Line Buddhism—and is the ultimate desacralization of Buddhist meditation. It removes the inconvenience of religious rites and rituals, so that Buddhist meditation conforms to "corporate time," accessible to anyone, anytime, anywhere. Religion, according to French sociologist Émile Durkheim, is by nature inconvenient to ordinary life. All religions distinguish between the sacred and the profane, Durkheim declared in his classic study *The Elementary Forms of Religious Life*. Nothing is inherently sacred. Things become sacred through religious rites, rituals, and rules that set them apart in time and space from the profane, or the ordinary. In most traditions of monastic Buddhism, monastics differentiate themselves from "householders," or the laity, by shaving their heads, wearing robes, living in monasteries, and abstaining from meat, alcohol, and sex. Lay Buddhists also observe the distinction between sacred and profane. They create separate, sacred spaces in their homes and communities such as household altars and temples, and they mark sacred time by abstaining from meat and alcohol on Buddhist holy days. All over the world, most people alter their behavior when they recognize the sacred—they speak in hushed tones, refrain from profanity, and wear modest clothes in sacred spaces.

But in order to fit into the workplace, Buddhist meditation must renounce the liturgy of the sacred and adopt the liturgy of efficiency.

Hidden, Whitened, Scientific, and Bottom-Line Buddhism make meditation universal, normal, legitimate, and profitable, but they don't solve the problem of fitting a time-consuming practice into a busy workday. Most workplace meditation sessions last from thirty minutes to one hour and are offered one to three times a week. Some companies offer meditation and mindfulness intensives—such as a one-hour workshop over six weeks, or a half-day, or one-day, or two-day workshop—in addition to, or in place of, regular weekly sittings. But it is difficult to find thirty minutes or more a day for meditation in companies where employees feel as though they barely have time to eat lunch. One engineer told me that although she loved attending the weekly workplace meditation, she had to stop because she just didn't have the time. Even executives who advocate for workplace meditation admit that meditation carries a high "productivity cost," one they can defend only as an "investment."

Companies want their employees to meditate, so long as it doesn't take too much time. The head of the mindfulness program at one tech firm calculated that, in the last year, employees had collectively spent over fifty thousand hours meditating. Laughingly putting his fingers to his lips, he stage-whispered, "Shhhh! Don't tell the company. They don't want to know that they are paying for their employees to spend so much time meditating and not working!" His "secret" gets at the problem that a time-consuming practice like meditation poses in the workplace: being mindful can be at odds with being productive.

Meditation entrepreneurs feel pressure to make meditation quick and convenient. One large tech company asked dharma teacher Samantha Lieberman if she could teach mindfulness in a fifteen-minute session. She declined, explaining to me that she was "not hungry enough" to accept those unappealing terms. But she knows that there are plenty of other meditation entrepreneurs who are "hungry enough." Teachers say they feel rushed when teaching in companies. "At the company, I have one hour," Gil Goldman says, "and then you got to get out of there because the next group is coming in to use the conference room. It's very limited in what we can do in corporate settings because of schedules and space constraints. At the temple, we schedule double the time to do the same module."

This time pressure is intensifying as competition grows among corporate meditation providers. Back when Michael King was one of the few people teaching meditation in companies, he taught it as a one-hour session, twice a week for three weeks. Now, he says, there is much competition, and there are many people who are willing to teach faster and in less depth. Still, teaching in his retirement, Michael refuses to compromise the teaching. But not everyone can afford to teach meditation on their own terms.

The point of the workplace, after all, is work and not meditation. So when mindfulness takes too much time from work, it fails. A couple of years ago a large firm instituted "Meditation Mondays," offering weekly ninety-minute meditation training sessions every Monday, then reduced it to one hour after managers complained that ninety minutes was too long. Apparently one hour was still too long, and the number of attendees dwindled until the company eventually ended the program, replacing it with an online meditation module for employees to access at their convenience.

Meditation entrepreneurs adapt meditation to the fast-paced tech world by "taking the practice off the cushion into real life": "micropractices" that can calm and focus the mind but are quick and convenient enough to be easily integrated into everyday office behavior. These practices enhance work engagement without the disruption of a thirty-minute sitting meditation.

Meditation entrepreneurs play up the convenience of meditation by calling it a "practical habit" or "tool" rather than a "practice." These are monikers that suggest functionality, handiness, and ordinariness. "Practice" connotes a dedicated behavior that is intentionally set apart in time and space. Some teachers call them "stealth practices," implying that they are easily disguised as "ordinary" office behavior.

"Stealth practices" and "micropractices" allow tech workers to access a meditative state without disrupting their normal workday. One example is "breathe, smile, let go": on the first breath, take a deep breath; on the second breath, smile; and on the third breath, "let go" of worries. Then there is the "three-breath connection exercise": on the first breath take a deep breath; on the second, think of someone; and on the third, mentally send good wishes to that person. By infusing breathing with intentionality, practitioners claim they transform a normal bodily function into a "practice" that shifts tech workers into more "productive" states of focus, equanimity, compassion, and creativity, as we saw in chapter 4.

Mindfulness instructors encourage their students to develop the "practical habit" of mindfulness by pairing practices with all sorts of routine behaviors, walking to the bathroom, say, or walking to lunch. At one company mindfulness retreat, the teacher instructed the attendees to focus on their breath while walking by inhaling for four steps, and exhaling for four steps. While people who practice walking meditation are usually identifiable because they walk very slowly, these tech workers are able to conceal their meditation by counting their breath as they walk at a normal pace. In one company's mindfulness program, the teacher instructed the participants, "Look for opportunities for mindful moments throughout the day." Employees shared their "mindful moments." One engineer volunteered that he practiced focused breathing every time he went to the bathroom. Another person said she focuses on her breath every time she pulls a paper towel from the dispenser in the bathroom, and pauses, once again before leaving the bathroom. Note that these tech employees did not mention meditating in the company's meditation rooms. There may be no better example of the desacralization of Buddhist meditation than the fact that so many tech workers must catch a "mindful moment" in the bathroom.

But the apps give the bathroom a run for its money. To make meditation even more convenient, many companies offer employees free access to meditation apps as a part of their wellness benefits. Mindfulness apps such as Headspace, Calm, and Buddhify have taken meditation to a whole new level of convenience. These meditation applications treat meditators as user-consumers who can access the meditation experience "on demand," making meditation not only more convenient to employees, but more scalable and cost-effective to the firm.

Apps change the meaning of Buddhist meditation. The practitioner is no longer a member of a religious community who is guided by its collective wisdom and tradition. Instead, meditation is a consumer product, and the practitioner is an individual user-consumer who navigates through a menu of choices regarding time, function, and instructor to design the ideal meditation experience for his or her present need. Instead of a traditional sitting meditation that may take one hour, users can choose how long they want to meditate, ranging anywhere from one minute to twenty-five minutes.

Rather than following the meditation practice the tradition or priest prescribes, users choose the appropriate meditation "tool" depending on what they need at that moment. For example, Headspace users can choose meditations based on whether they want to be "finding calm," "less stressed," or "more focused." Similarly, Whil users can choose meditations from a menu of functions: "improve performance," "boost emotional intelligence," "manage your emotions," and "career well-being." These apps train users to think of meditation as a consumable tool with discrete functions, like a hammer, a screwdriver, or a wrench. With many meditation apps, meditators aren't limited to one teacher as they might be if they belonged to a sangha (Buddhist community) or a workplace meditation program. As user-consumers, they pick from a variety of "trainers," each with a different style. Flipping through the menu of trainers on the website, users can easily choose their teachers on the basis of race, gender, and age.

Finally, meditation apps allow users to monitor their "progress" while meditating, turning meditation—a practice closely associated with the ideal of nonattainment—into a goal-oriented activity. For example, the app Buddhify tracks how long users meditate. Whil goes further, allowing companies to track how long employee users are meditating and why they are meditating, as well as to measure employees' self-reported levels of stress and sleep quality, all while somehow complying with HIPAA privacy guidelines. Furthermore, meditation apps help users keep their goals by reminding them to be mindful, compassionate, and grateful, and to take deep breaths. Phone pings replace collective rituals, such as the ringing of bells or the lighting of incense, that mark the beginning of shared sacred time. All these apps are designed to accommodate to the busy lifestyles of modern professionals who want to meditate anytime and anywhere. Rohan Gunatillake, founder of the app Buddhify, explicitly positions "mobile mindfulness" as a way to fit "mindfulness techniques alongside the activities we are already doing rather than having to find a special time and space for it."[70]

On-the-Go Buddhism is indeed more accessible and convenient than a religious Buddhism, which is practically defined by its adherents' willingness to "find a special time and space for it." Most meditation entrepreneurs think it is worth sacrificing the inconvenience of "religious" meditation and make it accessible to anyone at all times and in all places. But desacralizing meditation and subjecting it to the logic of the ordinary workplace has its own cost. This became clear at a mindfulness event at a large tech company that featured a prominent psychologist's research on the emotion of awe, an emotion that is fundamental to religious experience across traditions.

The psychologist talked about awe in the instrumental manner of meditation entrepreneurs speaking about meditation—as a tool that reduces inflammation and stress and induces positive qualities like compassion and helpfulness. He too, invoked the legitimacy of science, presenting his case on slides of his data organized into neat tables and graphs. At the end of his talk, an audience member in a company t-shirt raised his hand. "Where can I get this awe?" he asked. "Is there something I can buy, or download?" The psychologist was flummoxed, and people in the audience chuckled nervously, turning their heads to see who would ask such a ludicrous question. After gaining his composure, the psychologist tried to answer the question, stammering his way through: "Well, you can take a walk in nature, or you can read poetry . . . uh . . . or you can buy my book."

The psychologist was puzzled. But he shouldn't have been. The question was perfectly sensible in a world where virtuous and sublime states have become instrumental "skills" that optimize work performance. Judging from his face, the questioner was disappointed with the answer. And why not? The psychologist's scientific and utilitarian presentation of awe had implied that awe was a "skill" that he could learn with a simple purchase or download.

But, much like the sacred, what makes something awesome is that it is *not* ordinary. If the experience of awe is rendered ordinary and convenient, it ceases to be awesome. The inconvenient truth about both awe and the sacred is that you have to step out of ordinary time, place, and consciousness to experience it. Awe cannot be reduced to a trainable and marketable skill that you can master and possess. Awe possesses you.

The awkward encounter between the psychologist and the awe-seeking tech employee captures the incompatibility between the inconvenience of the sacred and the efficiency of the workplace. Contrary to what most meditation entrepreneurs claim, making Buddhist meditation convenient is not just a cosmetic disguise. How, when, where, and why you do something changes the meaning of it. This is why the Users associate meditation with productivity and efficiency and not mystical experience. On-the-Go Buddhism seeks to capture and tame the sacred but ends up killing it. And when the sacred dies, religion loses its transformative power to produce awe.

A Buddhist meditation teacher once told me that teachers must put a Buddhist hand in a corporate glove, and not the other way around. Most meditation entrepreneurs think they are doing this by hiding, scientizing, Whitening, instrumentalizing, and making Buddhism quick and convenient for tech workers. They have discarded its religious trappings, and whittled meditation down to the "fundamentals" of "just breathing." The "corporate glove," they believe, is merely cosmetic, a way to get the dharma in the door. But there is a more powerful hand at play here than the Buddhist hand or the corporate hand. It is the "invisible hand" of capitalism that silently shapes all of life, including religion, in Silicon Valley.

Since the ninth century, when Chan Master Linji Yixuan instructed his disciple, "If you meet the Buddha, kill him," Buddhists have sought to remove religious fetishism from the dharma. But when meditation entrepreneurs "kill the Buddha," they replace the Buddha with something else. They don't get rid of religious rituals, rites, and devotions. They just swap them for the rituals, rites, and devotions of another religion—the religion of work.

What must Buddhism renounce when tech companies become temples? In Silicon Valley, "killing the Buddha" means renouncing a sacred, separate, Asian, otherworldly, and ethical "religious Buddhism"—one that is at odds with the needs of the tech industry—and replacing it with a universalized, Whitened, scientized, profitable, and efficient Buddhism that is in service to it. It means turning Buddhist meditation into a practice that promotes mental training and leadership rather than liberation or enlightenment. In the dharma according to Silicon Valley, virtuous states of calm, focus, and joy liberate *productive beings* from habits that hold back their productive potential, rather than liberate sentient beings from habitual tendencies that tie them to *samsara*, the cycle of rebirth. Religious practices bind practitioners closer to their religious communities and traditions. So too, corporate meditation binds workers more tightly to their companies in the religion of work. A Buddhism that is at home in the tech company is an ethically hollow Buddhism, one that must practice detachment from its own ethical teachings and turn its mind's eye away from the karmic consequences of the tech industry—extreme inequality, employment insecurity, and a crisis in housing, to name just a few. Without a "religious Buddhism" that honors a separate and sacred ethics, teaching, time, space, practice, and community apart from tech and its goals, this brave new Silicon Valley Buddhism becomes just another one of tech's service providers.

Silicon Valley indeed killed the Buddha. But they have replaced the Buddha with another religion's leader: the productivity guru in the religion of work. Like the dry cleaners, chefs, masseuses, and executive coaches, he's there to "awaken" tech workers to their full productivity.

CONCLUSION

Techtopia

PRIVATIZED WHOLENESS AND PUBLIC BROKENNESS

What happens to society when its members worship work? Silicon Valley offers us an answer. The tech industry has created what I call *Techtopia,* one of its most disruptive innovations yet. Techtopia is Silicon Valley's upgraded social "operating system"—an engineered society where people find their highest fulfillment in the utopian workplace. It promises high-skilled Americans a new kind of "wholeness." Professionally managed, data-driven, meritocratic, and designed to scale, Techtopia gives tech workers what their families, religions, neighborhoods, unions, and civic organizations have failed to deliver in the last forty years: meaning, purpose, recognition, spirituality, and community. It is the twenty-first century American Dream.

Techtopia's promise of fulfillment may feel distant, even comical to most Americans. But in fact, it addresses a silent and growing absence in the American soul, an absence of belonging. Social institutions that once nurtured belonging and fulfillment no longer serve Americans well. In the last forty years, Americans have withdrawn not only from religion, but from marriage and civic associations that at one time offered "wholeness." Rates of marriage and civic participation are at an all-time low.[1] Few Americans are members of unions any longer.[2] Many people don't even have a sense of attachment to the companies they work for because they are subcontracted labor, including many of the people who make the tech companies thrive. Even a sense of national belonging is in crisis. In 2018, a record low number of Americans reported being "extremely proud to be American."[3] What institutions do we turn to now for belonging and purpose in life? Where do we go for "wholeness?"

The media pathologizes people who worship work, calling them "workaholics." But what is the alternative? In American society today, there is no single institution that so faithfully aspires to meet the material, social, and spiritual needs of its members as work does for its highly skilled workers. Tech workers are worshipping work because work has become worthy of worship.

Techtopia is a cautionary tale for the rest of America. It may be making an elite group of tech workers "whole," but it is leaving the rest of society broken. What kind of society do we become when human fulfillment is centered in the workplace? What happens to our families, religions, communities, and civil society when work satisfies too many of our needs? Silicon Valley is a bellwether of what happens when we worship work—when we surrender our time, our identities, our resources, and even our cherished traditions in service to work. It is what will happen if we don't invest in building and sustaining social institutions and traditions that nurture community, identity, and purpose outside of work.

Techtopia and the Monopolization of Human Energy

Techtopia seeks to monopolize the collective energies of communities, channeling them away from religions, families, neighborhoods, and civic associations, and into the tech workplace. To illustrate tech's relationship to the community, imagine social institutions represented as a variety of magnets spaced out on a tabletop. And let's say we have a bucket of metal filings that symbolize the energy (time, effort, attention) of people in the community. If we scattered the bucket of metal filings onto the table, the filings would cluster around the most powerful magnets. And even if we tried to distribute the filings evenly across the table, they would naturally migrate toward the most powerful magnets. The piles of filings show us where the energy of the community gravitates.

The metaphor of magnets and metal filings illustrates the relationship between work and human energy in Silicon Valley. Workplaces are like big and powerful magnets that attract the energy of individuals away from weaker magnets such as families, religious congregations, neighborhoods, and civic associations—institutions that we typically associate with "life" in the "work-life" binary. The magnets don't "rob" or "extract"—words that we use to describe labor exploitation. Instead they *attract* the filings, monopolizing human energy by exerting an attractive rather than extractive force. By creating workplaces that meet all of life's needs, tech companies attract the energy and devotion people would otherwise devote to other social institutions, ones that, traditionally and historically, have been sources of life fulfillment.

Consider how the "life" provisions of the workplace attracted the devotion of Sheba Nair, the tech worker and single mother we met in chapter 2. She chose to take a more senior position at a new firm even though it would mean longer hours, leaving her less time to spend with her seven-year-old daughter. Despite the longer hours, the new job had perks that made her life easier as a single mother. The company had an after-school child-care facility and a big playground that stayed open late. In the past, Sheba had struggled to pick up her daughter by six from her school's aftercare program. Now, Sheba can work late knowing that her daughter is safe and well cared for. On top of that, the new company's cafeteria serves dinner. Now, instead of hastily heating up a microwaved frozen dinner, Sheba and her daughter have stress-free healthy dinners at work, where she enjoys "quality time" with her daughter.

If Sheba lived in a different time or place, she would have called on other institutions and individuals to care for her daughter: the watchful eyes of neighborhood adults, a neighborhood youth center, or extended kin. But all the other families in her neighborhood are like hers. They, too, work long hours in tech and send their kids to after-school programs away from the neighborhood. Moreover, as a "tech migrant" who moved to Silicon Valley from India, Sheba has no extended kin to rely on.

In Techtopia, companies replace all other potential providers of social support—families, local businesses, neighborhoods, and public services. Indeed, the company's professional, managed care is so efficient that the services of other social institutions pale in comparison. One woman marveled at the perks of her daughter's tech job—the meals, laundry service, wellness benefits. "I could never give her all that," she admitted.

Companies are also stepping in where religions have failed. "I was talking to a guy at work the other day about mindfulness," Jim Ward, the mindfulness director at one firm, recalls. "And he said, 'I want to do more of this. Are there groups where you can get together and do this?' And I said, 'Yeah, it's called church.' [laughing] And he says, 'Oh yeah, but I don't want church.'" Jim delivers the all-too-serious punch line with a grin: the company's mindfulness program is "having church at work without having church."

People are hungry for spirituality, Jim says, but they "are turned off by religion." Although he is an active member of a faith community outside of his company, Jim doesn't see religious institutions meeting people's spiritual needs in Silicon Valley. The workplace, in his view, is the answer: "I think we can create that place at work, where they can be spiritual without even knowing they are being spiritual. . . . They can feed that part of themselves that wants to be fed in a way that's completely secular."

Carrie Hawthorne, a former human resources director at a large tech firm, also sees the depth of people's unmet needs and the company willingness to take the place of religion:

> People don't really go to church the way they used to. They're not really rooted in their communities the way they used to be. There is this deep need for being a part of something larger than themselves, so feeling connected to the other people in the company, to the mission of the organization . . . what I see is it's taking the place of some of these other institutions that we used to have. . . . People are wanting more out of their work. They're not actively volunteering or in a spiritual community. They're expecting to be fulfilled in that way and to make a contribution through their work.

Most of us can agree that eating well, being physically fit, experiencing spiritual growth, and having a purpose in life are all good things. Why should we care if people fulfill these needs through their workplaces, especially if work provides them more efficiently than families, neighborhoods, and faith communities?

The problem is that tech companies increasingly operate like the most extreme of religious organizations—cults. They channel the energy of their employees inward and cut them off from things outside. As I've discussed, tech companies do this by hoarding so much of their employees' time, energy, and passions that they have nothing left for anything else. And they provide for so many of their employees' needs that tech workers can do without the public. As a result, Techtopia is corroding the collective capacity to build and sustain a common good.

Peter Kim, a tech entrepreneur in his late forties, has witnessed the breakdown of community and civic participation as tech workers took over his Silicon Valley suburb. Fifteen years ago, Peter had neighbors with diverse occupations—one neighbor was in real estate, one in finance, another a plumber, and another a small business owner. Peter would see them walking their dogs and mowing their lawns, and their children playing in the yards. The neighborhood felt to him like a community, he says. There was a sense of mutual concern for each other and the neighborhood as a whole. They *belonged* to the neighborhood. The previous owner of Peter's house used to run a day-care center from the home, drawing in many of the children and families from the neighborhood. When issues arose, they'd organize community meetings and post flyers around the neighborhood. Peter, who is now running for elected office in his city, credits his start in city politics to the activism of this earlier neighborhood. If it weren't for those neighbors, he believes, he wouldn't be running for political office today.

Today, he says, "a lot of those people are gone." Many moved because of the rising cost of living. Others sold their homes at unthinkable profits and retired early somewhere else. What do his neighbors do for a living now? Peter goes down the list: "software engineer, software engineer, software engineer." None of them, in his view, care about the neighborhood. They live there, but there's no sense of belonging. The town was closing small neighborhood parks to cut costs, he complained. That was something his old neighbors would have fought. But now, his neighbors don't do anything. I asked him why engineers are different. "They're busy," he answered. Peter rarely sees his neighbors anymore. They're not around enough to see the town notices about the impending shut-down of their neighborhood park. And even if they see the notices, they don't seem to care. "They don't go to the park, so it just disappears," Peter explained.

Peter's story made me think of Sheba. What if Sheba had lived in Peter's old neighborhood when it was rich with social relations? Sheba and her daughter's life might have been different. Her daughter might have attended a child-care center run out of a neighbor's house, instead of the company program. The child would have been able to walk to the neighborhood park instead of relying on her mother to drive her to the company playground. Between the neighbors, whose work schedules were different from Sheba's, there would usually have been some adult to keep an eye on the kids at the park. Her daughter's playmates would have been neighborhood children with parents from different walks of life—as realtors, small business owners, and plumbers—and not just the children of other tech workers. The swing set and the monkey bars in the neighborhood park wouldn't be as new and flashy as the ones at Sheba's company, but one could imagine such a community fighting the city tooth and nail if it tried to take the park away from them.[4]

Richard Grant, a longtime Protestant minister in Silicon Valley, notices that church participation has declined as tech has grown. People, he says, now live at "a breathless pace." Thirty years ago, the typical member of his church attended both Sunday service and Sunday school most weeks. Today, the average member of his church attends only Sunday service once a month. This has caused a "volunteer challenge" in his church. Time and energy that people used to devote to church is now going to work.

In Techtopia, people don't belong to neighborhoods, churches, or cities. They belong to work.[5] Instead of building friendships, trust, and goodwill within their communities, they develop the social capital of their companies. Not only does this hurt the communities they live in; it weakens the foundations for participatory democracy.

Silicon Valley's public officials, who know the tech world well, think tech workers are extraordinarily disengaged from public concerns.

Grace Hsieh, a Bay Area public official and former tech entrepreneur, blames Techtopia for tech workers' notorious political apathy. When she worked in the tech bubble, she says ruefully, she ate, exercised, socialized, worked, and played at the company and then returned home in the company bus.

Now, as a public official, Grace and others in the Bay Area are finding "it's very hard" to engage tech companies and workers in community issues. Tech workers are especially "uninvolved" in city politics, far less involved than professionals from industries such as health, real estate, or banking. It's not a generational thing, Grace insists. Millennials actually make up the backbone of civic participation in San Francisco. But tech workers are "very apolitical. They don't get involved. They don't vote. They don't know their local representatives."[6] Peter Kim, a rare tech worker active in city politics, confirmed Grace's observations. Tech workers show up so rarely at city events, he says, that when he first started attending city meetings years ago, one woman asked him, "Where are you visiting from?" When Peter replied that he lived in the city and asked why she thought otherwise, she said, "Well, you know, 'cause you're a young guy. They don't come to meetings like this."

It isn't just the engineers. Tech companies and their leaders exhibit the same public disinvestment as their employees.[7] According to Grace, the relationship between tech and Bay Area cities is tense. It wasn't always so. Before tech's dominance, business leaders from finance, textiles, and real estate were many of San Francisco's civic leaders, she observes. CEOs of major corporations served on the boards of local community organizations and were engaged in civic life. But with the exception of people like Mark Benioff, Grace says that today's tech CEOs are much less civically engaged.[8] Tech companies show interest in the public only when the public gets in its way, she says. Rules and laws designed to protect the public don't matter to tech companies who want to "change the world," Grace explains. "Their policy is 'break the rules.' They create business models that are potentially illegal, and when they get big and they bump up against laws, that's when they get involved in civil society, and they call me. This leads to political fight after political fight where citizens want to regulate the hell out of them. They don't understand the value of laws," Grace concludes with a sigh.

The conflict between the tech industry and the public interest is now a familiar story. Time and time again, we see tech's business models collide with the public good, jeopardizing the safeguards to our democracy, privacy, and labor protection. Big Tech has the power to change laws and bend public will in its interest. For instance, in the 2020 elections, Uber and Lyft challenged a new California labor law that required app-based transportation companies to treat their drivers as employees and provide them with benefits and bargaining rights. Uber and Lyft spent over $200 million to propose and successfully pass Proposition 22, a ballot measure that classifies app-based drivers the way that Uber and Lyft had always done, as independent contractors. For many observers, Proposition 22 shows that tech companies engage the public only when they want to defend and widen their market share.

Servicing the Techtopian Economy

Tech companies have hoovered up so much of the wealth and resources in Silicon Valley that local businesses and organizations must cater to their needs in order to survive. We might call this concentration of resources in tech, with its enthralled local economy, the *Techtopian economy*, and it has been brewing a long time.[9]

In 1958, the British sociologist Michael Young predicted these developments in his book *The Rise of Meritocracy*.[10] In it, he described a future society organized around optimizing the mental labor of a technocratic elite. Employers would consider it their "duty" to "provide the best possible conditions for mental activity, during the whole of every twenty-four hours, on the job and off the job."[11] Companies, Young wrote, would provide their employees with meals and arrange domestic servants, chauffeurs, and even trips "wintering" in "Montego Bay . . . Caracas . . . Palm Beach . . . wherever the industrial psychologist recommended."[12] Society would be divided according to "mental aptitude," with those who lacked the mental aptitude dedicated to creating a "total environment conducive to high performance" for a technocratic elite.[13]

Young's portrait of a stratified society organized around servicing the productivity needs of a technocratic elite describes Silicon Valley with eerie precision. Anyone who wants a share of the region's wealth must either cooperate with it or join it. Henry Henessy, the head chef at an upscale restaurant, knows this all too well. Every day, he drives an hour and a half from his home in Menlo Park across the Golden Gate Bridge to his job in Marin County. His commute is long because, he says, "Silicon Valley is a food desert." No one wants to open restaurants in Silicon Valley, he explains, because they can't compete with tech companies and their cafeterias, which offer free, high-quality food right there at the office. Even if diners did show up, all the good chefs are opting for the easier hours and higher pay of the tech company. So Henry, who dreams of opening his own restaurant one day, commutes an hour and a half to get the work experience that he needs. Calling Menlo Park a "food desert" may be an exaggeration, but tech companies' relentless effort to colonize their employees' mealtimes has crippled the public good that is the local food scene.[14]

Tech companies are flush not only with money, but with something even more scarce in the valley: the time and attention of their employees. In order to attract the time, energy, and souls of tech workers, religions, which are, after all, in the business of enlightenment and salvation, must bring their wares to the workplace. Watching the temples and churches empty out, religious leaders of many faiths are now supplicants at the company gates. Traditional Sunday service, say Christian leaders, isn't working for this new population of tech workers who live at work. Why not bring church to work? Local churches have established "workplace ministries" in tech firms that offer weekly gatherings for tech workers to worship, pray, and study the Bible together, without leaving the office.[15]

But when the church moves to work, it diverts resources away from those who don't work in tech. This creates tensions between those who want to preserve the church as a refuge for families in a work-obsessed world, and those who think that a workplace ministry best serves the local population of tech professionals. Church members agree that they cannot do both things well.

Workplace ministries also leave out another group of people who work in tech firms—low-paid contract workers like janitors and food-service workers who don't control their own work time. Some firms allow janitors to join the fellowship, but many do not, to the frustration of Mike Lansing, pastor of a local Protestant church, who leads a "workplace ministry." In comparison to workplace ministries, churches in the community are more diverse across occupational, class, and racial lines. For instance, Jack Sunland, a White retired tech executive, attends a church whose pastor is Black and has a "middle-class" congregation that includes teachers, secretaries, and janitors alongside tech workers like him. Bringing church to work ends up infecting the church with what some call tech's "caste system": the "core" skilled full-time employees who enjoy security, benefits, and perks, versus "peripheral" contract workers who don't.[16] It turns praying and studying the Bible with fellow Christians at work into just another "perk" reserved for "core" company employees, not much different from bus rides, smoothies, and massages. Workplace ministries are offering to make tech workers "whole." But who is looking out for the souls of the janitors and food-service workers?

Getting Google Money

It's hard to get by in the Bay Area unless you're getting "Google money." It is one of the most expensive metro areas in the country. In 2019, a family of four living in Silicon Valley needed to earn *more than* $131,600 just to meet their basic needs.[17] Even though about only a quarter of Silicon Valley jobs are in tech, the salaries of well-paid tech workers have driven up the cost of living for everyone.[18] In 2019, the median compensation for a Google employee was $246,804.[19] In contrast, the median income for individuals in San Francisco was $74,841.[20] That puts the median home cost in San Francisco at $1.35 million, out of reach for most people.[21]

But to get Google money, businesses and organizations must align their services to tech's particular vision of productivity and efficiency. They must shift what they do and who they serve. I saw this very clearly among meditation teachers who had to "kill the Buddha" in order to pay rent, and who lament that they cannot afford to teach in the schools and community centers where their hearts feel called. I saw this in a nursing school, turning from training nurses to teaching tech workers about wellness, health, and diet. I saw it in a Christian seminary, agonizing over whether to embark on a spiritual and ethical training program for tech executives even if it siphoned off precious resources from its traditional mission of training ministers. Tech companies have monopolized the services of meditation teachers, nurses, and ministers into making their tech workers "whole," but who is tending the bodies, minds, and souls of the rest of society?

The most poignant examples of getting Google money came when I interviewed executive coaches. Many were middle-aged former tech workers. They'd been unhappy working in the "toxic" tech workplace and wanted to escape. In the end, their companies pushed them out. They'd become old, obsolete, and expensive, they told me. No longer yoked to these "toxic" workplaces, they dreamed of creating careers more aligned to their spiritual paths. But to make ends meet in the Bay Area, they could never escape tech. They remade themselves into executive coaches, became service providers in the Techtopian economy. The great irony is that they are now tasked with making tech workers happy and whole in the same companies that broke them.

Living on the Margins of Techtopia

Some people never find a way to be useful to tech. Linda Taylor, a middle-aged woman looking for a job in human resources, is one of the many living on the margins of Techtopia. I met Linda at a mindfulness and tech networking event. She tried hard to fit in, but in her pantyhose, pumps, and a tailored dress that was just a little too small, Linda looked like an interloper in the jeans-and-wool-sneakers crowd of millennials. All evening, Linda hovered on the margins of different groups, trying to get a word in, then giving up, and moving on to the next group. The young hipsters eyed her suspiciously. Finally, at the end of the evening, she found herself next to me. Once that she realized that I was another outsider and that she no longer had to perform, Linda burst into tears and told me her story. She'd gotten laid off over a year and a half ago and had been looking for work ever since. Linda was the sole breadwinner in her family. She supported her two teenage boys and her disabled husband. Their health-care costs had gone through the roof, and they were down to the last penny of their savings. If she didn't find a job fast, Linda said, she and her family, all Bay Area natives, would have to sell their home of fifteen years and leave California. But they have no idea where they would go.

Linda's experience reveals the limits of Techtopia: it is a place where wholeness is the privilege of those with the right skills and credentials, and of the right age, race, and gender. Silicon Valley's businesses and organizations are so busy getting Google money and making tech workers happy and productive that people like Linda get left behind, not to mention the whole army of janitors, food-service workers, bus drivers, housecleaners, dry cleaners, gardeners, and dog walkers who make the valley hum. Wholeness, for them, would begin with basics like job security and health benefits that have become the privilege of a select few in the new economy.

Techtopia creates social inequality by turning public goods and services into private company perks. Consider, for example, the Bay Area's public transit system, which is staggering under the influx of hundreds of thousands of tech workers. Tech companies have "solved" the problem for their employees by creating private transportation systems. But the multiplying "Google buses" and their ilk have starved Bay Area cities of the political will to expand the region's beleaguered public transit system.[22] On top of that, tech companies' aggressive tax-avoidance tactics have strangled cities' and counties' capacity to build it.[23] That leaves everyone except tech workers with longer commutes.

The social disparities of Techtopia have only heightened during Covid-19. Most fully employed tech professionals have kept their jobs. Companies have adjusted their perks to the home office, offering $1,500 stipends to create home workspaces, expanding free access to meditation apps and therapists, and distributing monthly cash "wellness benefits." Some companies are mailing employees snacks to make up for the free meals they've come to expect at work. One engineer told me that he's gotten so many snacks that he's had to give them away to his friends. Moreover, companies are continuing to look after their employees' social lives by organizing book clubs and happy hours. One manager said that her team is working even harder now. Without their daily commute, and with nowhere else to go, they are channeling even more of their energy into work. Other tech workers have treated working from home as an opportunity to move their burnout-inducing hours to Hawaii or Bali.

While some tech workers are getting mailed snacks, those at the margins are waiting in thousand-car lines to get donated food at the Oakland Coliseum.[24] Low-income workers in the Bay Area are also moving, but not to Hawaii. Instead they're getting evicted and moving to a friend's couch or a shelter because they can't pay the rent. According to a Bay Area survey taken in June 2020, 15 percent of renters had "slight confidence" or "no confidence" that they could pay the next month's rent.[25] While tech workers have watched their productivity and company stocks rise during Covid-19, janitors, food-service workers, and bus drivers whose work has been curtailed are wondering when they will be laid off.[26]

Today, the Bay Area has one of the highest levels of income inequality in the country. The top tenth of earners makes 11.5 times more than those in the bottom tenth.[27] The Bay Area is a bellwether of not only the economic but also the social, physical, and spiritual disparities that are playing out across the United States between high-skilled and low-skilled workers. Those at the margins of the new economy are not happy, healthy, and whole. Mortality rates from suicide, drug overdose, and alcoholism have risen to an all-time high among non-college-educated Whites.[28] They have inferior health and mental health outcomes compared to college-educated Whites. They socialize less and relax less than their college-educated counterparts. They are less likely to marry, have children, or participate in their communities than college-educated Whites. In short, they have been left behind in the new knowledge economy, where the basic stuff of a good life—health, family, community, status, economic means—is reserved for the highly skilled.[29]

An America in which the physical, social, and spiritual health of its citizens is contingent on scarce good jobs is a precarious place. The Techtopia of Silicon Valley and the "deaths of despair"[30] one witnesses in the deindustrialized heartland of the country appear to be worlds apart, but they are really two sides of the same coin: they represent the haves and the have-nots in a society whose material, social, and spiritual wealth is concentrated in work. Techtopia delivers the promise of "good work"—"wholeness" of body, mind, and spirit. Deaths of despair happen when good and fulfilling work, and the sense of belonging, meaning, and self-worth that goes with it, disappear. Both realities, however, reveal an America whose hollowed-out communities, institutions, and traditions are quickly eroding—everywhere, that is, except work.

Silicon Valley shows what happens when we worship work—when we surrender our time, our identities, our resources, and even our cherished traditions in service to work. How, then, can we *not* worship work? How do we break the theocracy of work?

"In the day-to-day trenches of adult life," the late writer David Foster Wallace observed, "there is actually no such thing as atheism. There is no such thing as not worshipping. Everybody worships. The only choice we get is what to worship."[31] We stop worshipping work, Wallace suggests, by choosing to worship something else. But we cannot do it alone, in the private sanctuary of our personal prayers and devotions. Since worshipping work is a social enterprise, choosing not to worship work must also be a collective endeavor. We can do this by intentionally building shared places of worship, fulfillment, and belonging that attract our time, energy, and devotion. These are our families, neighborhoods, clubs, and civic associations, as well as our faith communities. We need to recharge these "magnets" that have grown weak. Contrary to what time management pundits tell us, we do this by letting these magnets attract *more and not less of* our time, energy, and passion. This is not a call to end work; it's a call to energize non-workplaces. It's an invitation to reflect on how we as a society expend our collective energy. It's an appeal to redistribute our devotion into the institutions that we want to shape our desires and fulfill us. And it's a proposition to invest in institutions that share resources equitably across society.

Among our civic institutions, religions are especially well positioned to respond to the challenges of our time. Religion is one of the last spheres of social life to offer cohesive and communal traditions that resist marketized forms of logic and exchange. Unfortunately, most organized religions in the United States today seem to regard the worship of work not as a problem to change, but rather as something to accommodate. In places like Silicon Valley, religion has become a therapeutic salve to heal the inner self in a work-obsessed world. Religions as varied as Buddhism and evangelical Christianity offer "personal freedom" and "personal salvation" but leave the worship of work intact.

Religions can do much more, of course. Their liturgies, practices, and teachings reorient the human heart, mind, and body away from the world of work and markets. Religious traditions can offer a powerful and distinct set of ethics, communities, and rituals to counter the morally bereft religion of work. They can teach virtues such as justice, stewardship, kinship, and compassion, qualities that help us determine how, why, and when to work; how and what to produce; and what to do with the profits of our work. Religion can show us that values such as efficiency, productivity, and growth are means and not ends in themselves. Now more than ever, we need the prophetic voices of our religious traditions and communities to help us restore a collective wholeness.

As I write, we are in the middle of the Covid-19 pandemic, during a time of great transition. The future of work is uncertain for Silicon Valley and the rest of the world. Most tech workers in Silicon Valley work from home during this time. They no longer live their lives at work. Instead, work now lives with them at home. It's become the newest family member and has settled in, like a newborn, requiring constant attention and devotion.

There's no telling how work will change for Silicon Valley tech workers and other high-skilled professionals after the Covid-19 pandemic. Some companies, such as Twitter, claim that they are going completely remote for good. Others are so invested in their infrastructures and cultures that they'll want to return to the way things were. But once we reopen our workplaces, neighborhoods, churches, temples, and gyms, we will have to learn to be with one another again. We will have to re-create our communities. What will we do? The philosopher Alasdair MacIntyre writes that our actions and ethics emerge from our sense of belonging: "I can only answer the question 'What am I to do?' if I can answer the prior question 'Of what story or stories do I find myself a part?'"[32] To whom and to what will we choose to belong? What will we choose to worship?

APPENDIX A

Finding the Sacred in a Secular Valley

If work is replacing religion, how do we know religion when we see it? The challenge in studying religion in a highly secular place like Silicon Valley is identifying the object of study—religion—when it is purportedly absent or in very short supply. In Silicon Valley, most people aren't "religious"—they don't identify with a religion or belong to a religious community, and they seldom participate in communal religious practice. Finding religion is a problem for scholars studying religion not only in Silicon Valley, but also in places such as the Cambridges, Berkeleys, and Portlands of the United States. To find "religion" in Silicon Valley, I realized that I'd have to reexamine my assumptions about what is "secular" and what is "religious."

There are two ways of studying religion empirically in a secular age—through the "religious" and through the "sacred." This first and more common way to study religion is to study "religious things"—traditions, practices, texts, aesthetics, laws, communities, and people—that associate with religious traditions such as Hinduism, Buddhism, Christianity, Islam, and so on.

The second way is to look at what Émile Durkheim calls "the sacred"—the institutions, ideas, practices, spaces, and things that a community sets aside as special and worthy of worship. Something is sacred because of the power it has over the members of the community. Durkheim describes in vivid language how the sacred is coercive and even violent, bending the wills of those under its power. Something is sacred because people submit and surrender to it, according to Durkheim. The warm and fuzzy words that we in the twenty-first-century West use to describe religion—love, compassion, authenticity, meaning—don't pass muster to him.

We tend to think of the religious and the sacred as the same. But they are often two different things. Let me give you an example. When I started this project, I took the first approach of studying religion through "religious" things. I went to yoga studios, because they contained religious, in this case Hindu and Buddhist, things. Yoga studios were full of religious things—chants, images of the Buddha and Hindu deities, incense, and ritual bows—but the *sacred* was nowhere to be found. This was plainly evident in the behavior of yoga students. To be sure, some people were obsessed with yoga. But they didn't worship yoga or Hinduism. No one sacrificed their familial relations or deprived themselves of necessary sustenance—rest or food—as I had witnessed among devout Taiwanese American Buddhists and Christians that I once studied. Nor did yoga studios have the power of religious communities to organize and order people's lives—their time, resources, desires, identities, priorities, and social worlds. No yoga practitioner I met in Silicon Valley was about to deprive him- or herself of food, sleep, sex, money, and family for yoga—the traditional renunciatory practices among the religious.

Yet in the course of my interviews, I learned that there was something that most yoga practitioners were willing to sacrifice for: work. They held work "sacred" in their lives, even though they didn't use that term. They paid homage to it by chronically depriving their bodies of rest and exercise and their families of time and attention. Devotion to work filled their lives with purpose and meaning, even as it manifested in headaches, anxiety, insomnia, depression, and divorce. Yoga, they explained, was how they restored and healed themselves, so that they could fully devote themselves again to work. In the late capitalist sacred cosmos, yoga was worship, but not in the Hindu or "religious" sense. Rather, yoga was how they worshipped work.

I realized that to *really* understand religion in a place like Silicon Valley, I'd have to look beyond religious places—churches, temples, synagogues, and even yoga studios, retreat centers, and meditation centers—and look for the sacred in the places and things where people sacrificed, renounced, and surrendered themselves, and where they experienced sacred emotions of awe and transcendence by becoming one with a big and awesome power. In Silicon Valley, I found the sacred at work.

APPENDIX B

Studying the Souls of Tech Folk

I began my study in the summer of 2013 when I moved from Evanston, Illinois, to Palo Alto, California, for one year to research Asian religions in secular spaces. The Bay Area, with its abundance of yoga studios and meditation centers, seemed like an ideal field site. As I discussed in appendix A, my focus quickly shifted to the workplace. Two years later, I moved from Evanston, Illinois, to Berkeley, California, permanently, and spent the next four years delving into Silicon Valley's world of spirituality and work.

My research took place between 2013 and 2019. Between 2013 and 2017, I conducted the majority of my 102 in-depth interviews with professionals in the tech industry, such as engineers, designers, entrepreneurs, executives, and venture capitalists, as well as the service providers who make them "whole," including human resources professionals, executive coaches, meditation and mindfulness teachers, yoga instructors, dharma teachers, Buddhist priests, and masseuses. When I interviewed them, half of my respondents were working as tech professionals and the other half as service providers. But actually, the categories were fluid. Twenty percent of the service providers had once worked as engineers in tech. And a few of the engineers and executives were expanding their roles to become providers. For instance, most executive coaches have business experience and worked in Silicon Valley, either in human resources or as a senior leader in another division.

Several human resources professionals were engineers who switched units because they claimed to be "people persons." A few Buddhist priests and meditation and yoga teachers were one-time engineers and executives in the tech industry. And the masseuse at one firm was a former tech entrepreneur who switched to bodywork after selling his start-up. I met some of my respondents at workshops and meetings on mindfulness and work. Others I recruited through snowball sampling.

The demographic makeup of my interview respondents reflects the larger composition of the Silicon Valley tech industry. The tech professionals (engineers, executives, entrepreneurs, venture capitalists) I interviewed were White and Asian American. All were men except for eleven women. People working in human resources were predominantly women, mostly White, with a few of Asian and Latinx descent. Executive coaches, meditation and yoga teachers, and dharma teachers were an even mix of men and women but overwhelmingly White, with a few of Asian and Latinx descent. My respondents ranged in age from twenty-two to seventy. Tech professionals tended to be younger, ranging from their mid-twenties to mid-forties. Some human resources professionals were in their thirties, but most, along with executive coaches, dharma teachers, and meditation teachers, were middle-aged, and some even of retirement age. The age variation helped me understand how work and religion had changed in Silicon Valley in the last forty years. The vast majority of my respondents were not religious. But since I was interested in the interaction between religion and work, I intentionally sought out more religious respondents, bringing them to 15 percent of my sample. Although I spoke to Jews, Hindus, Muslims, and Catholics, the majority of my respondents were Buddhist and Protestant.

In addition to the interviews, I visited fifteen tech companies, which varied in size from as few as ten employees to as many as ten thousand. In these companies, I participated in meditation and mindfulness sessions, yoga classes, well-being workshops, and retreats. I also spent time with tech workers, enjoying the beneficence of their companies—we shared meals in their cafeterias, snacked in their lounges, and exercised in their gyms. Becoming more mindful and "well" was one of the unanticipated benefits of my research.

Outside of the companies, I participated in various meetups, workshops, conferences, and trainings that intersect with spirituality and work in the Bay Area. The majority of these events were sponsored by the coaching industry. Tech companies paid for their employees in management positions to attend these events. In them, I met start-up founders, human resources professionals, and managers in engineering, design, sales, and product development. These workshops taught them practices that promised to "liberate" their employee potential by "connecting" employees to their "authentic selves." I fully participated in these meetings, even though I was clear about my role as a researcher. Contemplative practices such as meditation and journal reflection were a central part of these workshops. We often formed small groups to discuss personal topics such as where "the universe" is leading us, our life's purpose, what brings us joy, what we need to let go to move forward. Together, we meditated, reflected, and chanted. We also danced, hugged, and cried. These meetings cultivated a spirt of openness, intimacy, and authenticity, one that participants hoped to bring back to their own companies. I didn't hold back in these meetings, but "showed up," as they say, as real and authentic as I could. I wanted to experience what "wholeness" and "connection" felt like in these settings.

Finally, to get a sense of how the culture of tech shapes the surrounding community and its organizations, I spoke to people who don't work in tech but live in the area, such as teachers, ministers, priests, child-care providers, local elected officials, and small business owners.

Notes

Introduction. How Work Is Replacing Religion

1. "Where Americans Find Meaning in Life," Pew Research Center, November 20, 2018, https://www.pewforum.org/2018/11/20/where-americans-find-meaning-in-life/.

2. Don Grant, Kathleen O'Neil, and Laura Stephens, "Spirituality in the Workplace: New Empirical Directions in the Study of the Sacred," *Sociology of Religion* 65, 3 (2004): 265–83.

3. Tom W. Smith, Michael Davern, Jeremy Freese, and Stephen Morgan, General Social Surveys, 1972–2018 (machine-readable data file), principal investigator Tom W. Smith, co-principal investigators Michael Davern, Jeremy Freese, and Stephen Morgan, sponsored by National Science Foundation—NORC ed. (Chicago: NORC, 2018), NORC at the University of Chicago (producer and distributor), data accessed from the GSS Data Explorer website at gssdataexplorer.norc.org.

4. Ibid.

5. Max Weber develops these ideas in *The Protestant Ethic and the Spirit of Capitalism*, trans. Talcott Parsons (1930; London: HarperCollinsAcademic, 1991), and *The Sociology of Religion* (1922; Boston: Beacon, 1993).

6. Claude S. Fischer and Michael Hout, *A Century of Difference: How Americans Changed in the Last One Hundred Years* (New York: Russell Sage Foundation, 2006).

7. C. Wright Mills, *White Collar: The American Middle Classes* (1951; New York: Oxford University Press, 2002), 225.

8. Ibid., xii.

9. Ibid., 229.

10. Ibid., 228.

11. Fischer and Hout, *Century of Difference*.

12. Mills, *White Collar*, xv.

13. Robert D. Putnam, *Bowling Alone: The Collapse and Revival of American Community* (New York: Simon and Schuster, 2000).

14. Robert Ellwood, *The Fifties Spiritual Marketplace: American Religion in a Decade of Conflict* (New Brunswick, NJ: Rutgers University Press, 1997).

15. For religion in American suburbs in the middle of the twentieth century, see Ellwood, *Fifties Spiritual Marketplace*; William H. Whyte, *The Organization Man* (Garden City, NY: Doubleday Anchor, 1957); Herbert Gans, *The Levittowners: Ways of Life and Politics in a New Suburban Community* (New York: Columbia University Press, 1967); Will Herberg, *Protestant, Catholic, Jew: An Essay in American Religious Sociology* (Chicago: University of Chicago Press, 1955).

16. Putnam, *Bowling Alone*.

17. See Juliet B. Schor, *The Overworked American: The Unexpected Decline of Leisure* (New York: Basic Books, 1992); Jerry Jacobs and Kathleen Gerson, *The Time Divide: Work, Family, and Gender Inequality* (Cambridge, MA: Harvard University Press, 2004); Youngjoo Cha and Kim A. Weeden, "Overwork and the Slow Convergence in Gender Gap in Wages," *American Sociological Review* 79, 3 (2014): 457–84.

18. Fischer and Hout, *Century of Difference*.

19. Peter Kuhn and Fernando Lozano, "The Expanding Workweek? Understanding Trends in Long Work Hours among U.S. Men, 1979–2006," *Journal of Labor Economics* 26, 2 (April 2008): 311–43.

20. Leslie A. Perlow, *Sleeping with Your Smartphone: How to Break the 24/7 Habit and Change the Way You Work* (Boston: Harvard Business Review Press, 2012).

21. Heather Boushey, *Finding Time: The Economics of Work-Life Conflict* (Cambridge, MA: Harvard University Press, 2016), 108.

22. The decline of unions explains the increase in work hours and work intensity among blue-collar workers in the late twentieth century. In the first half of the twentieth century, labor unions successfully advocated for a shorter work week. Benjamin Hunnicutt explains that by the mid to late twentieth century, labor unions, who were already in decline, abandoned the goal of a shorter work week for full-time employment. See Benjamin Kline Hunnicutt, *Free Time: The Forgotten American Dream* (Philadelphia: Temple University Press, 2013).

23. Fischer and Hout, *Century of Difference*, 109.

24. See Jill Andresky Fraser, *White-Collar Sweatshop: The Deterioration of Work and Its Rewards in Corporate America* (New York: W. W. Norton, 2001); Peter Cappelli et al., *Change at Work* (New York: Oxford University Press, 1997); Michael Useem, *Investor Capitalism: How Money Managers Are Changing the Face of Corporate America* (New York: Basic Books, 1996).

25. Perlow, *Sleeping with Your Smartphone*, 6.

26. Since 1980, income grew for the top 10 percent of the American population by 120 percent. In comparison, the incomes of those in the bottom half stayed flat. Thomas Piketty, Emmanuel Saez, and Gabriel Zucman, "Distributional National Accounts: Methods and Estimates for the United States," *Quarterly Journal of Economics* 133, 2 (May 2018): 553–609; Thomas Piketty, *Capital in the Twenty-First Century* (Cambridge, MA: Harvard University Press, 2014).

27. Elise Gould, "State of Working America: Wages 2018," Economic Policy Institute, February 20, 2019, https://www.epi.org/publication/state-of-american-wages-2018. Between 2000 and 2018, the hourly wages of the top ninety-fifth percentile of earners has increased by 25.1 percent; top ninetieth percentile by 20.3 percent; top seventieth percentile by 8.2 percent; top fiftieth percentile by 6.9 percent.

The uneven compensation reflected in the national patterns are particularly prominent in a place like the Bay Area because of its high concentration of tech/knowledge workers. In 2019, the median salary was $246,804 for Google workers and $228,651 for Facebook workers (not including contract workers), placing them comfortably within the top ninety-fifth percentile of earners, who have accrued the large share of financial benefits of work. See Scott Thurm, "What Tech Companies Pay Employees in 2019," *Wired*, May 21, 2019, https://www.wired.com/story/what-tech-companies-pay-employees-2019/.

28. Neil Fligstein and Taekjin Shin, "The Shareholder Value Society: A Review of the Changes in Working Conditions and Inequality in the United States, 1976 to 2000," in *Social Inequality*, ed. Kathryn M. Neckerman (New York: Russell Sage Foundation, 2004), 401–32.

29. Neil Fligstein and Ofer Sharone, "Work in the Postindustrial Economy of California," in *The State of California Labor, 2002*, Working paper, Russell Sage Foundation, 2002.

30. Arne L. Kalleberg, *Good Jobs, Bad Jobs: The Rise of Polarized and Precarious Employment Systems in the United States, 1970s to 2000s* (New York: Russell Sage Foundation, 2011).

31. See Francis Green, *Demanding Work: The Paradox of Job Quality in the Affluent Economy* (Princeton, NJ: Princeton University Press, 2013); Karen Legge, "Human Resource Management," in *The Oxford Handbook of Work and Organization*, ed. Stephen Ackroyd et al. (Oxford: Oxford University Press, 2005); Eileen Appelbaum et al., *Manufacturing Advantage: Why High-Performance Systems Pay Off* (Ithaca, NY: ILR / Cornell University Press, 2000).

In practice, companies adopt a combination of strategies—often taking high-road strategies with their "core" skilled workers such as engineers, physicians, lawyers, and scientists—while taking low-road strategies with "peripheral" workers such as janitors and food-service workers, although skilled workers may also be contracted. For instance, at Google, highly skilled engineers are compensated handsomely and enjoy a panoply of perks, while janitors, Google maps drivers, and some skilled workers are subcontracted with no job security, retirement benefits, or sick leave.

32. Kuhn and Lozano, "Expanding Workweek?"

33. Green, *Demanding Work*.

34. For instance, see William G. Ouichi, *Theory Z: How American Business Can Meet the Japanese Challenge* (Reading, MA: Addison-Wesley, 1981); Anthony G. Athos and R. T. Pascale, *The Art of Japanese Management* (New York: Simon and Schuster, 1981).

35. Ouichi, *Theory Z*; Stephen R. Barley and Gideon Kunda, "Design and Devotion: Surges of Rational and Normative Ideologies of Control in Managerial Discourse," *Administrative Science Quarterly* 37, 3 (1992): 363–99; Bruce E. Kaufman, "The Development of HRM in Historical and International Perspective," in *The Oxford Handbook of Human Resource Management*, ed. Peter Boxall, John Purcell, and Patrick M. Wright (New York: Oxford University Press, 2009), doi:10.1093/oxfordhb/9780199299249.003.0012.

36. Scholars in management and organizational behavior started focusing on spirituality in the 1990s. Spirituality in businesses, they've argued, contributes to organizational and individual performance. It makes employees more loyal and attached to their companies. But there are also scholars who are critical of spirituality in business, pointing out its potential to manipulate employees. See Ian I. Mitroff and Elizabeth A. Denton, *A Spiritual Audit of Corporate America: A Hard Look at Spirituality, Religion, and Values in the Workplace* (San Francisco: Jossey-Bass, 1999); Robert A. Giacalone and Carole L. Jurkiewicz, eds., *Handbook of Workplace Spirituality and Organizational Performance* (Armonk, NY: M. E. Sharpe, 2010); Arménio Rego and Miguel Pina e Cunha, "Workplace Spirituality and Organizational Commitment: An Empirical Study," *Journal of Organizational Change Management* 21, 1 (February 2008): 53–75. For a more critical interpretation of spirituality in organizations, see Peter Case and Jonathon Gosling, "The Spiritual Organization: Critical Reflections on the Instrumentality of Workplace Spirituality," *Journal of Management, Spirituality and Religion* 7, 4 (2010): 257–82; Emma Bell and Scott Taylor, "The

Elevation of Work: Pastoral Power and the New Age Work Ethic," *Organization* 10, 2 (2003): 329–49; Catherine Bailey, Adrian Madden, Kerstin Alfes, Amanda Shantz, and Emma Stone, "The Mismanaged Soul: Existential Labor and the Erosion of Meaningful Work," *Human Resource Management Review* 27, 3 (September 2017): 416–30.

37. No book captures how modern management harnesses the religious needs of workers better than the 1982 classic *In Search of Excellence*, one of the best-selling management books of the twentieth century. In it, authors Thomas J. Peters and Robert Waterman Jr. instruct readers that it is management's responsibility to make work meaningful for employees because when they do, they can elicit the *full* effort of workers: "We desperately need meaning in our lives and will sacrifice a great deal to the institutions that will provide meaning for us." According to Peters and Waterman, "America's best-run companies" are like religions: they offer employees "guiding beliefs," "superordinate goals," "transforming purpose," "faith," and even "transcendence." See Thomas J. Peters and Robert H. Waterman Jr., *In Search of Excellence: Lessons from America's Best-Run Companies* (New York: Harper and Row, 1982), 56.

38. See Robert Wuthnow, *Poor Richard's Principle: Recovering the American Dream through the Moral Dimension of Work, Business, and Money* (Princeton, NJ: Princeton University Press, 1996); Kathi Weeks, *The Problem with Work: Feminism, Marxism, Antiwork Politics, and Postwork Imaginaries* (Durham, NC: Duke University Press, 2011); David G. Bromley, "Transformative Movements and Quasi-religious Corporations: The Case of Amway," in *Sacred Companies: Organizational Aspects of Religion and Religious Aspects of Organizations*, ed. N. J. Demerath III, Peter Dobkin Hall, Terry Schmitt, Rhys H. Williams (New York: Oxford University Press, 1998), 349–63

39. John Coleman, "Six Components of a Great Corporate Culture," *Harvard Business Review*, May 6, 2013, https://hbr.org/2013/05/six-components-of-culture.

40. James L. Heskett, *The Culture Cycle: How to Shape the Unseen Force That Transforms Performance* (Upper Saddle River, NJ: Pearson, 2011).

41. Shawn Achor, Andrew Reece, Gabriella Rosen Kellerman, and Alexi Robichaux, "9 Out of 10 People Are Willing to Earn Less Money to Do More Meaningful Work," *Harvard Business Review*, November 6, 2018, https://hbr.org/2018/11/9-out-of-10-people-are-willing-to-earn-less-money-to-do-more-meaningful-work.

42. Tammy Erickson, "Meaning Is the New Money," *Harvard Business Review*, March 23, 2011, https://hbr.org/2011/03/challenging-our-deeply-held-as.

43. Mary Blair-Loy, "Work Devotion and Work Time," in *Fighting for Time: Shifting Boundaries of Work and Social Life*, ed. Cynthia Fuchs Epstein and Arne L. Kalleberg (New York: Russell Sage Foundation, 2006), 288; see also Mary Blair-Loy, *Competing Devotions: Career and Family among Women Executives* (Cambridge, MA: Harvard University Press, 2003).

44. Mary Blair-Loy, "Work Devotion and Work Time," 293.

45. Ibid., 298.

46. Gideon Kunda, *Engineering Culture: Control and Commitment in a High-Tech Corporation* (Philadelphia: Temple University Press, 1992), 88.

47. Ibid.

48. "Where Americans Find Meaning in Life," Pew Research Center, November 20, 2018, https://www.pewforum.org/2018/11/20/where-americans-find-meaning-in-life/.

49. "The State of American Jobs," Pew Research Center, October 6, 2016, https://www.pewsocialtrends.org/2016/10/06/3-how-americans-view-their-jobs/.

50. Deborah Petersen, "How to Bring Your Spiritual Side to Work Every Day," Insights by Stanford Business, February 10, 2015, https://www.gsb.stanford.edu/insights/how-bring-your-spiritual-side-work-every-day.

51. Weeks, *Problem with Work*, 60.

52. Maria T. Poarch, "Ties That Bind: U.S. Suburban Residents on the Social and Civic Dimensions of Work," *Community, Work and Family* 1 (1998): 125–47.

53. Ibid., 130.

54. Laura Nash and Scotty McLennan, *Church on Sunday, Work on Monday: The Challenge of Fusing Christian Values with Business Life* (San Francisco: Jossey-Bass, 2001).

55. See Putnam, *Bowling Alone*; Gideon Kunda and Galit Ailon-Souday, "Managers, Markets and Ideologies: Design and Devotion Revisited," in *Oxford Handbook of Work and Organization*, ed. Stephen Ackroyd et al.; Jeffrey Pfeffer, "What Ever Happened to the Idea of Organizations as Communities," Working paper, Stanford School of Business, 2005; Peter Cappelli, *The New Deal at Work: Managing the Market Driven Workforce* (Boston: Harvard Business School Press, 1999).

56. Jeffrey Boase, John B. Horrigan, Barry Wellman, and Lee Rainie, "The Strength of Internet Ties," Pew Internet and American Life Project, January 25, 2006, https://www.pewresearch.org/internet/2006/01/25/the-strength-of-internet-ties/.

57. Ruben J. Thomas, "Source of Friendship and Structurally Induced Homophily across the Life Course," *Sociological Perspectives* 62, 6 (2019): 822–43.

58. Jean M. Twenge, Stacy M. Campbell, Brian J. Hoffman, and Charles E. Lance, "Generational Differences in Work Values: Leisure and Extrinsic Values Increasing, Social and Intrinsic Values Decreasing," *Journal of Management* 36, 5 (2010): 1117–42; Lori Goler, Janelle Gale, Brynn Harrington and Adam Grant, "The 3 Things Employees Really Want: Career, Community, Cause," *Harvard Business Review*, February 20, 2018, https://hbr.org/2018/02/people-want-3-things-from-work-but-most-companies-are-built-around-only-one.

59. Martin Carnoy, *Sustaining the New Economy: Work, Family, and Community in the Information Age* (Cambridge, MA: Harvard University Press, 2002). J. A. English-Leuck, *cultures@siliconvalley* (Stanford, CA: Stanford University Press, 2002).

60. See Reinhard Bendix, *Work and Authority: Ideologies of Management in the Course of Industrialization* (New York: Wiley, 1956); Catherine Casey, *Work, Self and Society after Industrialism* (London: Routledge, 1995).

61. See Casey, *Work, Self and Society after Industrialism*; Arlie Russell Hochschild, *The Time Bind: When Work Becomes Home and Home Becomes Work* (New York: Metropolitan Books, 1997); Robert Howard, *Brave New Workplace* (New York: Viking Penguin, 1985).

62. Rodd Wagner and Jim Harter, "The Tenth Element of Great Managing: Executives Who Don't Think Friendships Are None of Their Business Don't Understand Human Nature," *Gallup Business Journal*, February 14, 2008, https://news.gallup.com/businessjournal/104197/Tenth-Element-Great-Managing.aspx.

63. Zameena Mejia, "Why Having Friends at Work Is So Crucial for Your Success," CNBC Make It, March 30, 2018, https://www.cnbc.com/2018/03/29/why-having-friends-at-work-is-so-crucial-for-your-success.html.

64. Hochschild, *Time Bind*.

65. Ibid., 45.

66. Putnam, *Bowling Alone*, 86.

67. Goler, Gale, Harrington, and Grant, "3 Things Employees Really Want" (emphasis in the original).

68. Peters and Waterman, *In Search of Excellence*, 261.

69. See Hochschild, *Time Bind*; Jacobs and Gerson, *Time Divide*; Blair-Loy, *Competing Devotions*; Boushey, *Finding Time*.

70. See Mark Chaves, *American Religion: Contemporary Trends* (Princeton, NJ: Princeton University Press, 2017).

71. See Herberg, *Protestant, Catholic, Jew*; Robert N. Bellah, Steve M. Tipton, Ann Swidler, William M. Sullivan, and Richard Madsen, *Habits of the Heart: Individualism and Commitment in American Life* (Berkeley: University of California Press, 1985).

72. Herberg, *Protestant, Catholic, Jew*.

73. Gerhard Lenski, *The Religious Factor: A Sociological Study of Religion's Impact on Politics, Economics, and Family Life* (Garden City, NY: Doubleday, 1961).

74. Smith, Davern, Freese, and Morgan, General Social Surveys, 1972–2018. Protestants lost the largest proportion to the unaffiliated category.

75. See Chaves, *American Religion*.

76. Smith, Davern, Freese, and Morgan, General Social Surveys, 1972–2018.

77. Ibid.

78. Chaves, *American Religion*.

79. In 2003 Americans on average spent 0.30 hours on weekends attending religious services. In 2018, that number had declined to 0.22 hours. See United States, Bureau of Labor Statistics, American Time Use Survey (ATUS), https://www.bls.gov/tus/.

80. Chaves, *American Religion*.

81. Putnam, *Bowling Alone*.

82. Data based on author's own calculations from Smith, Davern, Freese, and Morgan, General Social Surveys, 1972–2018.

83. Harold L. Wilensky and Jack Ladinsky, "From Religious Community to Occupational Group: Structural Assimilation among Professors, Lawyers, and Engineers," *American Sociological Review* 32, 4 (August 1967): 541–61.

84. C. Corry, C. Azzi, and Ronald G. Ehrenberg, "Household Allocation of Time and Church Attendance," *Journal of Political Economy* 83, 1 (1975): 27–56; Jody W. Lipford and Robert D. Tollison, "Religious Participation and Income," *Journal of Economic Behavior and Organization* 51, 2 (June 2003): 249–60; Sedefka V. Beck, "Wage Differentials in the United States: Does Religious Participation Matter?," *Journal for the Scientific Study of Religion* 55, 5 (September 2016): 558–78.

85. "Income Distribution," 2014 US Religious Landscape Study, Pew Research Center, accessed June 11, 2020, https://www.pewforum.org/religious-landscape-study/income-distribution/.

86. Robert J. Barro and Rachel M. McCleary, "Religion and Economic Growth across Countries," *American Sociological Review* 68, 5 (October 2003): 760–81.

87. Richard Florida, *The Rise of the Creative Class, Revisited* (New York: Basic Books, 2011).

88. Richard Florida, "America's Most and Least Religious Metro Areas," Citylab, April 4, 2013, https://www.citylab.com/equity/2013/04/americas-most-and-least-religious-metro-areas/5180/.

89. Adam Okulicz-Kozaryn, "The More Religiosity, the Less Creativity across US Counties," *Business Creativity and the Creative Economy* 1, 1 (July 2015): 81–87, https://ssrn.com/abstract=2672330.

90. Kathryn Lofton, *Consuming Religion* (Chicago: University of Chicago Press, 2017), 9.

91. Work is an important source of recognition and status in American society. But as high-skilled workers have gained in status, low-skilled workers have lost in recognition for the value of their work. See Cecelia L. Ridgeway, "Why Status Matters for Inequality," *American Sociological Review* 79, 1 (2014): 1–16; Anne Case and Angus Deaton, *Deaths of Despair and the Future of Capitalism* (Princeton, NJ: Princeton University Press, 2020); Michael J. Sandel, *The Tyranny of Merit: What's Become of the Common Good?* (New York: Farrar, Straus and Giroux, 2020).

92. See also Wendy Cadge and Mary Ellen Konieczny, "'Hidden in Plain Sight': The Significance of Religion and Spirituality in Secular Organizations," *Sociology of Religion* 75, 4 (2014): 551–63.

93. Tainya C. Clarke, Patricia M. Barnes, Lindsey I. Black, Barbara J. Stussman, and Richard L. Nahin, "Use of Yoga, Meditation, and Chiropractors among U.S. Adults Aged 18 and Over," National Center for Health Statistics Data Brief No. 325 (November 2018), https://www.cdc.gov/nchs/products/databriefs/db325.htm.

94. Pew Research Center, "America's Changing Religious Landscape," May 12, 2015, https://www.pewforum.org/2015/05/12/americas-changing-religious-landscape/.

95. Jeff Wilson, *Mindful America: Meditation and the Mutual Transformation of Buddhism and American Culture* (New York: Oxford University Press, 2014); Stef Aupers and Dick Houtman, "Beyond the Spiritual Supermarket: The Social and Public Significance of New Age Spirituality," *Journal of Contemporary Religion* 21, 2 (2006): 201–22.

96. Jeremy Carette and Richard King, *Selling Spirituality: The Silent Takeover of Religion* (New York: Routledge, 2004).

97. Dick Houtman and Stef Aupers, "The Spiritual Turn and the Decline of Tradition: The Spread of Post-Christian Spirituality in 14 Western Countries, 1981–2000," *Journal for the Scientific Study of Religion* 46, 3 (September 2007): 305–20.

98. Tess Taylor, "22% of Companies Now Offering Mindfulness Training," HR Dive, August 16, 2016, https://www.hrdive.com/news/22-of-companies-now-offering-mindfulness-training/424530/.

99. See Wilson, *Mindful America*; Joseph Cheah, *Race and Religion in American Buddhism: White Supremacy and Immigrant Adaptation* (New York: Oxford University Press, 2011); Kimberly J. Lau, *New Age Capitalism: Making Money East of Eden* (Philadelphia: University of Pennsylvania Press, 2015); Andrea Jain, *Selling Yoga: From Counterculture to Pop Culture* (New York: Oxford University Press, 2015); Paul Heelas, *Spiritualities of Life: New Age Romanticism and Consumptive Capitalism* (Malden, MA: Blackwell, 2008).

100. See Wilson, *Mindful America*; David L. McMahan, *The Making of Buddhist Modernism* (New York: Oxford University Press, 2008).

Chapter 1. Losing My Religion . . . and Finding It at Work

1. For instance, see Robert N. Bellah, Steve M. Tipton, Ann Swidler, William M. Sullivan, and Richard Madsen, *Habits of the Heart: Individualism and Commitment in American Life* (Berkeley: University of California Press, 1985).

2. Whitney Cross, *The Burned-Over District: The Social and Intellectual History of Enthusiastic Religion in Western New York, 1800–1850* (Ithaca, NY: Cornell University Press, 1950).

3. Robert Wuthnow, *Experimentation in American Religion: The New Mysticisms and Their Implications for the Churches* (Berkeley: University of California Press, 1978).

4. Timothy L. Smith, "Religion and Ethnicity in America," *American Historical Review* 83, 5 (December 1978): 1155–85.

5. For instance, see Carolyn Chen, *Getting Saved in America: Taiwanese Immigration and Religious Experience* (Princeton, NJ: Princeton University Press, 2008).

6. See Richard Florida, *The Rise of the Creative Class, Revisited* (New York: Basic Books, 2011); Richard Florida, "America's Most and Least Religious Metro Areas," Citylab, April 4, 2013, https://www.citylab.com/equity/2013/04/americas-most-and-least-religious-metro-areas/5180/.

7. Robert Wuthnow, *After the Baby Boomers: How Twenty and Thirty Somethings Are Shaping the Future of American Religion* (Princeton, NJ: Princeton University Press, 2010).

8. Keeping quiet about one's religion at work is not just a Silicon Valley thing. D. Michael Lindsay finds that only half of evangelical elites are open about their faith at work. See D. Michael Lindsay, *Faith in the Halls of Power: How Evangelicals Joined the American Elite* (New York: Oxford University Press, 2007).

9. For more on tech culture and community, see Daniel Marschall, *The Company We Keep: Occupational Community in the High-Tech Network Society* (Philadelphia: Temple University Press, 2012).

10. William H. Whyte, *The Organization Man* (New York: Simon and Schuster, 1956).

11. Mary Blair-Loy, *Competing Devotions: Career and Family among Women Executives* (Cambridge, MA: Harvard University Press, 2003).

12. Robert Howard, *Brave New Workplace* (New York: Viking Penguin, 1985).

13. For instance, see Chen, *Getting Saved in America*; R. Stephen Warner and Judith G. Wittner, eds., *Gatherings in Diaspora: Religious Communities and the New Immigration* (Philadelphia: Temple University Press, 1998).

14. Pew Research Center, "The State of American Jobs: How the Shifting Economic Landscape Is Reshaping Work and Society and Affecting the Way People Think about the Skills and Training They Need to Get Ahead," October 2016, https://www.pewsocialtrends.org/2016/10/06/3-how-americans-view-their-jobs/.

15. Ibid.

16. The 2016 Gallup report "How Millennials Want to Work and Live" found the rates of disengagement from work to be: Millennials, 55 percent; Generation X, 50 percent; Baby Boomers, 48 percent; Traditionalists, 41 percent.

17. "How Much do Millennials in Silicon Valley Really Make?" March 4, 2016, *KSBW Action News*, https://www.ksbw.com/article/how-much-do-millennials-in-silicon-valley-really-make/1296632.

18. Sociologist Daniel Marschall describes technologists similarly in his study of a tech company: "A hardcore developer is someone who writes code as a hobby, a person who would spend time programming regardless of whether a paycheck was involved." See Marschall, *Company We Keep*, 58.

19. See Max Weber, *The Protestant Ethnic and the Spirit of Capitalism*, trans. Talcott Parsons (1930; London: HarperCollinsAcademic, 1991). By secular age, I refer to Charles Taylor's understanding of a world where the transcendent can no longer be assumed: "a move from a society where belief in God is unchallenged and indeed, unproblematic, to one in which it is understood to be one option among others, and frequently not the easiest to embrace" (3). The secular, Taylor argues, opens the possibility for "exclusive humanism," "a humanism accepting no final goals beyond human flourishing, nor any allegiance to anything else beyond this flourishing" (18). The distance between seventeenth-century Calvinist and twenty-first-century Silicon Valley notions of salvation and work illustrates the radical shift from what Taylor would describe as a "transcendent" to "immanent" orientation toward salvation that occurs between early and late capitalism. See Charles Taylor, *A Secular Age* (Cambridge, MA: Belknap Press of Harvard University Press, 2007).

20. In recent years, the tech industry has come under wide criticism for issues such as privacy and misinformation. Given this change, it's questionable whether tech can continue to maintain the idealism and culture of faith among its employees. I cannot fully answer this question since I conducted most of my interviews before 2018, when many of these issues surfaced in the public consciousness. But I did get a sense of different ways that tech workers dealt with the morality of their products. Most tech workers did not experience moral dilemmas with their work. They thought of their products as amoral "tools" that they compared to fire. It can nurture or destroy life, depending on the user. How people use the technology is not their business. This is analogous to Mark Zuckerberg's approach with Facebook. The app is merely a medium of communication. How people use it is not the company's responsibility. A minority of tech workers expressed moral doubts about their work. They tended to be older and have families. But they suppressed their feelings, like one engineer and manager who admitted, "I try not to think about it." The dilemma for them was not only moral but financial. They were living in one of the most expensive regions of the world. How could they provide a home for their families unless they worked in tech?

The walkouts and employee protests at Google and Facebook surrounding the Me Too movement and President Trump's dubious and inflammatory posts might suggest cracks in the company culture of faith. Once considered the best place to work, Facebook has slipped a few notches in recent years. That most employees are not leaving, but choosing to stay and through protest change their companies, suggests that perhaps the culture of faith is changing but still intact. People are not abandoning their companies when they go off course, but staying and investing the time and energy to redirect them to the "right" direction.

21. Tech workers used the phrase "drinking the Kool-Aid" to refer to having extreme faith in their companies, rather than to the doom that can result from extreme faith as exemplified in the 1978 Jonestown mass suicide from which the term originates.

22. This is a biblical reference to James 2:14.

23. Religious studies scholar Kathryn Lofton argues that "corporation and religion frame very similar enterprises." Kathryn Lofton, *Consuming Religion* (Chicago: University of Chicago Press, 2017), 7.

24. Will Herberg, *Protestant, Catholic, Jew: An Essay in American Religious Sociology* (Garden City, NY: Doubleday, 1955).

25. See Robert Wuthnow, ed., *I Come Away Stronger: How Small Groups Are Shaping American Religion* (Grand Rapids, MI: Wm. B. Eerdmans–Lightning Source, 2001).

26. Arlie Russell Hochschild, *The Time Bind: When Work Becomes Home and Homes Becomes Work* (New York: Metropolitan Books, 1997).

27. Lewis Coser, *Greedy Institutions: Patterns of Undivided Commitment* (New York: Free Press, 1974), 4.

28. Max Weber, "Religious Rejections of the World and Their Directions," in *From Max Weber: Essays in Sociology*, ed. H. H. Gerth and C. Wright Mills (1920; London: Routledge, 2013), 323–53.

29. For further reading, see ibid.; Max Weber, *The Sociology of Religion* (1922; Boston: Beacon, 1993); Ernst Troeltsch, *The Social Teachings of the Christian Churches* (1912; Louisville, KY: Westminster John Knox, 1992); Lawrence Iannaconne 1994, "Why Strict Churches Are So Strong," *American Journal of Sociology* 99, 5 (March 1994): 1180–211; Christian Smith et al. *Evangelicals in America: Embattled and Thriving* (Chicago: University of Chicago Press, 1998).

30. It is no coincidence that so many of Protestant tech workers are Asian American. There is a racial-ethnic pattern to Protestant religiosity. Asian Americans have the highest rates of weekly church attendance compared to Protestants of other races. They also are the disproportionate majority of members in tech-company-sponsored Christian fellowship groups, I was told. No doubt this pattern is related to the prevalence of Asian American college students joining Christian fellowships at elite universities. See Carolyn Chen and Jerry Z. Park, "Secularization and the New Religious Assimilation: Religious Retention and Religiosity among Second-Generation Asian Americans," *Journal for the Scientific Study of Religion* 58 (2019): 666–88; Rebecca Y. Kim, *God's New Whiz Kids: Korean American Evangelicals on Campus* (New York: New York University Press, 2006).

31. See Coser, *Greedy Institutions*; Rosabeth Moss Kanter, *Men and Women of the Corporation* (New York: Basic Books, 1977).

32. I don't know whether all successful Protestant tech professionals are like Ed Baratheon and Howard Chen and shun material wealth. It is notable, however, that they brought it up without my prompting. D. Michael Lindsay, however, found that only a minority of evangelical executives embraced an ascetic lifestyle. See Lindsay, *Faith in the Halls of Power*, 193.

33. Religion may have been a way for people to resist the overwhelming pull of work on their lives. But they never expressed religion as a vehicle for changing or reforming business. Bradley Smith also found this in his study of evangelical executives. Smith, *Baptizing Business*.

34. Tom Wolfe, "The Tinkerings of Robert Noyce: How the Sun Rose on Silicon Valley," *Esquire*, December 1983, 346–74.

Chapter 2. Corporate Maternalism: Nurturing Body and Soul

1. Not all meditation rooms are dedicated spaces. Many are multipurpose spaces. But these rooms still evoke a sense of what sociologist Émile Durkheim, would call the "sacred." See Émile Durkheim, *The Elementary Forms of Religious Life*, trans. Karen E. Fields (1912; New York: Free Press, 1995). Out of respect for the "sacred," people alter their behavior when entering into a meditation space. They enter quietly, not engaging in eye contact or seeking interaction with others. In many companies, people removed their shoes before entering the meditation room—a sign of respect that one is entering a sacred space.

2. See Youngjoo Cha and Kim A. Weeden, "Overwork and the Slow Convergence in the Gender Gap in Wages," *American Sociological Review* 79, 3 (June 2014): 457–84.

3. See Marianne Cooper, "Being the 'Go-To Guy'": Fatherhood, Masculinity, and the Organization of Work in Silicon Valley," *Qualitative Sociology* 23, 4 (2000): 379–405; Gideon Kunda, *Engineering Culture: Control and Commitment in a High-Tech Corporation* (Philadelphia: Temple University Press, 1992).

4. See Francis Green, *Demanding Work: The Paradox of Job Quality in the Affluent Economy* (Princeton, NJ: Princeton University Press, 2013); Arne L. Kalleberg, *Good Jobs, Bad Jobs: The Rise of Polarized and Precarious Employment Systems in the United States, 1970s to 2000s* (New York: Russell Sage Foundation, 2011); Karen Legge, "Human Resource Management," in *The Oxford Handbook of Work and Organization*, ed. Stephen Ackroyd et al. (Oxford: Oxford University Press, 2009), doi:10.1093/oxfordhb/9780199299249.003.0012; Eileen Appelbaum et al., *Manufacturing Advantage: Why High-Performance Systems Pay Off* (Ithaca, NY: ILR / Cornell University Press, 2000).

5. Peter F. Drucker with Joseph A. Maciariello, *Management* (New York: HarperCollins, 2008), 52.

6. For example, the website for Whil, a company that provides web-based training to improve employee mental health, quantifies the cost of stress. https://www.whil.com/why-whil.

7. Karl Marx, *Capital: A Critique of Political Economy, Volume I* (1867; London: Penguin Books, 1990), 199.

8. It might appear that wellness directors are absolving companies of overworking their employees by attributing overwork to tech workers' "aspirational" and "passionate" personalities. But their characterization of tech workers gets at the general neoliberal condition of overwork in what Korean-born German philosopher Byung-Chul Han calls the "achievement society." He argues that the compulsion to achieve makes the contemporary worker a slave who exploits his own labor to the point of self-destruction: "Although the achievement-subject deems itself free, in reality it is a slave. In so far as it willingly exploits itself without a master, it is an *absolute slave*. There is no master forcing the achievement-subject to work." See Byung-Chul Han, *Psychopolitics: Neoliberalism and New Technologies of Power*, trans. Erik Butler (London: Verso Books, 2017), 2; Byung-Chul Han, *The Burnout Society* (Stanford, CA: Stanford University Press, 2015).

9. In her memoir, Anna Weiner offers an eye-opening account of women's experiences in tech. Although she worked in customer relations and not human resources, Weiner describes taking on the tasks of corporate maternalism as one of the few women at the firm: "I was always

trying to be everyone's girlfriend, sister, mother," she writes. Anna Weiner, *Uncanny Valley: A Memoir* (New York: MCD / Farrar, Straus and Giroux, 2020), 104.

10. Rosabeth Moss Kantor, *Men and Women of the Corporation* (New York: BasicBooks, 1977).

11. See ibid.; Bruce E. Kaufman, "The Development of HRM in Historical and International Perspective," in *The Oxford Handbook of Human Resource Management*, ed. Peter Boxall, John Purcell, and Patrick M. Wright (Oxford: Oxford University Press, 2008), 1–30.

12. Andrea Tone, *The Business of Benevolence: Industrial Paternalism in Progressive America* (Ithaca, NY: Cornell University Press, 1997).

13. See Tamara K. Hareven, *Family Time and Industrial Time: The Relationship between Family and Work in a New England Industrial Community* (New York: Cambridge University Press, 1982); Richard Snow, *I Invented the Modern Age: The Rise of Henry Ford* (New York: Scribner, 2013).

14. Sanford M. Jacoby, *Modern Manors: Welfare Capitalism since the New Deal* (Princeton, NJ: Princeton University Press, 1997).

15. See Han, *Burnout Society*; Han, *Psychopolitics*.

16. Rosabeth Moss Kantor, *Commitment and Community: Communes and Utopias in Sociological Perspective* (Cambridge, MA: Harvard University Press, 1972).

17. See Michael Buroway, *Manufacturing Consent: Changes in the Labor Process under Monopoly Capitalism* (Chicago: University of Chicago Press, 1979); Robin Leidner, *Fast Food, Fast Talk* (Berkeley: University of California Press, 1993); Kunda, *Engineering Culture*; John Van Maanen, "The Smile Factory," in *Reframing Organizational Culture*, ed. P. Frost et al. (Newbury Park: Sage, 1991), 58–76.

18. Jacoby, *Modern Manors*.

19. Robert Howard, *Brave New Workplace* (New York: Viking, 1985); Catherine Casey, *Work, Self and Society after Industrialism* (London: Routledge, 1995); Arlie Russell Hochschild, *The Time Bind: When Work Becomes Home and Home Becomes Work* (New York: Metropolitan, 1997).

20. Andrea Rees Davies and Brenda D. Fink, "The Origins of the Ideal Worker: The Separation of Work and Home from the Market Revolution to 1950," *Work and Occupations* 41, 1 (2014): 18–39.

21. Priya Krisna, "There Is Free Lunch, After All. It's at the Office," *New York Times*, January 7, 2019, https://www.nytimes.com/2019/01/07/dining/free-food-employees.html.

22. The city of Mountain View has banned company cafeterias in new construction, affecting Facebook's expanding campus. But that doesn't stop companies from subsidizing meals that are delivered or consumed off-campus. See Olivia Solon, "Facebook's Free Food Banned as Silicon Valley Restaurants Hit Back," *Guardian*, July 25, 2018, https://www.theguardian.com/technology/2018/jul/25/facebook-free-lunch-banned-silicon-valley-restaurants.

23. Neither the office-as-home aesthetic nor the rambling lifestyle provisions of the corporate campus are new or unique to Silicon Valley. With the rise of white-collar workers in the mid-twentieth century, corporate offices became increasingly homelike. Companies attracted urban workers to their new suburban corporate campuses in postwar America with recreational amenities such as bowling alleys, swimming pools, movie theaters, and cafeterias. See Nikil Saval, *Cubed: A Secret History of the Workplace* (New York: Anchor, 2014); Louise A. Mozingo, *Pastoral Capitalism: A History of Suburban Corporate Landscapes* (Cambridge, MA: MIT Press, 2011).

24. See Christina DesMarais, "5 Silicon Valley Companies We All Want to Work For," *PC World*, October 12, 2012, http://www.pcworld.com/article/2012775/5-silicon-valley-tech-companies-we-all-want-to-work-for.html.

25. Kathleen Elkins, "A 23-Year-Old Google Employee Lives in a Truck in the Company's Parking Lot and Saves 90% of His Income," *Business Insider*, October 20, 2015, https://www.businessinsider.com/google-employee-lives-in-truck-in-parking-lot-2015-10; Annabel Pasarow, "I Make $122,000 in California's Tech Industry—and I Live in My Car," *Business Insider*, April 20, 2018, https://www.businessinsider.com/i-make-work-in-californias-tech-industry-and-i-live-in-my-car-2018-4; Shirin Gaffary, "Even Tech Workers Can't Afford to Buy Homes in San Francisco," Vox, March 19, 2019, https://www.vox.com/2019/3/19/18256378/tech-worker-afford-buy-homes-san-francisco-facebook-google-uber-lyft-housing-crisis-programmers.

26. David Streitfeld, "Welcome to Zucktown Where Everything Is Just Zucky," *New York Times*, March 21, 2018, https://www.nytimes.com/2018/03/21/technology/facebook-zucktown-willow-village.html.

27. This monk spoke during the event "A Day of Compassion," at Dreamforce, San Francisco, CA, October 7, 2016.

28. See Paul J. DiMaggio and Walter W. Powell, "The Iron Cage Revisited: Institutional Isomorphism and Collective Rationality in Organizational Fields," *American Sociological Review* 48, 2 (April 1983): 147–60; Walter W. Powell and Paul J. DiMaggio, eds., *The New Institutionalism in Organizational Analysis* (Chicago: University of Chicago Press, 1991).

29. "Q&A with Chef Charlie Ayers," One World, July 22, 2019, http://www.chefcharlieayers.com/whats-up/index.html.

30. C. Wright Mills, *White Collar: The American Middle Classes* (1951; New York: Oxford University Press, 2002), 233.

31. Yuval Noah Harari, *Homo Deus: A Brief History of Tomorrow* (New York: HarperCollins, 2017).

32. To this point, Steve Jobs said the following to an audience at Stanford in 1982: "A lot of people ask if Silicon Valley is ever going to be unionized. I say everybody's unionized. . . . There's much greater union here than I've seen anywhere. What we're starting to see is the redefinition of the corporation in America." See Howard, *Brave New Workplace*, 4. But with the recent Me Too movement, employees in Silicon Valley have been organizing.

33. Jacoby, *Modern Manors*.

34. Sara Ahmed, *The Promise of Happiness* (Durham, NC: Duke University Press, 2010).

35. Casey Newton, "Yoga Teacher Fired over Cell Phone Ban at Facebook," *SF Gate*, July 11, 2012, https://www.sfgate.com/technology/article/Yoga-teacher-fired-over-cell-phone-ban-at-Facebook-3694293.php.

Chapter 3. Managing Souls: The Spiritual Cultivation of Human Capital

1. Local coaching schools such as New Ventures West or Co-active Training Institute heavily integrate spirituality and religion into their curriculum. They train students in spiritual practices, often originating from Asian religions, to help clients "connect" to their "authentic selves." For instance, the Co-active Training Institute website claims to teach "new techniques and strategies

that help you discover the wisdom and creativity you already have inside of you." See https://coactive.com/#events. One executive coach described her coaching training by saying, "it's an ontological program which is really about the study of the nature of being. . . . It's like who are we at the core beyond the swirl of thoughts and feeling? It's very much a spiritual program without any particular tradition."

2. Stratford Sherman and Alyssa Freas, "The Wild West of Executive Coaching," *Harvard Business Review*, November 2004, https://hbr.org/2004/11/the-wild-west-of-executive-coaching.

3. Stephen R. Barley and Gideon Kunda, "Design and Devotion: Surges of Rational and Normative Ideologies of Control in Managerial Discourse," *Administrative Science Quarterly* 37, 3 (1992): 363–99; Bruce E. Kaufman, "The Development of HRM in Historical and International Perspective," in *The Oxford Handbook of Human Resource Management*, ed. Peter Boxall, John Purcell, and Patrick M. Wright (New York: Oxford University Press, 2008), 1–30.

4. For instance, see William G. Ouichi, *Theory Z: How American Business Can Meet the Japanese Challenge* (Reading, MA: Addison-Wesley, 1981); Anthony G. Athos and R. T. Pascale, *The Art of Japanese Management* (New York: Simon and Schuster, 1981).

5. Barley and Kunda, "Design and Devotion"; Kaufman, "Development of HRM in Historical and International Perspective."

6. For instance, see Arlie Russell Hochschild, *The Managed Heart: Commercialization of Human Feeling* (Berkeley: University of California Press, 1983); Arlie Russell Hochschild, *The Time Bind: When Work Becomes Home and Home Becomes Work* (New York: Metropolitan Books, 1997); Gideon Kunda, *Engineering Culture: Control and Commitment in a High-Tech Corporation* (Philadelphia: Temple University Press, 1992); Catherine Casey, *Work, Self and Society after Industrialism* (London: Routledge, 1995).

7. C. Wright Mills, *White Collar: The American Middle Classes* (1951; New York: Oxford University Press, 2002), 233.

8. Making companies a place where employees can be authentic and bring their "whole selves" to work was a central premise of the management scholarship on spirituality that emerged in the 1990s. For instance, management scholars Ian I. Mitroff and Elizabeth A. Denton write that employees in companies that address spiritual needs "bring significantly more of their complete selves to work, specifically their creativity and intelligence—two qualities that are especially needed if organizations are to succeed in today's hypercompetitive environment" (xv). Ian I. Mitroff and Elizabeth A. Denton, *A Spiritual Audit of Corporate America: A Hard Look at Spirituality, Religion, and Values in the Workplace* (San Francisco: Jossey-Bass, 1999), xv.

9. Catherine Bailey, Adrian Madden, Kerstin Alfes, Amanda Shantz, and Emma Stone, "The Mismanaged Soul: Existential Labor and the Erosion of Meaningful Work," *Human Resource Management Review* 27, 3 (September 2017): 416–30.

10. In *White Collar*, C. Wright Mills writes, "Underneath virtually all experience of work today, there is a fatalistic feeling that work *per se* is unpleasant" (229).

11. See Francis Green, *Demanding Work: The Paradox of Job Quality in the Affluent Economy* (Princeton, NJ: Princeton University Press, 2013); Arne L. Kalleberg, *Good Jobs, Bad Jobs: The Rise of Polarized and Precarious Employment Systems in the United States, 1970s to 2000s* (New York: Russell Sage Foundation, 2011); Karen Legge, "Human Resource Management," in *The*

Oxford Handbook of Work and Organization, ed. Stephen Ackroyd et al. (Oxford: Oxford University Press, 2006); Eileen Appelbaum et al., *Manufacturing Advantage: Why High-Performance Systems Pay Off* (Ithaca, NY: ILR / Cornell University Press, 2000).

12. See Mitroff and Denton, *Spiritual Audit of Corporate America*; Emma Bell and Scott Taylor, "The Elevation of Work: Pastoral Power and the New Age Work Ethic," *Organization* 10, 2 (2003): 329–49.

13. Treating the soul as a source of human capital is an example of how deeply neoliberalism saturates Silicon Valley life. Neoliberalism, according to political theorist Wendy Brown, is a "governing rationality that disseminates market values and metrics to every sphere of life. . . . It formulates everything, everywhere, in terms of capital investment and appreciation, including and especially humans themselves." Wendy Brown, *Undoing the Demos: Neoliberalism's Stealth Revolution* (Brooklyn: Zone Books, 2015), 176.

14. See Leigh Eric Schmidt, *Restless Souls: The Making of American Spirituality* (New York: HarperSanFrancisco, 2005).

15. Robert N. Bellah, Steve M. Tipton, Ann Swidler, William M. Sullivan, and Richard Madsen, *Habits of the Heart: Individualism and Commitment in American Life* (Berkeley: University of California Press, 1985), 33–35, 221.

16. Charles Taylor, *Sources of the Self: The Making of Modern Identity* (Cambridge, MA: Harvard University Press, 1989), 368–69.

17. Rick Warren, *The Purpose Driven Life* (Grand Rapids, MI: Zondervan, 2002).

18. Explaining the purpose behind spiritual practice at the Wisdom 2.0 Conference (San Francisco, CA, February 21, 2016), Jack Kornfield said, "the practice is not to escape the world, but to remember who you are."

19. Stephen R. Covey, A. Roger Merrill, and Rebecca R. Merrill, *First Things First: To Live, to Love, to Learn, to Leave a Legacy* (New York: Simon and Schuster, 1994).

20. Stephen R. Covey, *The 8th Habit: From Effectiveness to Greatness* (New York: Free Press, 2004), 37–94.

21. Bill George, *True North: Discover Your Authentic Leadership* (San Francisco: Jossey-Bass, 2007), 219.

22. Bill George, "The Spirituality of Authentic Leadership," accessed July 14, 2020, http://www.billgeorge.org/articles/the-spirituality-of-authentic-leadership/.

23. Quoted in Tony Schwartz, "Companies That Practice 'Conscious Capitalism' Perform 10 × Better," *Harvard Business Review*, April 4, 2013, https://hbr.org/2013/04/companies-that-practice-conscious-capitalism-perform.

24. Fred Kofman, *Conscious Business: How to Build Value through Values* (Boulder, CO: Sounds True, 2006), 279.

25. Wisdom 2.0 Conference, San Francisco, CA, February 28, 2015.

26. Ibid.

27. Wisdom 2.0 Conference, San Francisco, CA, February 21, 2016.

28. Kofman, *Conscious Business*, 12.

29. Wisdom 2.0 Conference, San Francisco, CA, February 28, 2015.

30. Ibid.

31. Ibid.

32. "Start-Ups That Work: Investing in the New Leader," Wisdom 2.0 New Leader Summit, Mountain View, CA, May 4, 2017.

33. Even though Amy Cuddy's findings have been discredited by academics in recent years, the power pose and the more general idea that certain physical postures can activate confidence-inducing hormones are still widely circulated in the coaching community. For an example of how businesses have embraced Cuddy's findings, see Shana Lebowitz, "The 'Power Poses' That Will Instantly Boost Your Confidence Levels," *Inc. Magazine*, December 22, 2015, https://www.inc.com/business-insider/amy-cuddy-the-poses-that-will-boost-your-confidence.html.

34. See Kevin O'Brien, *The Ignatian Adventure: Experiencing the Spiritual Exercises of St. Ignatius in Daily Life* (Chicago: Loyola Press, 2001).

35. Miya Tokumitsu, *Do What You Love and Other Lies about Success and Happiness* (New York: Regan, 2015); Bethany Moreton, *To Serve God and Wal-Mart: The Making of Christian Free Enterprise* (Cambridge, MA: Harvard University Press, 2009).

36. Daniel Pink, *Drive: The Surprising Truth about What Motivates Us* (New York: Riverhead Books, 2011), 137.

37. "LinkedIn's Jeff Weiner: How Compassion Builds Better Companies," Knowledge@Wharton, May 17, 2018, https://knowledge.wharton.upenn.edu/article/linkedin-ceo-how-compassion-can-build-a-better-company/.

Chapter 4. The Dharma according to Google

1. See Robert Wuthnow, *Experimentation in American Religion: The New Mysticisms and Their Implications for the Churches* (Berkeley: University of California Press, 1978); Steven M. Tipton, *Getting Saved from the Sixties: Moral Meaning in Conversion and Cultural Change* (Berkeley: University of California Press, 1982); Charles Y. Glock and Robert N. Bellah, eds., *The New Religious Consciousness* (Berkeley: University of California Press, 1976).

2. "San Jose, California Population," World Population Review, accessed June 10, 2020, http://worldpopulationreview.com/us-cities/san-jose-population.

3. See David Weil, *The Fissured Workplace: Why Work Became So Bad for So Many and What Can Be Done to Improve it* (Cambridge, MA: Harvard University Press, 2014); Arne L. Kalleberg, *Good Jobs, Bad Jobs: The Rise of Polarized and Precarious Employment Systems in the United States, 1970s to 2000s* (New York: Russell Sage Foundation, 2011).

4. High-skilled workers in sociologist Allison Pugh's study also "embraced insecurity culture at work as the conduit to the flexibility they prize." Allison Pugh, *The Tumbleweed Society: Working and Caring in an Age of Insecurity* (New York: Oxford University Press, 2015), 50. In Silicon Valley, only some employees have the benefit of enjoying "flings": young tech workers with degrees from elite universities. Middle-aged workers who are not in upper management are particularly vulnerable because they are expensive to keep and may lack skills to work with cutting-edge technology. Immigrants on H1B status are also particularly vulnerable because of the difficulty of obtaining a visa.

5. Ilana Gershon, *Down and Out in the New Economy* (Chicago: University of Chicago Press, 2017), 9.

6. Philosopher Byung-Chul Han argues that the ethos of self-optimization is a dimension of the twenty-first-century neoliberal "achievement society," where we deem ourselves as "projects" who are "always refashioning and reinventing ourselves" and engaged in "compulsive achievement and optimization." See Byung-Chul Han, *Psychopolitics: Neoliberalism and New Technologies of Power*, trans. Erik Butler (London: Verso Books, 2017), 1.

7. Wendy Brown, *Undoing the Demos: Neoliberalism's Stealth Revolution* (Brooklyn: Zone Books, 2015), 33.

8. Anna Weiner describes her experience with Silicon Valley's "fetish for optimization culture and productivity hacking" in her memoir. See Anna Weiner, *Uncanny Valley: A Memoir* (New York: MCD / Farrar, Straus and Giroux, 2020), 165.

9. Nellie Bowles, "Jack Dorsey Is Gwyneth Paltrow for Silicon Valley," *New York Times*, May 2, 2019, https://www.nytimes.com/2019/05/02/fashion/jack-dorsey-influencer.html.

10. Olivia Solon, "The Silicon Valley Execs Who Don't Eat for Days: 'It's Not Dieting, It's Bio-hacking,'" *Guardian*, September 4, 2017, https://www.theguardian.com/lifeandstyle/2017/sep/04/silicon-valley-ceo-fasting-trend-diet-is-it-safe.

11. See John Markoff, *What the Dormouse Said: How the Sixties Counterculture Shaped the Personal Computing Industry* (New York: Penguin Books, 2005); Fred Turner, *From Counterculture to Cyberculture: Stewart Brand, the Whole Earth Network, and the Rise of Digital Utopianism* (Chicago: University of Chicago Press, 2006).

12. Sara Solovitch, "Tweaking Brains with 'Smart Drugs' to Get Ahead in Silicon Valley," *Washington Post*, June 11, 2017, https://www.washingtonpost.com/national/health-science/tweaking-brains-with-smart-drugs-to-get-ahead-in-silicon-valley/2017/06/09/5bc9c064-0b35-11e7-93dc-00f9bdd74ed1_story.html.

13. Wuthnow, *Experimentation in American Religion*.

14. See Jamie Kucinskas, *The Mindful Elite: Mobilizing from the Inside Out* (New York: Oxford University Press, 2018); Jeff Wilson, *Mindful America: Meditation and the Mutual Transformation of Buddhism and American Culture* (New York: Oxford University Press, 2014).

15. Melissa Gregg argues that mindfulness is "the work of recalibration needed when brain and body so regularly fall out of attunement in the intensified conditions of cognitive capitalism." See Melissa Gregg, *Counterproductive: Time Management in the Knowledge Economy* (Durham, NC: Duke University Press, 2018), 120.

16. Csikszentmihályi defines flow as "a state in which people are so involved in an activity that nothing else seems to matter; the experience is so enjoyable that people will continue to do it even at great cost, for the sheer sake of doing it." Mihaly Csikszentmihályi, *Flow: The Psychology of Optimal Experience* (New York: Harper and Row, 1990), 4.

17. The Buddhist term "monkey mind" has grown so mainstream that even *Forbes* has an article about it. Alice G. Walton, "8 Science-Based Tricks for Quieting the Monkey Mind," *Forbes*, February 29, 2017, https://www.forbes.com/sites/alicegwalton/2017/02/28/8-science-based-tricks-for-quieting-the-monkey-mind/?sh=6dfef411af6c.

18. See Matthew MacKenzie, "Buddhism and the Virtues," in *The Oxford Handbook of Virtue*, ed. Nancy E. Snow (New York: Oxford University Press, 2017), doi:10.1093/oxfordhb/9780199385195.001.0001. In *The Bodhicaryāvatāra*, the eighth-century Indian Buddhist monk, Santideva writes "a person whose mind is distracted stands between the fangs of the

defilements." See *The Bodhicaryāvatāra*, ed. Paul Williams, trans. Kate Crosby and Andrew Skilton (New York: Oxford University Press, 1996), 88.

19. For more on studies like this, see Daniel Goleman and Richard J. Davidson, *Altered Traits: Science Reveals How Meditation Changes Your Mind, Brain, and Body* (New York: Avery, 2017).

20. MacKenzie, "Buddhism and the Virtues."

21. Chade-Meng Tan, *Search Inside Yourself: The Unexpected Path to Achieving Success, Happiness (and World Peace)* (New York: HarperOne, 2012), 100.

22. Ibid., 89.

23. David's exercise is an adaptation from the teaching of one of the most popular Zen Buddhist teachers to White Americans in the 1960s and 1970s, Shunryu Suzuki, who coined the term "beginner's mind."

24. I didn't encounter many people that I would have considered "on the spectrum," but this may be because of the bias in the population that I studied—people who are especially attuned to their emotions through mindfulness and meditation.

25. Tenzin Gyatso, the Fourteenth Dalai Lama, *The Compassionate Life* (Boston: Wisdom, 2001), 17.

26. Ibid., 23.

27. Markoff, *What the Dormouse Said.*

28. Wilson, *Mindful America*, 106.

Chapter 5. Killing the Buddha

1. Jeff Wilson, *Mindful America: Meditation and the Mutual Transformation of Buddhism and American Culture* (New York: Oxford University Press, 2014).

2. This figure comes from a 2016 study conducted by the National Business Group on Heath (NBGH) and Fidelity Investments. See Tess Taylor, "22% of Companies Now Offering Mindfulness Training," HR Dive, August 16, 2016, https://www.hrdive.com/news/22-of-companies-now-offering-mindfulness-training/424530/.

3. For instance, see Marissa Levin, "Why Google, Nike and Apple Love Mindfulness Training and You Can Easily Love It Too," *Inc.*, March 12, 2016, https://www.inc.com/marissa-levin/why-google-nike-and-apple-love-mindfulness-training-and-how-you-can-easily-love-.html; Jen Weiczner, "Meditation Has Become a Billion-Dollar Business, *Fortune*, March 12, 2016, https://fortune.com/2016/03/12/meditation-mindfulness-apps/.

4. See Wilson, *Mindful America*; Ann Gleig, *American Dharma: Buddhism beyond Modernity* (New Haven, CT: Yale University Press, 2019); Jamie Kucinskas, *The Mindful Elite: Mobilizing from the Inside Out* (New York: Oxford University Press, 2018); Ronald E. Purser, *McMindfulness: How Mindfulness Became the New Capitalist Spirituality* (London: Repeater Books, 2019).

5. Some religious studies scholars argue that what constitutes religion is in the eye of the beholder. For instance, Winnifred Fallers Sullivan argues that religion cannot be coherently defined by the law today because everyone has a different understanding of what religion is. In his study of psychotherapy and Buddhism, religious studies scholar Ira Helderman argues that the boundaries that therapists draw between what is religious and secular are inherently unstable, inconsistent, and subject to revision. Similarly, Jeff Wilson writes that Buddhism, reli-

gion, and the secular are socially constructed categories whose labels are strategically applied. Candy Gunther Brown, on the other hand, argues that organizations such as schools and hospitals must treat secularized yoga and mindfulness as religious practices and offer students and patients opt-in informed consent. She writes that even when secularized, practices such as yoga and meditation often produce spiritual experiences. Moreover, Brown argues that some providers are motivated by religious evangelization. See Winnifred Fallers Sullivan, *The Impossibility of Religious Freedom* (Princeton, NJ: Princeton University Press, 2007); Winnifred Fallers Sullivan, "We Are Religious Now. Again," *Social Research* 76, 4 (Winter 2009): 1181–98; Ira Helderman, *Prescribing the Dharma: Psychotherapists, Buddhist Traditions, and Defining Religion* (Chapel Hill: University of North Carolina Press, 2019); Candy Gunther Brown, *The Healing Gods: Complementary and Alternative Medicine in Christian America* (New York: Oxford University Press, 2013); Candy Gunther Brown, *Debating Yoga and Mindfulness in Public Schools: Reforming Secular Education or Reestablishing Religion?* (Chapel Hill: University of North Carolina Press, 2019); Wilson, *Mindful America.*

6. Jan-Philipp Martini, "Unleashing the Power of Mindfulness in Organizations," Boston Consulting Group, April 26, 2018, https://www.bcg.com/en-us/publications/2018/unleashing-power-of-mindfulness-in-corporations.

7. "The Science," Headspace, accessed May 17, 2021, https://www.headspace.com/science.

8. See Brown, *Debating Yoga and Mindfulness in Public Schools*; Alia Wong, "Why Schools Are Banning Mindfulness," *Atlantic*, September 20, 2018, https://www.theatlantic.com/education/archive/2018/09/why-schools-are-banning-yoga/570904/.

9. The attempt by meditation entrepreneurs to frame meditation as a universal rather than a Buddhist practice is an example of *areligious secularism*. Religion studies and law scholar Winnifred Fallers Sullivan describes it as "a form of the secular" that is a "still emerging post-Christian space where religion is honored as a human universal and religious pluralism can be creatively negotiated in sites of cultural exchange" (230). Areligious secularism emphasizes the "universality of 'spiritual' practices" (232). See Winnifred Fallers Sullivan, *Prison Religion: Faith-Based Reform and the Constitution* (Princeton, NJ: Princeton University Press, 2009). Wendy Cadge refers to a similar phenomenon that she calls *spiritual secularism.* In her study of hospital chaplains, Cadge argues that many Western therapeutic practices adapt religious traditions that are seen as "secular" because of their universal appeal. Spiritual secularism is a "broad approach to meaning-making rather than something explicitly connected to religious traditions" (200). See Wendy Cadge, *Paging God: Religion in the Halls of Medicine* (Chicago: University of Chicago Press, 2013), 200.

10. Mary Douglas, *Purity and Danger: An Analysis of Concepts of Pollution and Taboo* (London: Routledge, 1966).

11. "Meditation," Headspace, accessed May 17, 2021, https://www.headspace.com/meditation/meditation-101.

12. Kucinskas, *Mindful Elite.*

13. Paradoxically, it is precisely when senior leaders bring meditation into the workplace that companies need to be concerned about religion being coercive. One engineer told me that the many employees who attend the company meditation class do so in order to find favor with the teacher, a senior leader. At another company, an engineer told me that it was "important" that employees attend the company meditation because the CEO showed up regularly.

14. This is an example of the subjectivity and indeterminacy of the labels "religion" and "secular." See Sullivan, *Impossibility of Religious Freedom*; Helderman, *Prescribing the Dharma*; Wilson, *Mindful America*.

15. Some scholars call this "Western Buddhism," "convert Buddhism," "American Buddhism," or even "modern Buddhism" or "Buddhism without beliefs." But none of these terms capture the obvious racial dimension of this kind of Buddhist experience. The terms conflate White Buddhist experience with "Western," "convert," "American," and so on. Asian American Buddhists, who are also "Western," "converts," and "American," practice a very different kind of Buddhism that is ostensibly more "religious" with devotional and ritual dimensions.

16. Richard Hughes Seager, *Buddhism in America* (New York: Columbia University Press, 2012).

17. For further reading on the San Francisco Zen Center and the history of Anglo-American Zen, see James William Coleman, *The New Buddhism: The Western Transmission of an Ancient Tradition* (New York: Oxford University Press, 2002); Rick Fields, *How the Swans Came to the Lake: A Narrative History of Buddhism in America* (Boston: Shambhala, 1992); Michael Downing, *Shoes Outside the Door: Desire, Devotion, and Excess at San Francisco Zen Center* (Washington, DC: Counterpoint, 2001).

18. Joseph Cheah, *Race and Religion in American Buddhism: White Supremacy and Immigrant Adaptation* (New York: Oxford University Press, 2011).

19. Steve Batchelor, *Buddhism without Beliefs: A Contemporary Guide to Awakening* (New York: Riverhead Books, 1997).

20. Marion Goldman, *The American Soul Rush: Esalen and the Rise of Spiritual Privilege* (New York: New York University Press, 2012).

21. Claiming that the dharma is universal does not make it secular. Religious studies scholar Jeff Wilson writes, "Defining dharma as universal and above or beyond any particular religion is, of course, itself a religious statement about the nature of dharma." See Jeff Wilson, "The Religion of Mindfulness," *Tricycle*, Fall 2016, https://tricycle.org/magazine/mindfulness-jeff-wilson/.

22. Anne Harrington, *The Cure Within: A History of Mind-Body Medicine* (New York: W. W. Norton, 2008).

23. Gil Fronsdal, "Life, Liberty and the Pursuit of Happiness in the American Insight Community," in *The Faces of Buddhism in America*, ed. Charles S. Prebish and Kenneth K. Tanaka (Los Angeles: University of California Press, 1998), 167 (emphasis added).

24. Cheah, *Race and Religion in American Buddhism*; Seager, *Buddhism in America*.

25. See Cheah, *Race and Religion in American Buddhism*; Wilson, *Mindful America*.

26. For the proportion of Asian American professionals in the Bay Area workforce, see Buck Gee and Denise Peck, "The Illusion of Asian Success: Scant Progress for Minorities in Cracking the Glass Ceiling in 2007–2015," Ascend, https://www.ascendleadershipfoundation.org/research/the-illusion-of-asian-success. For the proportion of Asian Americans among Buddhists in the United States, see "Asian Americans: A Mosaic of Faiths, Pew Research Center, Religion and Public Life, August 2012, https://www.pewforum.org/2012/07/19/asian-americans-a-mosaic-of-faiths-religious-affiliation/.

27. On the invisibility of Asian Americans in American Buddhism, see Cheah, *Race and Religion in American Buddhism*; Funie Hsu, "We've Been Here All Along," *Lion's Roar*, May 17, 2017,

https://www.lionsroar.com/weve-been-here-all-along/; Chenxing Han, "The Invisible Majority," *Lion's Roar*, September 5, 2019, https://www.lionsroar.com/the-invisible-majority-2/; Chenxing Han, *Be the Refuge: Raising the Voices of Asian American Buddhists* (Berkeley, CA: North Atlantic Books, 2021); Edwin Ng and Ron Purser, "White Privilege and the Mindfulness Movement," Buddhist Peace Fellowship, October 2, 2015, http://www.buddhistpeacefellowship.org/white-privilege-the-mindfulness-movement/.28; George Yancey and Emily McRae, eds., *Buddhism and Whiteness: Critical Reflections* (Lanham, MD: Lexington Books, 2019).

28. Harrington, *Cure Within*.

29. Herbert Benson, *The Relaxation Response* (New York: HarperCollins, 1975).

30. Laura Efron, "Neuroscientist Richie Davidson Says Dalai Lama Gave Him 'A Wake-Up Call' That Changed His Research Forever," ABC News, July 27, 2016, https://abcnews.go.com/Health/neuroscientist-richie-davidson-dalai-lama-gave-total-wake/story?id=40859233.

31. Harrington, *Cure Within*, 236.

32. Efron, "Neuroscientist Richie Davidson says Dalai Lama Gave Him 'A Wake-up Call.'"

33. Kathy Gilsinan, "The Buddhist and the Neuroscientist: What Compassion Does to the Brain," *Atlantic*, July 4, 2015, https://www.theatlantic.com/health/archive/2015/07/dalai-lama-neuroscience-compassion/397706/.

34. His Holiness the Dalai Lama, *The Universe in a Single Atom: The Convergence of Science and Spirituality* (New York: Three Rivers, 2006), 3.

35. Tsering Tsomo, "Buddhism Is a Science of the Mind," His Holiness the 14th Dalai Lama of Tibet, November 5, 2006, https://www.dalailama.com/news/2006/buddhism-is-a-science-of-the-mind-dalai-lama.

36. I bring up the Dalai Lama's strategic use of science not to discredit the validity of meditation research—I don't offer any evidence to this end, but rather, to highlight the political, religious, and cultural interests that shape the development of scientific knowledge. Scientific knowledge is not produced in a vacuum.

37. Daniel Goleman, *Emotional Intelligence: Why It Can Matter More Than IQ* (New York: Bantam Books, 2005), 18.

38. J. A. Brefcsynski-Lewis et al., "Neural Correlates of Attentional Expertise in Long-Term Meditation Practitioners," *Proceedings of the National Academy of Science of the United States of America* 104, 27 (2007): 11483–88; Sara Lazar et al., "Meditation Experience Is Associated with Increased Cortical Thickness," *Neuroreport* 16, 17 (2005): 1893–97.

39. Matthew Lieberman et al., "Putting Feelings into Words: Affect Labeling Disrupts Amygdala Activity in Response to Affective Stimuli," *Psychological Science* 18, 5 (2007): 421–28.

40. Richard Davidson et al., "Alterations in Brain and Immune Function Produced by Mindfulness Meditation," *Psychosomatic Medicine* 65, 4 (2003): 564–70.

41. Heleen Slagter et al., "Mental Training Affects Distribution of Limited Brain Resources," *Plos Biology* 5, 6 (2007): e138.

42. "Science," Wisdom Labs, accessed May 17, 2021, https://wisdomlabs.com/science/.

43. "The Science," Headspace, accessed May 17, 2021, https://www.headspace.com/science.

44. James Paine, "11 Famous Entrepreneurs Who Meditate Daily," *Inc.*, September 16, 2016, https://www.inc.com/james-paine/11-famous-entrepreneurs-who-meditate-daily.html.

45. Nicholas T. Van Dam et al., "Mind the Hype: A Critical Evaluation and Prescriptive Agenda for Research on Mindfulness and Meditation," *Perspectives on Psychological Science* 13, 1

(2017): 36; see also Linda Heuman, "Don't Believe the Hype," *Tricycle*, October 11, 2014, https://tricycle.org/trikedaily/dont-believe-hype/; Evan Thompson, "Looping Effects and the Cognitive Science of Mindfulness Meditation," in *Meditation, Buddhism, and Science*, ed. David L. McMahan and Erik Braun (New York: Oxford University Press, 2017), 47–61. For a summary of studies, see Purser, *McMindfulness*, 115–30.

46. "The Science," Headspace, accessed May 17, 2021, https://www.headspace.com/science.

47. Chade-Meng Tan, *Search Inside Yourself: The Unexpected Path to Achieving Success, Happiness (and World Peace)* (New York: HarperOne, 2012), 3.

48. "Our Methodology," Search Inside Yourself Leadership Institute, accessed May 17, 2021, https://siyli.org/approach/methodology.

49. I am indebted to one of my clever respondents for the phrase "libertarian technological idealism." He is a tech entrepreneur and one of the few I met who is critical of this dimension in Silicon Valley culture.

50. Dreamforce, San Francisco, CA, September 18, 2015.

51. Gopi Kallayil, *The Internet to the Inner-net: Five Ways to Reset Your Connection and Live a Conscious Life* (Carlsbad, CA: Hay House, 2015).

52. Tan, *Search Inside Yourself*, 17.

53. Kucinskas, *Mindful Elite*, 94; Purser, *McMindfulness*, 153.

54. Van Dam et al., "Mind the Hype."

55. "Mindfulness Champions in Organizations," Search Inside Yourself Leadership Institute, accessed May 19, 2021, https://siyli.org/resources/mindfulness-champions?utm_campaign=wisdom2019.

56. Purser, *McMindfulness*, 133–34.

57. One mindfulness vendor proposed allowing me to observe her workshops if I would prepare a study proving the efficacy of meditation in the workplace. I politely declined.

58. For example, workplace mindfulness practice was no more beneficial to lowering cortisol, stress, or depression in nonobese employees than those participating in an "education control group." See William B. Malarkey, David Jarjoura, and Maryanna Klatt, "Workplace Based Mindfulness Practice and Inflammation: A Randomized Trial," *Brain, Behavior, and Immunity* 27 (January 2013): 145–54.

59. For example, see Agnes E. Ven Den Berg and Mariette H. G. Custers, "Gardening Promotes Neuroendocrine and Affective Restoration from Stress," *Journal of Health Psychology* 16, 1 (2010): 3–11; Mark Keith et al., "Team Video Gaming for Team Building: Effects on Team Performance," *AIS Transactions on Human-Computer Interaction* 10, 4 (2018): 205–31; Mark R. Rosekind et al., "The Cost of Poor Sleep: Workplace Productivity Loss and Associated Costs," *Journal of Occupational and Environmental Medicine* 52, 1 (2010): 91–98.

60. Gleig, *American Dharma*; see also Kucinskas, *Mindful Elite*.

61. Ronald E. Purser and David Loy, "Beyond McMindfulness," *Huffington Post*, August 31, 2013, https://www.huffpost.com/entry/beyond-mcmindfulness_b_3519289. Purser further developed the ideas from this article in a later publication, his book *McMindfulness*.

62. Purser and Loy write, "While a stripped-down, secularized technique—what some critics are now calling 'McMindfulness'—may make it more palatable to the corporate world, decontextualizing mindfulness from its original liberative and transformative purpose, as well as

its foundation in social ethics, amounts to a Faustian bargain." See Purser and Loy, "Beyond McMindfulness."

63. Ibid.

64. Ron Purser and Edwin Ng, "Corporate Mindfulness Is Bullsh*t: Zen or No Zen, You're Working Harder and Being Paid Less," *Salon*, September 27, 2015, https://www.salon.com/2015/09/27/corporate_mindfulness_is_bullsht_zen_or_no_zen_youre_working_harder_and_being_paid_less/; Slavoj Žižek, "From Western Marxism to Western Buddhism," *Cabinet Magazine* 2 (2001), http://www.cabinetmagazine.org/issues/2/western.php; Purser, *McMindfulness*.

65. The organizer of the Google protest at Wisdom 2.0, who is a member of Oakland's East Bay Meditation Center, posted a blog about the event. See Amanda Ream, "Why I Disrupted the Wisdom 2.0 Conference," *Tricycle*, February 19, 2014, https://tricycle.org/trikedaily/why-i-disrupted-wisdom-20-conference/.

66. Over time, Wisdom 2.0, whose sponsors include tech giants such as Google and LinkedIn, has expanded its stage to "safer" social justice issues such as racism and environmentalism. It's shied away, however, from issues such as class inequality, homelessness, and gentrification, social problems that are a direct result of the tech industry. Nor have subsequent meetings devoted any attention to issues of corporate governance highlighted by the Google walkout/strike in November 2018 in response to the company's handling of a top executive's sexual harassment. The closest attempt to examining the social suffering that the tech industry has caused was at the meeting in 2018, when Rich Fernandez, CEO of Search Inside Yourself Leadership Institute, asked the audience to ponder the uneven benefits of capitalism. That Fernandez felt comfortable only asking questions, but not offering answers, said volumes.

67. Wisdom 2.0 Conference, San Francisco, CA, March 2, 2019.

68. Wisdom 2.0 Conference, San Francisco, CA, March 29, 2018.

69. Kucinskas, *Mindful Elite*.

70. Rohan Gunatillake, "10 Things I Hate about Mindfulness," Medium, March 7, 2016, https://medium.com/@rohan_21awake/10-things-i-hate-about-mindfulness-2b9836f6bc9a.

Conclusion. Techtopia: Privatized Wholeness and Public Brokenness

1. Although voter participation in the 2020 presidential election was at an all-time high, general rates of civic participation have trended downward for the past fifty years. See Theda Skocpol, *Diminished Democracy: From Membership to Management in American Civic Life* (Norman: University of Oklahoma Press, 2003); Robert D. Putnam, *Bowling Alone: The Collapse and Revival of American Community* (New York: Simon and Schuster, 2000); Robert D. Putnam with Shaylyn Romney Garrett, *The Upswing: How America Came Together a Century Ago and How We Can Do It Again* (New York: Simon and Schuster, 2020).

For marriage rates, see Sally C. Curtin and Paul D. Sutton, "Marriage Rates in the United States, 1900–2018," National Center for Health Statistics E-Stat, April 29, 2020, https://www.cdc.gov/nchs/data/hestat/marriage_rate_2018/marriage_rate_2018.htm.

2. Putnam, *Upswing*, 51.

3. Jeffrey Jones, "In U.S., Record-Low 47% Extremely Proud to Be Americans," *Gallup News*, July 2, 2018, https://news.gallup.com/poll/236420/record-low-extremely-proud-americans.aspx.

4. To be sure, Silicon Valley was never as community oriented as its longtime residents remember it. It promoted land-intensive, spread-out tract housing long before Google showed up, and it relentlessly segregated Black and Latinx residents away from the park-rich neighborhoods people like Peter rightly cherished. But the tech companies' appetite for human energy has played a crucial role in the unravelling of civil society, whose consequences are only just beginning to be felt. For the history of suburbanization and racial segregation in Northern California, see Robert O. Self, *American Babylon: Race and the Struggle for Postwar Oakland* (Princeton, NJ: Princeton University Press, 2005).

5. Economist Paul Collier makes a similar argument to explain the rise of nationalism and the polarization between the working class and the highly skilled in Western democracies. In the last fifty years, the highly skilled have switched their identity from nation to work because work best "maximizes their esteem," he claims. The working class that got left behind in the new economy, on the other hand, turned to nationalism. Paul Collier, *The Future of Capitalism: Facing the New Anxieties* (Great Britain: Penguin Random House UK, 2018), 52.

6. Grace Hsieh shared those observations with me in May 2020. There is some evidence to suggest that tech workers may be becoming more politically involved. For instance, thousands of workers from Amazon, Google, and Microsoft walked out of work to join the Climate Strike on September 20, 2019. A survey conducted by sea.citi, a Seattle organization that promotes civic engagement among the city's tech workers, suggests that tech workers are more politically active than expected. See Monica Nickelsburg, "Do Tech Workers Vote," *GeekWire*, October 7, 2019, https://www.geekwire.com/2019/tech-workers-vote-new-survey-shows-top-issues-minds/; Erin Griffith and Nathaniel Popper, "To Do Politics or Not Do Politics? Tech Start-Ups Are Divided," *New York Times*, October 28, 2020, https://www.nytimes.com/2020/10/28/technology/politics-tech-start-ups-culture-war.html.

7. An example of this is the blog post that Brian Armstrong, CEO of Coinbase, wrote about wanting the company to avoid engaging in broader societal issues, because they would distract from their core mission of "creating an open financial system for the world." See Griffith and Popper, "To Do Politics or Not Do Politics?"

8. This generalization about the lack of civic involvement also extends to philanthropy. The mayor of Mountain View, Lenny Siegel, once said, "new wealth doesn't give as much money as old wealth." See Alana Semuels, "Tech Billionaires' Obligation to the Cities around Them," *Atlantic*, November 4, 2018, https://www.theatlantic.com/technology/archive/2018/11/tech-billionaires-donations/574735/.

9. According to a 2012 study, one job in the high-tech sector is associated with the creation of 4.3 additional jobs in the local goods and services economy in the Bay Area. In contrast, the local multiplier for manufacturing is 1.4 additional jobs. See Ian Hathaway, "Technology Works: High-Tech Employment and Wages in the United States," Bay Area Council Economic Institute Report, December 2012, 5, http://www.bayareaeconomy.org/files/pdf/TechReport.pdf. But many of the new jobs created are low-wage/low-skill jobs. For instance, in 2019, 43 percent of new jobs were in high tech, and 41 percent were in low-skill/low-wage occupations. See Joint Venture Silicon Valley and the Silicon Valley Institute for Regional Studies, "2020 Silicon Valley Index," 20.

10. Michael Young, *The Rise of the Meritocracy 1870–2033: An Essay on Education and Equality* (New York: Penguin Books, 1958).

11. Ibid., 158.

12. Ibid.

13. Ibid., 157.

14. See Nicole Perlroth, "How Tech Companies Disrupted Silicon Valley's Restaurant Scene," *New York Times*, September 18, 2016, https://www.nytimes.com/2016/09/19/technology/how-tech-companies-disrupted-silicon-valleys-restaurant-scene.html.

Because tech company cafeterias hurt local restaurant owners, the city of Mountain View has banned companies from subsidizing meals inside their offices. See Wendy Lee and Roland Li, "Mountain View's Unusual Rule for Facebook: No Free Food," *San Francisco Chronicle*, July 23, 2018, https://www.sfchronicle.com/business/article/Mountain-View-s-unusual-rule-for-Facebook-No-13096100.php.

15. For more on workplace ministries, see David W. Miller, *God at Work: The History and Promise of the Faith at Work Movement* (New York: Oxford University Press, 2007). Unlike many workplace mindfulness programs that are officially organized by the company, workplace ministries are organized by employees and fall under the category of "employee resource groups." Because of this, Christian workplace ministries have more autonomy than mindfulness programs sponsored by the company. One pastor who heads a workplace ministry compared the relationship between these groups and the company to "underground churches in China." Not being tied to the HR or the company allows them "to be autonomous to submit to the authority of scripture."

16. Daisuke Wakabayashi, "Google's Shadow Work Force: Temps Who Outnumber Full-Time Employees," *New York Times*, May 28, 2019, https://www.nytimes.com/2019/05/28/technology/google-temp-workers.html.

17. Joint Venture Silicon Valley and the Silicon Valley Institute for Regional Studies, "2020 Silicon Valley Index," 39.

18. Nearly 30 percent of the population in Silicon Valley live below the "self-sufficiency standard" and are unable to meet basic needs without public or private assistance. Latinx, Blacks, single mothers, and those without a college degree are most likely to live below the self-sufficiency standard. See Joint Venture Silicon Valley and the Silicon Valley Institute for Regional Studies, "2020 Silicon Valley Index," 37–38.

19. Scott Thurm, "What Tech Companies Pay Employees in 2019," *Wired*, May 21, 2019, https://www.wired.com/story/what-tech-companies-pay-employees-2019/.

20. This figure is according to the US Census American Community Survey estimates for 2013–17.

21. Joint Venture Silicon Valley and The Silicon Valley Institute for Regional Studies, "2020 Silicon Valley Index," 80.

22. Zara Stone, "Inside a Secretive $250 Million Private Transport System Just for Techies," Medium, February 24, 2020, https://onezero.medium.com/only-the-elite-have-nice-commutes-in-silicon-valley-8b2761863925.

23. Nellie Bowles, "Cupertino Mayor Urges Apple to Pay More Tax: 'Where's the Fairness?'" *Guardian*, May 5, 2016, https://www.theguardian.com/technology/2016/may/05/apple-taxes-cupertino-mayor-infrastructure-plan; Charles Duhigg and David Kocieniewski, "How Apple

Sidesteps Billions in Taxes," *New York Times*, April 28, 2012, https://www.nytimes.com/2012/04/29/business/apples-tax-strategy-aims-at-low-tax-states-and-nations.html.

24. Rachel Swan, "One Family. $1200 a Month," *San Francisco Chronicle*, July 7, 2020, https://www.sfchronicle.com/bayarea/article/Financial-devastation-of-coronavirus-pushing-Bay-15375212.php.

25. Ibid.

26. Levi Sumagaysay, "How Long Will the Silicon Valley Employees Who Can't Work from Home Keep Getting Paid," *MarketWatch*, September 18, 2020, https://www.marketwatch.com/story/how-long-will-the-silicon-valley-employees-who-cant-work-from-home-keep-getting-paid-11600445242.

27. Sarah Bohn, Dean Bonner, Julien Lafortune, and Tess Thorman, "Income Inequality and Economic Opportunity in California," Public Policy Institute of California, December 2020,17.

28. See Anne Case and Angus Deaton, *Deaths of Despair and the Future of Capitalism* (Princeton, NJ: Princeton University Press, 2020).

29. Ibid.; see also Robert N. Putnam, *Our Kids: The American Dream in Crisis* (New York: Simon and Schuster, 2016).

30. The phrase comes from Case and Deaton, *Deaths of Despair and the Future of Capitalism.*

31. David Foster Wallace, *This Is Water: Some Thoughts, Delivered on a Significant Occasion, about Living a Compassionate Life* (New York: Little, Brown, 2009), 7.

32. Alasdair C. MacIntyre, *After Virtue: A Study in Moral Theory* (Notre Dame, IN: Notre Dame University Press, 1984), 250.

Index

Discussion Questions

1. What does it mean to "bring your full self to work"?

2. What happens when work replaces religion in our lives? What do we gain? What do we lose?

3. In Carolyn Chen's research, she learned that companies are actively bringing spirituality into the workplace. Does your workplace or the workplaces where you have previously been employed have any programs to help employees find meaning or purpose?

4. Do you want to find meaning and fulfillment in your work? Would it be a problem for you if you didn't?

5. In Chapter 4, Alex Stockton is a tech professional who uses meditation to help him at work. What are some other "tools" or ways of thinking that modern work draws from religious practices?

6. What does Carolyn Chen mean when she talks about "Whitened Buddhism" in Chapter 5? What are some of the ways that Buddhism is used differently than other religions in the workplaces of Silicon Valley?

7. Is the experience in Silicon Valley, as depicted by Carolyn Chen, atypical? In her conclusion, Carolyn Chen writes: "Techtopia is a cautionary tale for the rest of America." Do you think that more companies across America will operate like the tech companies in Silicon Valley?